Human–Computer Interaction Series

Editors-in-chief
Desney Tan, Microsoft Research, USA
Jean Vanderdonckt, Université catholique de Louvain, Belgium

HCI is a multidisciplinary field focused on human aspects of the development of computer technology. As computer-based technology becomes increasingly pervasive – not just in developed countries, but worldwide – the need to take a human-centered approach in the design and development of this technology becomes ever more important. For roughly 30 years now, researchers and practitioners in computational and behavioral sciences have worked to identify theory and practice that influences the direction of these technologies, and this diverse work makes up the field of human-computer interaction. Broadly speaking it includes the study of what technology might be able to do for people and how people might interact with the technology. The HCI series publishes books that advance the science and technology of developing systems which are both effective and satisfying for people in a wide variety of contexts. Titles focus on theoretical perspectives (such as formal approaches drawn from a variety of behavioral sciences), practical approaches (such as the techniques for effectively integrating user needs in system development), and social issues (such as the determinants of utility, usability and acceptability).

Titles published within the Human–Computer Interaction Series are included in Thomson Reuters' Book Citation Index, The DBLP Computer Science Bibliography and The HCI Bibliography.

More information about this series at http://www.springer.com/series/6033

John N.A. Brown

Anthropology-Based Computing

Putting the Human in Human-Computer Interaction

 Springer

John N.A. Brown
Department of Informatics Systems
Alpen-Adria Universität Klagenfurt
Klagenfurt, Austria

ISSN 1571-5035
Human–Computer Interaction Series
ISBN 978-3-319-24419-8   ISBN 978-3-319-24421-1   (eBook)
DOI 10.1007/978-3-319-24421-1

Library of Congress Control Number: 2016933778

Printed on acid-free paper

Springer International Publishing AG Switzerland is part of Springer Science+Business Media
(www.springer.com)

[This book] is unavoidably affirmative and therefore unavoidably autobiographical. The writer has been driven back upon somewhat the same difficulty as that which beset Newman in writing his Apologia; he has been forced to be egotistical only in order to be sincere. While everything else may be different the motive in both cases is the same. It is the purpose of the writer to attempt an explanation...

G.K. Chesterton,
from his introduction to Orthodoxy, 1909

To all of my teachers and students,
past, present, and future…
…deliberate, incidental, accidental,
and inverse

Introduction

This book is an attempt to share the thinking that went in to developing a new theory of how interaction with computers should be designed. As a result, the reader will be presented with information coming from a wide variety of fields. This work offers an overview of those fields, pulling up some details from one or the other in turn, but not the incisive and definitive work of an expert.

It might help to consider the method as a guided walk through fields of grain, and to consider your guide a baker, rather than a proprietary farmer. I will walk you from field to field, choosing handfuls of varied grains to grind into a mixed flour. Again, I am not an expert on triticale or secale cereale, or even triticum aestivum. It's just that I've lived long enough, and travelled far enough, and studied in enough varied fields, to want to go back and sample from them when I bake. If the readers are curious and would like to consult an expert in any of these fields, they can find references at the end of each chapter.

The first section of this book explains a little bit about the history of each of the different fields, and how they have been cultivated, The second section proposes a new way of cooking, based on others, but original and possibly not to your taste. The final section of the book contains recipes for you to try at home. Should you try those recipes, I would love to know how they come out. If you choose to go further and to learn more about any combination of these fields, with this small tour as your inspiration, then I will count the tour a success. If you decide that none of these fields are for you, then I hope we can at least spend a few hours breaking the bread that I offer you here and now.

November 2014   John
Lisbon, Portugal

Foreword

I am pleased to be able to write the foreword to *Anthropology-Based Computing: Putting The Human In Human Computer Interaction* as it gives me the opportunity to introduce you to the mind of Dr. John NA Brown and tell you to be prepared for a most eclectic journey.

I first met John Brown 15 years ago. He was a professional animator and used computers and a computer mouse to develop animated features. He was frustrated by the inefficient design of the traditional mousing devices as they substantially limited control and accuracy afforded by one's hand and wrist in writing and drawing. This led to him to invent his own wireless mousing device with a dual purpose of being a device that could still point and click but also afforded the full range of anatomical freedom needed to draw and sketch with accuracy in a digital medium free from the confines of the desk. John contacted me to discuss the possibility of enrolling in a graduate program in ergonomics, so that he could learn more about the science, and to do so while immersing himself in research related to his newly invented device.

It did not take long during our first casual meeting, at a local coffee shop, to realize that I was being introduced to a person who perceives the world differently – that is he takes the time not only to stop and smell the roses, but to sketch them from every vantage point, learn from where they originated, read poetry about their relationship to romance and learn their names in several languages. This is because John has an eclectic background and spectrum of interests. He has academic degrees in anthropology, linguistics, education, biomechanics and human factors, and computer science, but more interestingly he is an accomplished artist, writer, musician and inventor as well as a self-proclaimed historian, sociologist, and world traveler. When you mash these characteristics together you get a person who can challenge you to see the world through a completely different set of lenses and help you travel down a path of thought you never before imagined navigating. Added to this, is John's ability to simplify complex issues through imaginative and metaphorically clear storytelling.

From the first chapter, you are sucked into the eclectic and thought-provoking mind of John Brown. He puts the reader at ease in his informal style, feeling like you are sitting with him in a café enjoying a latte – but he quickly challenges you to become aware of the world around you. This is not a traditional textbook where each chapter provides a theoretical concept, but rather a journey of understanding technology and how disruptive it can be in our lives, and if not attended to can be dominant and even harmful. As I read the opening chapters, I was reminded of the disturbing statistics presented in Brigid Shulte's book *Overwhelmed*. In it she enlightens the reader on how the technology designed to make us more productive and networked is actually disruptive and rendering us less productive. She highlights research that indicates that global information consumption exceeds 9.5 zettabytes/year; 1.3 trillion hours are spent reading and writing emails; that workers change tasks every 3 min using approximately 17 programs and visiting 40 websites per day. The real disruption is realized when it is understood that for every interruption it takes 10–20 times the interruption time to return to the original task. This may result in under 30-min of uninterrupted time per day! The stats presented are only the tip of the iceberg as they represent only how our computers, emails, web browsing and cell phones are far from being calm technology. But these are but merely a few of the technologies we deal with in our daily lives.

The second and third sections of the book provide countless examples of how proper ergonomic design can lead to better efficiency but more importantly how the lack of attention to human-centred design can be disruptive and in the worst cases deadly. John provides real-life examples and entices you to try exercises that require you to think about the world around you, not superficially, but have you look from different vantage points. I promise that you will not agree with all the theories put forth, but that is alright as this is part of the ultimate goal of the book – to make you question whether the design of current technology is calm, assistive or destructive in our lives.

To enjoy the book, you need to 'Keep Calm' and take the journey through a wonderfully told story, complete with original illustrations, humour and a wealth of academic, historical, and anthropological references to defend the thesis that human-centred design needs to have human interest and calm technology as its core.

Professor and Dean in the Faculty of Kinesiology   Wayne J. Albert, PhD
University of New Brunswick
Fredericton, Canada
Fellow of the Canadian Society of Biomechanics

Preface

Aren't There Already Enough Books About Computers?

Yes, yes there are… …but this book is about making them less harmful for the people who use them, and less harmful for innocent bystanders, too.

Have you ever looked up at the stars in the night sky? On a clear night, when there is little light pollution from relatively nearby sources like street lights or the moon, the view of the Milky Way can be awe-inspiring.

Have you ever looked at the night sky using a telescope? The use of the right technology enhances the experience to a phenomenal degree. It is a fantastic experience to see the rings of Saturn or to see details on the face of the moon. A telescope is very good for that, but its narrow field of view keeps you from seeing the rest of the night sky.

I'm not saying that's a bad thing. Telescopes were not designed to let you see a wide field of view – they were designed to allow you to focus in on one particular area. The limited field of view is just coincidental to the technology of aligned lenses and mirrors in a shaded tunnel that make up a telescope.

This only becomes a problem when someone decides to apply telescope design to a situation where a wide field of view is needed. Imagine that everyone around you is wearing telescopes strapped in front of their eyes. No one can see anything outside of the narrow field of view. No one can see immediately around their environment. Sure, they could learn to lip read, and so chat with distant friends, but then they'd have to learn to ignore the things in their immediate proximity. Unfortunately, the way the brain works, they would soon become convinced that they can focus on these distant interactions, quickly switching back and forth between far-away conversations, and still be aware of their surroundings. As a result, people would soon be living in a haze of incessant chatter, walking into fountains at shopping centers, and crashing their cars into obvious obstacles they hadn't even noticed.

What I'm trying to say is that even a tool that does exactly what it is designed to do should not be used in situations that do not suit every part of its design. It might be far better to design separate tools that are specifically suited to each task in question. It might be far better, but it is not what we usually do.

Even when it is possible to improve the tools, we mostly just make use of them as they are. Instead of making fundamental changes to the tool, we adapt ourselves to it, consciously or unconsciously adopting convoluted psychological, social, and physiological behaviors in order to make do.

In this book we will look at how we came to have these telescopes strapped in front of our eyes, and we will address some simple ways to improve our use of them by adapting the devices rather than ourselves.

So this isn't really a book about computers. This is a book about how to make your technology less likely to accidently interrupt, insult, injure, or kill you or anyone else.

Klagenfurt, Austria   John N.A. Brown

Contents

Index of Cartoons

Unless otherwise stated, all cartoons were created by the author for his own use and are included here with his express permission

Index of Figures

Unless otherwise stated, all figures were created by the author for his own use and are included here with his express permission

Glossary

ABC Ringtones These are ringtones that alert and inform the intended recipient without disturbing anyone else. This selective signal is achieved by using the individual's innate sensitivity to personally affective information as described in the Cocktail Party Effect.

Anthropogenic Describes anything initiated or caused by humans… you know, like Minamata Disease, the collapse of the Greek economy, and catastrophic climate change in the late 20th and early 21st Century.

Anthropology The study of humans, including the development of their physiology, their behaviour, and just about everything you can think of – so long as it is centered on humans.

Anthropology-Based Computing (ABC) The simple idea that computers should (and can) be designed to suit the abilities and limitations of the human body and mind. This simple idea requires that designers, computer scientists, and engineers seek the advice of ergonomists, anthropologists, psychologists, physiologists, and other experts in human factors when creating computerized tools for human use.

Ape Hominoidea, the superfamily of great apes (chimpanzees, bonobos, gorillas, orangutans, and us) and our cousins the lesser apes (like gibbons).

Bellman's Protocol In the same nonsense poem mentioned above, the captain of the ship and leader of the hunt is called the "Bellman". This is because of his unique manner of navigation. Without any knowledge of the relevant technology, the ship would simply go where it ought to when the Bellman would ring his bell. Given that the bell was an ubiquitous means of communication at the time, the name seemed appropriate for an interaction protocol that allowed the user to simply and intuitively use their phone to get what they wanted without having to learn any menus or command words.

Brown's Open Ontology for Joint User Management (BOOJUM) In the end [SPOILER ALERT] the Snark in Carrol's poem turns out to actually have been a Boojum, an invisible and unknowable creature that looks different to everyone that sees it. The seemingly simple SNARK circuit is greatly improved because –

unknown to the user – the ontology of the CASA TEVA system was designed to match user-specific phonemes and gestures to existing databases of commands and targets.

Brown's Representation of Anthropogenic Interaction in Natural Settings (BRAINS) The ABC model of three separate levels of human perception, processing, and response – by reflex, by reaction, and by reflection.

Calm Technology (CT) Calm Technology is technology with which humans can interact naturally – that is to say, technology that does not demand attention, but waits to provide service when needed and then disappears from one's attention once the service is no longer needed. To put it simply, calm technology allows you to perform your tasks without sparing any consideration for the tool.

Casa Vecchia The real-world project in which Leitner and Fercher's concepts of smart homes and wise homes were implemented in the family homes of seniors in rural and suburban Austria.

Cerebellum The "little brain" that seems to be involved in the coordination of complex reflex patterns such as the muscular activity involved in tying your shoes, riding a bicycle, or juggling. It sits in the bottom of the back of the skull.

Computerized Devices Devices that use imbedded computers – this includes most modern electronic devices: like digital watches, traffic lights, trains, planes and automobiles, and the same smartphone that just won't give you a moment's peace.

Computers The palmtop in your hand, the smartwatch on your wrist, the tablet on your table, the laptop in your backpack, the old desktop gathering dust in the corner, and the smartphone that keeps interrupting you as you try to read this glossary.

Customizable Activation of Smart-Home Appliances Through Enhanced Virtual Assistants (CASA TEVA) The Smart Home interface app that allows users to intuitively interact with any combination of embedded technologies through the exchange of peripheral and deliberate signals channeled through a smart phone, according to pre-existing mental models of either voice-centered interaction with an invisible butler or gesture-centered use of a magic wand. CASA TEVA worked overtop of the Casa Vecchia system. From the Catalan phrase: "casa meva és casa teva" (my home is your home).

Dynamic Environmental Focus (DEF) The natural human ability to gather and process multisensory peripheral information from one's environment – including one's peers – without losing the ability to concentrate on any one particular element.

Ergonomics The science of work, a field of fantastic depth combining the wide range of all the human and machine factors involved in any and every performed task. Ergonomics is the beginning of understanding what makes a tool (computerized or not) more or less useful. This is a very demanding field and, perhaps as a result, it is not uncommon for the word to be used even when the methods and standards have been ignored. The term *ergonomics* is often used interchangeably with the term *human factors*.

Evolution The process of incremental change over time in response to internal and/or external conditions. There are several theories concerning the specific means by which the change is affected, the most popular of which is Darwin's theory of natural selection.

Faith Belief without evidence – sometimes deliberately so. Strangely, *faith* is often confused with *knowledge*, even though the two of them may be considered antonyms.

General Human Interaction (GHI) Much of human interaction with computers is unconsciously based on our natural interaction with our environment – including other humans. GHI is my attempt to formalize the study and application of natural human interaction as a guideline for HCI.

Human A subdivision of Homininae, the term includes modern humans and our closest ancestors.

Human Factors Anything complex is made up of a number of different factors or contributing components. Some of these factors might be environmental, or they might be technical, or they might be categorized in many different ways. The term *human factors* embraces all of the contributing components that stem from human involvement. To put it a little too simply, rather than asking if the wheel turns, human factors asks if the wheel was made, attached, or used properly – and if it was not, then asks if the failure was due to issues of performance, training, intent, design, or anything else that is not purely mechanical or chemical. The term *human factors* is often used interchangeably with the term *ergonomics*.

Human-Centered Computing (HCC) HCC is supposed to describe HCI in which human requirements have been fundamental to the design and implementation of the system. Unfortunately, the term has been abused by those who do not sufficiently consider the mental and physical limitations of humans.

Human-Computer Interaction (HCI) The theory and practice of the cycle of communication between humans and computerized devices, encompassing software, hardware, and all of the human factors.

Intuitive Interaction Intuition is the feeling of knowledge without rational thought. It is the type of HCI that exploits the pre-existing mental models that would allow a user to perform a task without having to consciously consider the requirements of the hardware or software they are using.

Knowledge Contrary to popular belief, knowledge is the condition of *knowing* something – not *suspecting* it, or *believing* it, or *wanting it to be true,* or having faith that it simply must be so.

Limbic System Several parts of the brain at or near the edge (Latin: limbus) of the cortex. It is associated with emotion, pattern recognition, and fundamental drives for food and sex. This may be where we confound emotion with knowledge and where we generate false certainty, irrefutable opinions, and blind faith.

Natural Selection The process, according to Darwin's theory, by which the immediate adaptive value of a genotype or phenotype shapes the evolution of the species in which it appears.

Neocortex The newest part of the brain, this is where we think deliberately. It is the wrinkly "brain hat" that looks a bit like a six-layered sleeping bag that has been stuffed clumsily into its sack.

Peripheral Interaction (PI) Peripheral Interaction, in the context of HCI, relates to Weiser's call for CT. He wrote that a tool should sit unobtrusively at the periphery of the user's attention, waiting to be either ignored or brought to the center of attentive focus according to the user's decision. PI is the field of study centered on developing HCI tools that can be used (or not used) in this manner.

Prosimian *Primates prosimii*, the ancestor of our wet-nosed distant cousins the lemurs and lorises.

Protoprosimian The earliest primates with origins around 65 million years ago.

Reactive Brain According to the ABC BRAINS model, this is the part of the brain that reacts quickly, emotionally, and "without a second thought" in response to recognized patterns. It is the part of the brain that resists new information and seems to live in perpetual fear, boredom, joy, or lust. It is the part of the brain that biases us with unfounded certainty and unfounded fear. The reactive brain is the channel between the reflexive and reflective brains, filtering and reconstructing data according to established mental models. It is the part of the brain where we do most of our thinking.

Reflective Brain According to the ABC BRAINS model, this is the slowest and most expensive of our three processing systems. It is where we can think logically, perform tasks such as mathematics and reading, and take our time to develop new lines of thought. Under normal circumstances it has no direct link to the sensory system and relies almost entirely on the incomplete, poorly reconstructed, and emotionally distorted information from the *Reactive Brain*. It is the part of your brain that is reading these words, while your reactive brain is reminding you of all of the things you'd rather be doing, and your reflexive brain is insisting that your bladder is full.

Reflexive Brain According to the ABC BRAINS model, this is the part of the brain that reacts directly to simple or complex nervous stimuli. The reflexive brain is constantly in operation, perceiving and responding to internal and external stimuli and passing on only a very small amount of information to the other parts of the brain.

Scientific Method One of humanity's greatest achievements – a formal means of gathering, recording, examining, and sharing knowledge so that it can be evaluated impartially. It is difficult and requires that every participant behave ethically, setting aside their biases and preferences and ego in order to serve the advancement of human knowledge.

Scientist One who tries to apply the scientific method in their work and in their thoughts. This may or may not manifest as a paid position, depending on one's personal, academic, and professional experience, or – as we recently learned in Canada – on the political climate.

Simian From the Latin *simia*, or "ape".

Simple Hazard Identification through the Evaluation of Layered Displays (SHIELD) A modification of the CALMatrix intended for use in the identification and mitigation of hazards based on identifying mitigation strategies for each contributing factor.

Smart Home The idea that adding linked and embedded computerized devices – whether or not they are unified, and whether or not there is any artificial intelligence behind them – will improve one's living environment.

Synchronizing Natural Actions and Reacting Knowledgeably (SNARK) The model for using triple modular redundancy to resolve the issue of weak signals in natural human communication. Conscious and unconscious human linguistic output is used as input, including gestures, incidental noises, and deliberate commands. The near simultaneous occurrence of three pre-defined signals of equal value is read by the computer as a certain input. Two matching signals trigger a query. Single signals are ignored. The name is taken from Lewis Carrol's 1876 nonsense poem "The Hunting of the Snark", inspired by the fact that I had been told that there was no way to use current technology to facilitate natural, intuitive, multimodal interaction; that I was hunting for something that did not exist.

The Comparison of Attentional Levels Matrix (CALMatrix) A first useable step towards developing a scale for measuring "Calm", the *CALMatrix* is an ABC-based tool for measuring the demands made by a given task or combination of tasks on the three processing systems of the BRAINS model.

Triune Brain The idea, put forward by many theorists, that the brain can be usefully modelled as having three separate but related physical or conceptual regions, each of which is responsible for a separate type of information perception, processing, or response. The idea dates back to Aristotle's accounts of Plato's concept that each body has three souls and is reflected in the work of Freud and Jung.

Ubiquitous Computing (UC) Predicted by Mark Weiser in 1991, this is the computerized world as we know it – the state of having computers and computerized components embedded throughout our environment.

Wise Home Gerhard Leitner's concept that the next stage of the evolution of "smart" technology should be the goal of using those "smarts" wisely. A wise home will be considerate of its residents and sensitive to their changing needs and wants.

Part I
Everything You Always Wanted to Know About the Evolution of Computerized Technology, But Were Afraid to Ask

Being a Brief Summary of the Use of Tools Among a Particular Line of Great Apes over the Course of the Last 65 Million Years

Also Sprach Zarathustra, Jr.

Introduction

You are here, looking there…

It's all a question of perspective.

What you observe may appear to be different, depending on your vantage point. Once, on the southern edge of the Arctic Ocean, I decided to walk to a distant point on the shore and choose a walking stick from the driftwood jumbled haphazardly across the beach. After a walk that was much longer than I'd predicted, I found myself approaching a pile of trees, each three or four times my height.

Your understanding of what you observe is distorted by your perspective. I'm not saying that's always a bad thing, just that it is a thing, an observable fact, and that we should be aware of it.

So, before we start to look at how computers and people interact, let's take a few pages to establish just where exactly where we are.

Humans are apes. Like other apes, we enjoy organizing things into categories. I believe that we do this so that we can pretend to understand them better than we really do. What's more, we believe that we really do it well. Consider the examples of the labels "night" and "day". They are clearly different and mutually exclusive, so those seem like very good labels… but where do you draw the line between one and the other?

The real world does not have such clearly defined, completely opposed qualities, so we find greater precision by adding the terms morning and evening in order to shade the borders. Still, it is our habit to try to define and label the artifacts of the world around us.

For example, we distinguish ourselves and our immediate ancestors from all of the other apes by labelling ourselves with the family name "Homo" or "Human". We label our more distant ancestors for some minor distinction. One group of ancestors are labelled for their continent of origin (A. africanis) – even though other ancestors, both earlier and later, also came from Africa. Another group was named for being "handy" (H. habilis) – even though their great-grandparents also had very similar hands much, much further back.

In a fine display of ego over insight, we call ourselves the thinkers (H. sapiens). If you know any humans, you may have noticed that we are not actually great thinkers. We are pretty good at reacting to things, and we are very good at convincing ourselves that our reactions were actually the result of conscious and deliberate decision-making.

In fact, we are much better at jumping to conclusions and assuming we are right, than we are at thinking logically. That's why the scientific method is such a big deal: it is a totally unintuitive way of thinking that has been developed and refined to be even more unintuitive, and, it is based on the idea that you should get as many people as possible to check your work.

The first section of this book is intended to provide an overview of how humans and technology got to be where they are today, just where that is, and how deliberately applying a little more scientific method to our everyday lives helps to improve our own world, and the world in general.

Chapter 1
Everything Is Awesome!

Then   and   Now

...and "**C**" is for C-A-T, "*cat*",   ... and **that's** the record of
and "**D**" is for...   all your *downloads*.

JNAB '15   www.jnabrown.com
Based on an original illustration by an unknown engraver, from "A Gift Book of Stories and Poems for Children", 1850

Abstract This chapter presents two ideas for your consideration. The first is that perceiving the world through a device is different to perceiving it directly and, the second is that interacting with the world through a device is different to interacting with it directly.

These ideas may seem straightforward, but I am presenting them here in order to establish a common understanding of fundamental principles underlying our use of technology here and now, before broaching the more complex ideas presented in this book; the design of machines specifically for human use.

Now, you may be wondering why I am presenting these ideas for your consideration, and trying to explain the rationale so that we stand on equal footing, rather than simply telling you to accept these ideas as fact. The simple answer is that this just isn't that kind of book.

© Springer International Publishing Switzerland 2016
J.N.A. Brown, *Anthropology-Based Computing*, Human–Computer
Interaction Series, DOI 10.1007/978-3-319-24421-1_1

Fig. 1.1 Crowd watching their phones watch fireworks

If you had asked the people barely visible in Fig. 1.1, and I did, they would have told you that they were watching midnight fireworks to celebrate the new year, 2015, in downtown Lisbon, Portugal. If you ask me, they are watching their phones watch the fireworks. This chapter will discuss the fact that we now live in a world in which many people do not see a difference between those two activities, and whether or not the viewers might have lost some aspect of the experience by focusing on a screen instead of on the world around them.

Keep Calm and…

In 2000, Stuart Manley was sorting through a box of used books he'd picked up at an auction. This was a common task for Manley. He and his wife Mary operate Barter Books, a used book shop, out of an old Victorian railway station in Alnwick, England. On this particular day and in this particular box, Manley found an old poster that caught his eye.

They framed the poster and hung it at the front of the shop and, in response to customer interest, began to print and sell copies.

They released a 3-min video to tell their story about the sign, and how it was made, and how they found their copy, and what they think the sign means [1].

It's a pleasant video and a nice story, but that's not what I want to talk about. I want to ask you if you've seen the sign before. If you have, you may recall it based on this brief description. The poster is in two colours, with a crown at the top and five short words in large type:

Keep Calm and Carry On.

The key point here is that most of us who use the internet believe that we have seen this sign before. We believe that we have seen it, but we have not. In fact, almost none of us have ever seen the sign or ever will.

Two and a half million of the signs were printed for public distribution in 1939, but the design was held back and then later abandoned. Stocks of the poster were destroyed. It may be that only 13 of the original posters still exist: the 1 in the bookstore, and 12 others that were brought in to a television antiques show in 2012.

What we have seen is, at best, a digital recreation of a photograph of one or more of the signs (Fig. 1.2).

It has become so commonplace to see the world through a digitally-generated image on a screen that we don't even think of it as a distinct way of seeing anymore. You might say that display screens have become so ubiquitous that we no longer notice them, we just use them unthinkingly. If that is the kind of thing you might say, then you might also enjoy the rest of this book, because we are going to discuss in later chapters just how and why that happens, and how we might make deliberate use of it. So, yes, you might just enjoy the rest of this book. ...Or you might not. I make no promises.

Now, it's possible that you're reading this and thinking "So what? What's the difference between a sign I see hanging in a shop in Britain and a sign I see posted

Fig. 1.2 Reproductions of three versions of the sign that I have seen in shops. http://www.jnabrown.com

on-line? If anything the sign posted on-line is better, because it's not wrinkly, and I can download my own copy and look at it myself or share it around. I can even modify it and then share my version."

I'm not judging the value of the one over the other – that's not my purpose at all. I'm trying to say that there's a difference between them – that there's a difference between experiencing something directly and having it translated for you by someone or something else (Fig. 1.3).

I hope that difference is clear, and I'm going to take a few more minutes of your time now to try and be certain.

The world is vast and wide and we perceive much more than we process. Our senses are limited, but they detect much, much more information than they pass on to the part of our brain that is doing conscious processing.

This becomes really important when you're designing machinery for people to use, and I'll talk about it some more later on in this book. For now I just wanted to raise the idea with you: the idea that we don't actually perceive everything around us, and that we process even less of it. Because of that, what two people perceive can be different. What's more, the more different those two people are, in terms of personal and cultural background, in terms of experience and of taste, the more different their observations are likely to be. This is because, when we look out into the wide world, we each see the things we are prepared to see. I don't mean that in some new-age, spiritual kind of way, I'm talking about the way our brains work. Not that there's anything wrong with the spiritual – I just don't find any need of it in explaining something that is empirically true.

Our brains let us perceive less than our senses detect, and our senses detect less than is there, and each of us perceives differently. Because of that, we can deduce that you and I may look at the same thing, but see something different.

Fig. 1.3 Transmission deforms and reforms information

For some people, that seems obvious, and for others it is a very difficult concept to grasp. For the sake of both sorts of reader, here's an example that I hope you will find illustrative.

Sometimes, you can stare right at something and not see it. Like, when you lose your keys, search frantically, and then find them right where you looked the first time.

Now, it may be that after the first time you looked on the table, you experienced a quantum fluctuation and popped from your original universe (where the keys are in your jacket) into a parallel universe where you left them on the table all along. It *may* be so, but it's not likely. More likely, you were looking right at them, and your eyes were sensing the shapes and colours that could add up into an image of your keys, but your unconscious mind filtered out some or all of those details, and you couldn't see the keys.

Now, imagine if, before finding the keys, you painted a picture of the things on that table, strictly from memory. For the rest of its existence, anyone admiring your painting would see the other things there, but would not see the keys. The keys would have been lost in the translation between reality and your painting.

That is a bit of a crude example, but maybe there is a more subtle one waiting for us in that same painting. Even if you paint as well as Johannes Vermeer or Tim Jenison, the experience of looking at your painting will be different from the experience of looking at the real table. For example, when looking at the real table, one can move to the side or tilt their head, changing their perspective of the view and seeing new things.

That's why dogs tilt their heads to the side when they don't understand something, and why humans do, too. We're trying to gain a new perspective and the additional information that will come with it.

But you can't do that with a painting, or a photo, just like you can't choose to stand a little closer to the clarinet while listening to a recording of Rhapsody in Blue, or improve the quality of your mp4 by asking Huddie Ledbetter to lean in a little closer to the microphone.

Media-based experiences are different from reality (Fig. 1.4). Every time information is translated – translated from one person's perception to another, from one language to another, from one medium to another – there is a loss of quality. Some quality of the information will always be lost in translation. However great the experience might be second-hand, it must be different.

That's all I'm trying to say- that people who experience things directly experience them differently than the people for whom they translate the experience. If that is true, then what can we infer about information that comes to us through a computer? It simply cannot be as rich as the original.

I believe we all know that, but I think it might be hard to acknowledge if you currently do a lot of interaction through computers.

I hope you're not taking offence at what I've just told you. If you get most of your information through the Graphic User Interface (GUI) of a smartphone, tablet, or computer, then you might think that I'm insulting you. That was the impression fostered in two friends one time when we were talking about this. They thought

Fig. 1.4 The treachery of digital images

I was attacking them, personally, and all the rest of their entire circle of friends, and even their whole generation.

I wasn't and I'm not. I'm just trying to establish a common foundation of understanding with you, so that we might build upon it.

If you do find yourself taking offence at what I'm telling you, please under-stand that offending you is not my intent. I want you to read and enjoy this book, and I hope that it may help you learn to think differently than you do right now. If you become defensive that won't work.

So please, even if you disagree with my ideas, try to play along. They are only ideas, and ideas shouldn't seem like a threat.

So, if we can all agree that a direct experience is different to an experience translated through a screen, then what does it mean when most of our day-to-day experiences come to us through a graphical user interface?

It used to be that talking to someone had to mean actually being face-to-face with them. There were situations where face-to-face was replaced with signals that could be read at a distance, but those signals had to be codified – like a night watchman waving his lantern in a pattern that can be understood from a distance to mean that everything is quiet at his post. Writing allowed communication from a distance, but even in the midst of deep conversations, no one ever confused that with talking. You couldn't see your collocutor's face, or her body language, you couldn't read the rhythm of her speech, the tilt of her shoulders, or any of the other myriad non-verbal signals that help people understand each other. These signals are especially vital for emotional rather than intellectual communication. Consider nattering. All of the great apes, and some of our other cousins as well, natter to each other all of the time. It is a sort of verbal soothing; a reassurance that a friend is nearby, that we are part of a community.

Morse code, semaphore, horns, drums, and bagpipes, all made some degree of communication possible at greater distances, but only an adept could think of it as conversation, and I have never heard of anyone who deliberately used any one of them to replace simple nattering... ...until the advent and proliferation of instant messaging.

How will this effect social evolution? A child surrounded by adults must learn to interact with adults in order to feel included. A child who is never out of contact with her own social circle may not feel the need to learn how to socialize with adults. That may not seem like a big problem at first glance, but that kind of learned socialization is one of the roots of how we learn socially-acceptable behaviour, and of how we learn to adapt to new situations.

It will be interesting to see how this turns out.

I'm not saying that it is a bad thing to be able to be in constant contact with one's entire social circle, I'm just saying that it changes the nature of communication. As we have discussed, subtle aspects of communication are lost. On top of that, more simultaneous messages means less time and effort goes into creating and decoding each one – further increasing the chance of miscommunication. The predictable end result is either a constant state of confusion or a reduced depth of conversation. In the end, much of texting is just nattering, reassuring each other that we are not alone... even though we most demonstrably are.

Now that I've risked offending every reader fluent in thumb-typing, I'd like to return to our understanding that there is a difference between what we experience first-hand and what is translated for us by machines, because there is one more important step in that translation.

You are no doubt aware that, each time you experience translated information it has been shaped not only by the medium, but by the producer of that experience. That's why a comedy film by Charlie Chaplin is different to a comedy film by Woody Allen. The creator(s) of a piece of media shape it to their taste, but they are not the only ones shaping that piece of media. The designer of the hardware and software you are using has shaped the very nature of what can be created. This means that their conscious and unconscious biases shape what the media-maker can produce and, in turn, shape your experience. After all, your judgment of the experience cannot be based on any of the data that has been excluded by either the artists or their tools...

...except in as much as that every experience you have is shaped by the filters you use to reconstruct it.

I hope we have now reached the common understanding that our experience of the world is shaped by the technology that we use to perceive it and by the mind with which we deconstruct and reconstruct that experience. The rest of the chapters in the first section of this book will build on that to discuss where our minds and our technology came from, and how they got to be the way they are, and why the two of them – for the most part – do not work together very well at all. The second section will try to tie all of those ideas together into a coherent theory. The third section of the book will examine a number of the specific ways in which our technology is hurting, insulting or even killing us, and offer up both a human-centered explanation and a remedy that you can try at home. Each remedial strategy will be presented in a way that will enable you to empirically measure the changes you experience, just in case you want to formally track your progress. Personally, I hope that you'll choose to share your experiences with me and with the wide world at our associated website.

In the next two chapters we're going to discuss two ideas put forward by Mark Weiser and John Seeley Brown. They predicted that computers were going to be built into countless devices that surround us, and they warned of the dangers of not designing those computers to work well with humans.

Summary

Everything is Awesome! Really, it is! Science and Engineering have given you powers and abilities far beyond those of any of your ancestors. You are able to see and hear things that are far away, able to search out and retrieve selected visual, audial, and written information from the vast breadth and depth of human knowledge. You have access to millions of lectures and publications about the very cutting edge of every human endeavour from the battle to understand and control cancer, to the 50-year history of outrageous, cutting-edge fashion created and worn by the teenagers in Harajuku, Japan.

We have access to all of that knowledge, but it's very likely that we'd rather look up videos of the Harajuku fashionistas than watch a lecture on increasing our likelihood of avoiding cancer.

Yeah, everything is awesome…

Reference

1. The short video documentary reference for the Keep Calm and Carry On poster can be found at the website for Barter Books: www.barterbooks.co.uk. Or, it could as of July 11th, 2015.

Chapter 2
How Computing Became "Ubiquitous" and What That Means

Q.E.D.

Abstract This chapter is going to start with something you already know: that computers are everywhere around us, involved in our lives in many seen and unseen ways. One word for that is at is "ubiquitous". It's a very popular word these days among those who discuss the interaction between humans and computers. Once you know the word, you see it everywhere.

I hope that you can also see that we are surrounded by computers that we use without thinking. I'm going to try to help you notice them and, later in this book, I'm going to try to help you make better, safer, more comfortable use of them.

If you can't imagine what I mean, then please try to bear with me. The ubiquity of computers is measurably true, and should become obvious with only a little reflection. We'll do that reflection together in this chapter. What might be less obvious will be discussed in the chapters that follow.

The Prediction of Ubiquitous Computing

The most profound technologies are those that disappear. They weave themselves into the fabric of everyday life until they are indistinguishable from it [1].

With these words, Mark Weiser introduced the world to a new way to think about computers. His idea was based on the fact that, while some computers are tools unto themselves, the real value of computers would be their immersion into other devices. He predicted that computer technology would soon disappear into other technology, just as writing had done over the past few centuries.

It's a pretty big idea, and it's worth a few more lines to make it clear. If that seems pedantic, then I ask that you forgive me. It's just that I've worked with an awful lot of people who claim to understand the concept – and make that claim loudly and vehemently – and yet who seem to show in their work that they haven't the faintest notion about it. As is often the case when trying to avoid trouble with the loudly ignorant, let's take a look at a simple example. This way, you'll have a strategy to apply the first time you end up in the same kind of argument.

When you help a child learn to read a phrase in a schoolbook, are you helping them so that they will forever more be able to read any schoolbooks that come up in their day-to-day lives?

Visual images arranged as "writing" in order to convey meaning used to be very rare. For thousands of years, it was a tool used only by a small percentage of the population. Now, that tool – and the skill to use it – has become so ubiquitous, that it is very limiting to have to do without it.

Menus, whether provided by service establishments or by service providers, almost always require reading. Scrolling text on television, on satellite radio, or on a website, is put there to provide additional or supplementary information – to those who can read it. Even highway exit signs, street signs, and "no parking" signs require literacy and provide little or no help for those who cannot read.

I've lived in a half dozen countries where I was unable to read the language, and have visited a dozen more. I have personal experience in the value added when that skill is acquired. But you don't have to take my word for it. You could use your imagination – what Professor Einstein used to call a "thought experiment" – and try to imagine looking for the public toilets while visiting a small town in Not your native language istan, or trying to find a street address in I can't even tell if that's an alphabetovia.

If you'd rather gather a broad sample of evidence, like a good scientist should, I know where you can find it. Any candidate in any literacy programme will tell you that someone who learns to read will gain access to a lot more than school books. The same is true whether one is learning to read for the first time, or learning to read a new language – say as part of the process of immigration. I encourage you to look into this in greater depth and to assemble your data, whether you use it or not. In my limited experience, there are always literacy programmes looking for volunteers to help share our communal knowledge. As a pastime, I can honestly say that it will be a more enriching experience than reading schoolbooks.

The point is that, nowadays, people who can read don't even notice all of the small ways that writing has become embedded in our lives. The systems that allow us to read and write truly did "…weave themselves into the fabric of everyday life" and become "indistinguishable from it". Weiser predicted that computer technology would soon do the same thing.

The concept of Ubiquitous Computing meant much more to Weiser than just the ubiquity of computer technology. We'll deal with that a little more later in this chapter, and focus on it in the next chapter, but before we get to that let's do something that many professional computer scientists seem not to have done. Let's go through a few of the largely ignored issues raised in the original papers one by one, to try and build up a picture of Weiser's intent.

I know that this might seem a harsh criticism of my peers, and I hope that the reader can understand that I am not painting all computer scientists with a single brush when I stand by my statement. I have lectured about Weiser's writing on three continents, and at every venue there have been people who argue with me about the content of the original papers. Not about my interpretation of the content – I love to argue about that and invite you to do the same – but about whether or not Weiser actually mentioned some of the key points that I want to share with you.

Think of it this way: after reading this chapter, you will know things about the source material that are (somehow) completely unknown to both critics and adherents to Weiser's ideas. It will be a little bit like being able to quote the Bible at people who want to criticize it or praise it without really knowing the contents.

I mean, it won't be exactly like that but, depending on the specific make up of your family, it could still lead to a wonderful argument over dinner. Please remember that, in any argument, it is a good idea to have facts on your side. To that end, I recommend that you actually read all of Weiser's papers for yourself, rather than rely on this summary. It did me a world of good, and might do the same for you.

Of course, I've also read the Bible from cover to cover, in more than one translation of more than one edition, and that has never once helped me to win an argument with some people who haven't read it at all.

For some ideas on how to win arguments with unreasonable people, please refer to Chap. 12.

For a deeper than usual look at the original intent of Ubiquitous Computing, read on dear reader, read on.

A Few Things That Weiser Really Wrote About Ubiquitous Computing

As you can tell from the title of this book, I tend to focus on the human aspects of Human-Computer Interaction. This is a common idea in my line of work, but I am still met with scepticism when I mention that Weiser called for a humanistic approach. In that same paper that launched the idea of UC, Weiser said the following about how computers – or writing – manages to "vanish into the background".

> Such a disappearance is a fundamental consequence not of technology but of human psychology. Whenever people learn something sufficiently well, they cease to be aware of it. When you look at a street sign, for example, you absorb its information without consciously performing the act of reading [1].

Weiser then goes on to explain that he is not the first to express this idea, and refers to the nomenclature used to describe the same concept when experts have reported it in their respective fields. He cites Herbert A. Simon (the Nobel prize-winning computer scientist and economist, his colleague John Seeley Brown (no relation), the philosophers Micahel Polanyi, HG Gadamer, and Martin Heidegger, and psychologist JJ Gibson.

> It should be clear that what we mean by the periphery is anything but on the fringe or unimportant. What is in the periphery at one moment may in the next moment come to be at the center of our attention and so be crucial. The same physical form may even have elements in both the center and periphery [1].

Weiser's writing is clear, if a little fanciful – and who am I to complain about that? He is talking about the idea of how people and machines should interact, and he is saying that the human experience of technology is based on human psychology. That seems a little tautological, but I don't think I'm exaggerating when I say that the majority of computer scientists I know who consider themselves to be working in the area of Ubiquity, pay as little attention as possible to human psychology. In fact, I have seen colleagues treated with open contempt for making it a fundament of their own research. I'll share a story of my own experience with that a little later in this book.

Weiser's second paper on the topic is much more technical than the first [2]. It is generally considered a survey, or review, of the technological advances that had developed up to the date by the teams working at Xerox Parc, Weiser's professional home, and the home of UC. He describes it as "more akin to a tutorial than a survey" because his goal in writing the paper wasn't to provide a list of technologies that would eventually become outdated. His goal in writing the article is stated explicitly as follows:

> …to help others understand some of the new research challenges in ubiquitous computing, and inspire them to work on them [2].

Weiser explains the way that humans work is usually focussed on the experiences they are sharing with their co-workers, while the technology they are using is outside of their focus.

> The idea of ubiquitous computing first arose from contemplating the place of today's computer in actual activities of everyday life. In particular, anthropological studies of work life teach us that people primarily work in a world of shared situations and unexamined technological skills [2].

So Weiser refers to Anthropology as a means of measuring how people and their technology normally interact. He goes on to point out that the computer "as currently implemented and discussed for the future" is designed to be the focus of attention, rather than to behave like other tools and "…to get out of the way of the work." It's shocking to have to put this in writing, but I believe that, in direct contradiction to what Weiser observed and described, the majority of HCI design is still focussed on engaging the user rather than on getting out of his way. Now, I don't really blame young interaction designers for that – though I do think that they would benefit from reading original sources (hint. hint!); I blame their teachers. Yes it is easier to do things the way you have always done them, but that doesn't mean it is the right thing to do. Many designers working in computing want to treat it as though it should be a meaningful experience. Weiser said that it should not be any experience at all. Any engineers who are nodding their heads and gloating after reading that should stop. Most of the engineers I have worked with don't worry about design esthetics at all, but they also don't worry about how humans work. Their intent is to make the machine efficient. After that, well, the user should learn how to use it. That is not technology "getting out of the way", that is technology standing in the way and screaming and stamping its feet like a 2-year old throwing a tantrum. Engineers will tell you that their job is to make the hardware and software work well. As to the final product, well, the user will just have to learn how to work with the system as it is. I believe that Weiser stated the exact opposite, and did so very clearly.

> A key part of this evaluation is using the analyses of psychologists, anthropologists, application writers, artists, marketers, and customers. We believe they will find some features work well; we know they will find some features do not work. Thus we will begin again the cycle of cross-disciplinary fertilization and learning [2].

This idea of iterative cycles of learning is very important to my work, and will be addressed later in this book. As to the acceptance of feedback from these "cross-disciplinary cycles" by programmers and engineers, I'm afraid that I have witnessed much more fertilizer than learning. I'm going to attempt to expand on this discussion of tools in Chap. 5.

The last myth about Ubiquitous Computing that we are going to debunk simply by looking at this paper is the idea that Ubicomp supports the concept of digital assistants and autonomous agents. I admire much of the work being done in that field, but I do wish that they would not try to claim an affiliation with Ubiquitous Computing as conceived by Weiser. He wrote a short thought experiment to illustrate the difference between these ideas and "UC".

> Suppose you want to lift a heavy object. You can call in your strong assistant to lift it for you, or you yourself can be made effortlessly, unconsciously, stronger and just lift it. There are times when both are good. Much of the past and current effort for better computers has been aimed at the former; ubiquitous computing aims at the latter [2].

This differentiation is, I believe, vital to an understanding of Weiser's true intent, and to the reason that modern ubiquitous technology does not match up with the theory of Ubiquitous Technology.

Weiser wanted Ubiquitous Computing to empower humans by providing them with technological resources that they could access through their normal cognitive processes, without having to have any concern at all for the deliberate steps that the technology will have to follow in order to be of use.

Modern ubiquitous technology empowers machines by providing them with the technological resources that they can access through their normal computational processes, without having to have any concern at all for the deliberate steps that humans will have to follow in order to make use of the technology.

This is expressed every time you have to rediscover your favourite features when a familiar software updates its menu structure; every time you have to put off accessing some media until you can install a driver, or every time you find out that you need an extra 20 min to shut down your computer, because it needs to install updates.

Let's go on to Weiser's third paper on Ubicomp. We'll return to the second one at the end of this section, to deal with an issue that, though quite remote when Weiser was writing in 1992, has recently become one of the most contentious aspects of modern computer technology.

Fortunately for the sore eyes and distracted mind of the reader, and also for the nerve-damaged fingers of the author, Weiser's third and fourth papers on Ubicomp are each only two pages long.

Weiser starts the third paper by predicting a boring future based on a purely linear evolution of the computer systems from 1993 [3]. Unfortunately the computer industry in general has managed to give us the very tools that Weiser predicted: "…more laptops, possessing more power, more memory, and better colour displays." Fortunately, we have also experienced a dramatic increase in the kind of technology that Weiser foresaw: specifically the proliferation of cheap wireless networks and interconnected devices. Yes, that's right, those were not ubiquitous back in 1993.

Weiser uses this paper to discuss the intersection of "obtrusiveness" and "intrusiveness" in the implementation of our interaction with technology. While the technology is becoming more unobtrusive, outside information is intruding more in our lives. One need only look at texting to see how that has come to be. An expert thumbtypist doesn't look at the touchscreen to see where the keys are or to make sure that the words are building crrortl – sorry – correctly. But the same person, using the same device, expects to receive a nearly constant influx of messages.

Weiser once more raises the issue that, while an "intimate computer" (think of your smartphone) "responds to your voice and is a personal assistant", ubiquitous computing stays in the background and "gives you the feeling that you did it yourself". Where he goes wrong, at least so far, is in thinking that personal digital assistants (PDAs) would be replaced by dozens, hundreds, or even thousands of throwaway interfaces and display screens, hanging on walls and off wrists, and lying around like scrap paper.

That last seems ridiculous at face value, but every family I know that uses tablets and smartphones has some number of devices that have become communal property and so "…lay about to be used as needed."

Weiser had no doubt that researchers would solve all of the technical issues, leaving "only the psychological, social, and business challenges."

In the fourth paper on Ubicomp, Weiser criticises multimedia computing and intelligent agents, virtual reality and voice input [4]. He writes that all of these could be "good tools", but that all are implemented in a manner that makes them the centre of our attention. A "good tool" should become invisible in the context of use, like a pair of glasses which allow you to "focus on the task, not the tool." The comments are concise and yet well-written, and this short paper may be the best introduction to the idea of Ubicomp. My favourite part is at the end [spoiler alert!], when Weiser proposes the use of childhood as a metaphor and working mental model for how invisible technology might work.

> Our computers should be like our childhood-an invisible foundation that is quickly forgotten but always with us, and effortlessly used throughout our lives [4].

The final paper credited to Weiser was finished after his death [5]. Rich Gold, another polymath from Xerox PARC, finished the paper and John Seeley Brown wrote an afterword. Like the second paper, this one provides a history of the technological developments at PARC.

> In the end, ubi-comp [sic] created a new field of computer science, one that speculated on a physical world richly and invisibly interwoven with sensors, actuators, displays, and computational elements, embedded seamlessly in the everyday objects of our lives and connected through a continuous network [5].

At PARC, this was not purely theoretical research. They implemented their devices, and they implemented Ubicomp. In this final paper, there is an expression of surprise at how quickly it all came together and a clear and hopeful expression of the validity of Weiser's work.

> Once the infrastructure was up and running we clearly saw the vast potential of such a system for augmenting and improving work practices and knowledge sharing, by essentially getting the computers out of the way while amplifying human-to-human communication [5].

At the end of this paper, there is reference to "Calm Computing", the topic of the next chapter, and it might be structurally-clever to segue forward in that manner, but this paper also touches briefly on another issue – the last one I want to address here and now.

This last issue that I want to raise about Ubicomp requires that we turn back to Weiser's second paper [2]. As mentioned earlier, this is an issue that is of vital importance to the world today: the privacy of data. The first sentence of the following quote directly contradicts statements I have heard from a number of computer scientists. The second-last might just strike fear into the hearts of politicians and other profiteers.

> It is important to realize there can never be a purely technological solution to privacy, and social issues must be considered in their own right. In the computer science lab we are trying to construct systems that are privacy- enabled, giving power to the individual. But only society can cause the right system to be used.

In 2015, as I write this, Weiser's words sound like something that could have been written by Cory Doctorow or some other associate of the Electronic Frontier Foundation (EFF). I hope that anyone reading this book can see the inherent argument that we must take responsibility for the uses and misuses built into the devices we create. I hope that is a clearly-understood aspect of individual and professional maturity, regardless of political orientation, whether one is technically-minded, human-oriented, or inspired by the esthetics of design as personified by Mnemosyne and her daughter Thalia (to whom so much of this book may seem a burnt offering).

Weiser expressed concern that "future oppressive employers or governments" might to take away the individual's ability to control their own privacy, and proposed in his words and his actions that the solution to this would have to be in the "wide dissemination of information about [tracking systems] and their potential for harm."

This is why Weiser wrote popular articles about his work, and why he cooperated with reporters from the major newspapers of his country to inform the public about the technology they were developing at PARC, and about the potential for it to be used both to help the average person, and to harm them.

> The result, we hope, is technological enablement combined with an informed populace that cannot be tricked in the name of technology [5].

This book is also aimed at enabling its reader, and in much the same way. I hope that it is clear that I am expounding on history and theory in the first two sections of this book, so that the reader can understand the need to take the kind of personal actions described in the third and final section. Those actions are designed to help you take greater control of your interactions with the ubiquitous technology in your life. I hope that they are designed in a way that will inspire you to adapt and improve on my work, and to share your own work with the world.

Ubicomp Must Be More Than Ubiquitous

The real problem of badly-implemented HCI isn't the computer on your desk – it's the hidden computers everywhere else. You must have heard of the massive automobile recall in 2014 due to faulty ignition mechanisms. It seems that in these cars, if your knee should jostle the ignition system (the part of the dashboard just above your knee), the engine turns off. This, in turn, turns off the power-assisted breaks and the power-assisted steering. The resultant sudden lack of control has killed many people. It's not exactly a selling point for the ubiquity of computers, but I hope it is a selling point for the thesis of this chapter. Computers are everywhere now and we do have to start thinking about just what that means.

Let me tell you a story about my own experience with the influx of computers and computer technology in cars.

Some years ago, I took my car into the shop and they were kind enough to offer me a rental for a few days. When I first climbed into the car, I found that the seat was comfortable and had already been set at a good height and distance from the steering wheel and the pedals. The wheel itself was even set at an angel that suited me. The dashboard controls and displays of the new vehicle were different to those in my car, so I took a few minutes to familiarize myself with their locations and their functions. I checked my mirrors and started the engine.

There were lights everywhere!

There were lights all along the dashboard, but there was also a complex control panel that ran from the seatbelts to the sound system. There were illuminated controls in both arm rests, and similar lights winked at me from all around the steering wheel.

These weren't the soft green and orange lights of my familiar display, but a visual concatenation of turquoise and hot pink and yellow and red. When I blinked the afterimage painted a Jackson Pollock on the inside of my eyelids. The light pollution was enough to occlude my view through the windscreen.

I took a deep breath, found and adjusted the brightness, and took another deep breath. This was a beautiful car, and I would enjoy driving it.

With the lights on, but dimmed, I took another look around, noting the control systems I had missed and wishing I could remove half of them. I could tune the radio with the familiar controls on its face, but also with similar controls on the armrests and on the steering wheel. That just seemed to me to be unnecessarily repetitive and redundant over and over again – if you know what I mean.

But I could live with it, and maybe come to enjoy it. I fastened my belt, ran a visual check of my environs, and went on my way. I few hundred meters later, I stopped at a traffic light and decided to turn on the radio. As I did so, the traffic light turned green and I followed the other cars out into the intersection.

There was something moving in the bottom, right-hand side of my field of view – where nothing should have been moving at all! I glanced at it and was horrified. It was the small rectangular screen of the radio! There was something moving there and – it was scrolling text!

I know how scrolling text works – if you don't read it, it disappears!!

I pulled my eyes away from the nearly irresistible sight of letters rushing permanently out of view, of messages I did not know how to retrieve. With a massive effort of will, I focussed my concentration on the road around me, and made sure that I was still safe.

At the same time, I thumbed the radio power switch on the steering wheel. To my surprise, it had proven to be very useful after all.

So, there is much more to Weiser's idea of "Ubiquitous Computing" than just the ubiquity of computer technology. In the first Ubicomp paper we mentioned earlier, Weiser wrote:

> The constant background presence of these products of "literacy technology" does not require active attention, but the information to be transmitted is ready for use at a glance. It is difficult to imagine modern life otherwise [1].

While the idea of omnipresent, interconnected technology became one of the major focusses of the field of computer science, this aspect of ubiquity, the idea that the technology should be available without demanding attention, was misunderstood or ignored right from the start.

In the next chapter we're going to discuss another major idea put forward by Mark Weiser. The same scientist who predicted ubiquitous computers also warned of the dangers of not designing those computers to work well with humans.

Summary

Ubiquitous is a word often applied to computers. Like computers, that word is everywhere. Unlike the word ubiquitous, computers are a part of our daily lives. Each day we use computers in thousands of unseen ways.

Yes, yes, I am completely willing to believe that you do have a computer of your own, and I believe that -if you say so- you can see it easily... ...but that's not the kind of computer I'm talking about. If you're still confused about how computers can be unseen, you should really read this chapter... ...and probably Chap. 3, as well.

References

1. Weiser M (1991) The computer for the twenty-first century. Sci Am 265(3):94–104, Macmillan, New York
2. Weiser M (1993) Some computer science issues in ubiquitous computing. Commun ACM 36(7):75–84, ACM, New York
3. Weiser M (1993) Hot topics-ubiquitous computing. Computer 26(10):71–72
4. Weiser M (1994) The world is not a desktop. Interactions 1(1):7–8
5. Weiser M, Gold R, Brown JS (1999) The origins of ubiquitous computing research at PARC in the late 1980s. IBM Syst J 38(4):693–696

Chapter 3
Getting Excited About "Calm Technology"

Prof Weiser, you keep using the word 'calm'. I do not think it means what you think it does

Abstract So, as we saw in Chap. 2, Mark Weiser foresaw the change in our relationship with computers; a change that would come with the increased miniaturization, faster processing speeds, and wireless interconnectedness that was just starting to happen. Way back in 1991, in his first paper on Ubiquitous Computing Weiser cites a number of philosophers, a Nobel prize-winner, and a psychologist to try to explain how humans interact naturally with the world; to explain that most of our perception, and mental processing, and even most of our reactions don't happen consciously.

As he wrote, we can use familiar, well-designed tools without noticing them. Like a pair of glasses, once you start using them, you don't focus on them, you use them to focus on what you are trying to do.

Weiser called this kind of interaction "Calm", and he predicted that it would be necessary to design our increasingly ubiquitous computerized tools to disappear, rather than to demand our attention (Fig. 3.1). Along with John Seeley Brown (no relation), he produced two papers to try and explain this concept, and as guidelines for interaction designers.

In this chapter we'll look at those two papers and try to show that the astute reader is likely already familiar with both the concept and the practice of "Calm Technology".

Fig. 3.1 "Machines that fit the human environment instead of forcing humans to enter theirs will make using a computer as refreshing as taking a walk in the woods" – Mark Weiser

Keep Calm and Cite Primary Sources

As discussed in the previous chapter, Mark Weiser saw the coming era of Ubiquitous Computing and came up with a simple idea: that, as a default, all those computer-ised devices shouldn't be designed to treat us rudely – not through the ignorance of the programmers and designers, and not through the manipulative efforts of the marketing department.

> Calmness is a new challenge that UC brings to computing. When computers are used behind closed doors by experts, calmness is relevant to only a few. Computers for personal use have focused on the excitement of interaction. But when computers are all around, so that we want to compute while doing something else and have more time to be more fully human, we must radically rethink the goals, context and technology of the computer and all the other technology crowding into our lives. Calmness is a fundamental challenge for all technological design of the next fifty years. [1]

Weiser and Brown's idea surged in popularity by the end of the 1990s, and had been largely abandoned a decade later. This happens in science when one theory is disproven and replaced by another, but Weiser and Brown's theory had not been replaced by another, it had been replaced by misunderstanding and apathy, and by a desire to "search where the light is".

Let's go back and take a closer look at the two original papers on "Calm Technology". As in our previous discussion of Ubiquitous Computing, there is a lot to be gained from becoming familiar with the original work. As before, I hope that this summary will inspire the student to read the original papers, rather than giving them the false impression of an equivalency that should have been disproven in the first chapter.

The first paper focussed on Calm Technology started with the description of an installation at PARC that was at once technological and artistic: Natalie Jeremijenko's "Dangling String".

Dangling String was a brightly-coloured, 8-ft (~2.6 m) plastic filament that hung loosely from the ceiling in "an unused corner" of a common hallway where it could be seen from many offices. A small electric motor connected it to an Ethernet cable. Ethernet traffic caused the motor to peturbate the string, so that light traffic inspired the occasional twitch, while heavy traffic caused the string to spin wildly and cut audibly through the air.

Please remember that this was the 1990s and it was very common in those days for one's connection to the network to ebb and flow in time with the demands of unseen others. When your computer slowed down, you often could not tell if it was due to circumstances inside or outside of your terminal. If the reduction in process-ing speed interfered too strongly with your work, you would have to get up and go around and try to find out whether tech support was running tests or one of your co-workers was trying to download a photo. Otherwise, it might be a problem internal to your computer, and you would have to queue up for tech support tests of your own. Jeremijenko's project provided that information with no more than a glance, and maybe with less:

> Its output is so beautifully integrated with human information processing that one does not even need to be looking at it or near it to take advantage of its peripheral clues. [1]

Weiser and Brown proclaimed that Jeremijenko's string demonstrated that it was possible to deliberately design technology that would provide important information to the periphery of our senses without interrupting our work or play, a feature that they said might be "the most important design problem of the twenty-first century".

To them, it was vital to demonstrate that information technology could be informative without being demanding, and they pointed out that other forms of technology had made that step. To build a little on their examples, consider that the ability to tan and cure leather, and to cut and sew it into shoes resulted in comfort, not in a constant challenge. The technology of reading and writing and printing and transportation, combine with the successfully-met technological challenges behind pen-making and ink-mixing to enable a Professor in California to relax on a Sunday morning with the New York Times crossword puzzle. Those shoes, that pen, that puzzle, are comforting and encalming, while computers can be frustrating.

Weiser and Brown proposed that the key difference was the manner in which the technology engages with the attention of the person using it. If something demands your attention, then it takes control of your interaction – which means that sometimes it will interrupt you or frustrate you. They proposed that calm technology moves easily back and forth between the centre of our attention and the periphery of our perception.

They offered a bifurcate explanation of the calming value of that transition. The first is that, since Peripheral Interaction uses the peripheral senses to perceive and process information, it enables us to cope with much more information than we could hope to process consciously. "The periphery is informing without overburdening." The second is Centering, the ability to move items from the periphery to the centre and back.

"Without centering the periphery might be a source of frantic following of fashion; with centering the periphery is a fundamental enabler of calm through increased awareness and power."

They based the idea of "periphery" on James J. Gibson's concept of "affordances" as explained in Chapter 8 of his "Ecological Approach to Visual Perception" [2], and popularized by Don Norman in his first book "The Design of Everyday Things" [3] (both of which are or should be mandatory reading, not only for designers but for anyone who wants to build anything for human use). Affordances are relationships between people and the objects they use. The objects often have built-in cues that instruct, remind, or introduce that relationship – like the handle and spout on a teapot. The reader is encouraged to learn more about this, even though Weiser and Brown dismiss the idea by saying that "…it does not reach far enough into the periphery where a design must be attuned to but not attended to" [1].

Weiser and Brown go on to stress the central role that this understanding of the periphery should come into play when designing HCI, explaining that Centering makes us feel at home, connected to the world around us.

With the combination of Peripheral Interaction and Centering, increased information becomes encalming rather that stress-inducing. Though this is counterintuitive, and seems to fly in the face of most interaction design, that is because most design ignores our ability to be subconsciously aware of the vast amounts of information around us without having to give it any of our direct attention until we choose to move it from the periphery to the centre.

> But such designs are crucial. Once we are located in a world, the door is opened to social interactions among shared things in that world. As we learn to design calm technology, we will enrich not only our space of artifacts, but also our opportunities for being with other people. Thus may design of calm technology come to play a central role in a more humanly empowered twenty-first century. [2]

In their second and last collaboration, Weiser and Brown start by returning to the idea of the relationships between ourselves and our technology, and by describing our changing relationship with computers as it progressed from past trends to the then-present.

We are reminded of Weiser's earlier classification of the Mainframe Era, and the Era of the Personal Computer, and of how the time of writing was the transitionary Era of Distributed Computing. All of this is leading us to the Era of Ubiquitous Computing and the need for Calm Technology.

After a brief diversion into a discussion of specific technical matters that might now only be of interest to historians, they go on to talk about how "UC will bring information technology beyond the big problems like corporate finance and school homework, to the little annoyances like Where are the car-keys, Can I get a parking place, and Is that shirt I saw last week at Macy's still on the rack?" [4].

The reader is asked to remember that, even though the examples above seem commonplace in this day and age, at the time that Weiser and Brown were writing their work was so far ahead of the curve that most people considered it ridiculous fantasy. Perhaps most fantastic is the one change that they said would be more important than all of the others.

"The most potentially interesting, challenging, and profound change implied by the ubiquitous computing era is a focus on calm. If computers are everywhere they better stay out of the way, and that means designing them so that the people being shared by the computers remain serene and in control."

The paper then reframes the information from the previous one, offering up deeper explanations and a few more references.

We will end this review with their short illustration of the concepts of "Periphery" and "Centering".

> Ordinarily when driving our attention is centered on the road, the radio, our passenger, but not the noise of the engine. But an unusual noise is noticed immediately, showing that we were attuned to the noise in the periphery, and could come quickly to attend to it. [4]

We'll come back to the question of attention while driving a little later. For now, let's look at another example of calm technology.

What Time Is It?

Having seen the origins of the term, let's run a little thought experiment about "Calm" by following the development and use of an older technology.

Throughout most of the time that there have been humans or human-like creatures on earth, the passage of time during a day or a night could be measured by watching the change of the position of the sun and other stars in the sky or, more indirectly, by watching the changes to the shadows we cast under them. The world has always been replete with signs that can be easily perceived and interpreted for general information. Deeper knowledge or closer consideration can often decode greater information from the same signs either alone or in combination.

Monks in Europe began to mark their prayer times with the ringing of bells, intended to divide the day and night into equal measures. Their formal measurement and declaration of the hour of the day and the passage of time soon became the standard for surrounding communities. This despite the fact that the time between ringing was distorted by the changing period of the day/night cycle that occurs naturally across the changing seasons. There is also the possibly apocryphal story how hunger shaped the length of these "hours". It is said that monastic meals were to be taken at the ninth hour after the rising of the sun. The ninth hour ("nona hora" or "nones") gradually came earlier and earlier until the meal had moved to mid-day, and "nones" had become "noon".

Regardless of inaccuracy or the reasons therefore, about half a millennium ago, at around the same time that "noon" came to mean mid-day, some of the manual ringing of bells was supplanted by clockwork mechanisms. Both sorts of bells quantified the passage of time, and formalised that quantification throughout a community. The display of clock faces furthered the formality of that quantification, making it possible for people to refer to much more specific times throughout their day, and to do so with a glance.

This increase in precision should not be confused with an increase in accuracy. Towns went by their own clocks, often with deliberate indifference to the clocks of their neighbours, but with an increasingly shared sense of time's passage.

That was the case for hundreds of years and, by setting a standard, clocks became necessary. The market grew with necessity, and prices dropped, and components became smaller, and the device evolved into new forms more suited to occupy new landscapes. Clocks appeared in our workplaces and in our homes. Now workers and students could glance into the corner or at the wall and watch the seconds crawl by. Watches moved into our pockets too, and through a brief surge in women's fashion, onto our wrists.

Within a single generation wrist watches had become *de rigueur* among professionals of all genders, and within a century digitization made them ubiquitous. Now you could glance at your wrist instead of the wall. We had always had our own perspective of time, whether or not we shared some portion of that perspective with others. That personal perspective had traditionally been subjective, relying on qualitative measurements, as in T. S. Eliot's famous lament of the social limitations that come with old age, the Love Song of J. Alfred Prufrock:

For I have known them all already, known them all:
Have known the evenings, mornings, afternoons,
I have measured out my life with coffee spoons... [5]

Now you could carry your personal quantitative measurement of time with you, and you could measure it out in hours, minutes, seconds and even fractions of a second. The fact that greater precision creates an illusion of greater accuracy – while in fact reducing the possibility of accuracy – is a problem that can be discussed in more detail elsewhere. As to our discussions here and now, well, what time is it?

Please, look up the time right now.

Really, please do take a break from reading this to check the time right now.

Thank you.

Now, how did you check it?

Back on the farm, in my childhood, my father would have had me face North. The solar system is a clock, he would say, the earth is its face, your nose is pointing at 12, and your shadow is the hour hand. Depending on the time of year, he'd have me offset my shadow in one direction or another, but the method provided a quick answer that was both precise and accurate enough to suit our needs. Since then I have carried watches in my pocket, and I have worn them on my wrist and on my finger. These have usually been more accurate and more precise than the chronometry I learned from my father, but these newer methods never feel to me as though they are quite "right".

So, how did you check the time a moment ago? How many therbligs did it cost you? Therbligs are basic units of motion or action, a way of measuring how many steps must be performed to complete a task [6]. How many steps did you take to look up the time?

My father's method, once practiced, and when applied under conditions where cardinal directions were already known, served to keep me aware of the time, so that I never had to check it. This ongoing peripheral awareness cost me one therblig.

Like looking at the shadows around you, looking at a clock that is already within your line of sight is one therblig. Is that how you checked the time? Did you have to turn your head, or lean to the side, or move a window on your desktop? Each of those would add therbligs.

Please don't worry if you checked the time by leaning in your chair. In fact, it was probably good for you to stretch a little, and leaning doesn't really have to interrupt your work, depending on the task you were actually doing at the time. If you are familiar with the room in which you are reading, you might have been able to lean over so that the clock would be in view without even glancing up from these words until you were in place. Is that what you did, or did you glance at your wrist? If you did glance at your wrist, did you have to turn it so that you could see the clock face? If so, you probably did the turning and glancing quite unthinkingly, so that the four therbligs had hardly any impact at all on your reading...

…but is that what you did?

Or did you check the time on your phone?

Sales of wrist watches have dropped as mobile phones have become ubiquitous. Watches have gone back to being jewellery, because our phones keep track of the time and display it whenever we want to see it. Don't they?

If I want to check the time on my phone, I find that it is a little more complex than just glancing at something that is already on display. I have to:

1. Retrieve my phone from my pocket or from my desk,
2. Open the case,
3. Wake it, and wait a long second or two for that to happen, and then
4. Look at the display.

As I write this, I have just taken 17 therbligs to check the time on my phone. It would have been more if the phone had been in the pocket of my jacket.

Now, according to Weiser and Brown, the real problem isn't the therbligs – they're just a unit of measurement. The real problem is that going through all of those steps to check the time forcibly interrupted my work. In fact, unlocking my phone and reading the displayed time in amongst all of the other text on the screen really interrupted my train of thought.

I had to pay attention to the clock instead of to the time. As Robert Frost might have said, "…and that has made all the difference" [7].

Embracing Calm Technology, Then Deciding It's Easier Not to Worry About It

As discussed in the previous chapter Mark Weiser published a paper in 1991, predicting that the world was about to change into a place where humans would be surrounded at all times by countless seen and unseen computers. He called this the era of "Ubiquitous Computing". However, Weiser did more than predict the ubiquity of computers and computerized devices. He also stressed that, once we are surrounded by computers, those machines will unthinkingly shape our lives to suit the inputs and outputs fundamental to their designs, and we will unthinkingly adapt to them. Weiser called on the people building these smaller, faster, more interconnected computers to try to imagine computers that could provide and receive information in a more natural, human-centered way. He called this approach "Calm Technology".

Professor Weiser wrote:

> Machines that fit the human environment instead of forcing humans to enter theirs will make using a computer as refreshing as taking a walk in the woods [8].

Current issues with interoperability, product design and human factors prevent users from being able to see the forest for the trees, but this does not have to be the case. As mentioned earlier, Professor Weiser theorized that "Ubiquitous Computing" would eventually lead to an era of "Calm Technology" wherein computers would be embedded not only in our devices, but in our lives as well. As he put it:

> *...the most profound technologies are those that disappear. They weave themselves into the pattern of everyday life until they are indistinguishable from it.*

Calm Technology is based on the way that humans process information: the process of plucking things from the periphery of our attention and deciding how to prioritize them is a comforting activity that makes us feel at home and in control. Weiser described this concept of interaction on the very edge of perception by quickly citing the expressions used to describe it in the writing of experts from half-a-dozen different fields. One of those experts is his colleague from PARC, the mathematician and computer scientist John Seeley Brown. Brown was the one who referred to this region of unconscious-but-ready-to-use perception as the "periphery". This concept of the periphery is fundamental to the two papers that Weiser and Brown produced together, and also to the work that makes up the most part of this book. We'll discuss it in more detail soon, including the fact that a misunderstanding of the term led to the creation of the ubiquitous pop-ups and banner ads that plague us whenever we go on-line.

Weiser and the people he cited were not talking about the periphery of a monitor or of a workspace, but of the periphery of our attention – a conceptual space that has no real bearing to any particular region or amount of acreage on a GUI. They were talking about technology that is available for our use, but waits patiently to be noticed, without demanding our attention.

They were talking about making interaction intuitive and natural. In the same way that they had used the term "Ubiquitous" as a label to describe more than mere ubiquity, they tried to unify these concepts of intuitive and natural peripheral interaction under the label "Calm".

Calm Technology describes any tool that can be used with uninterrupted focus on a central task while new outside information is easily perceived and processed peripherally [9]. This dynamic allows the user to decide whether to divert their attention and change their focus at any time. This is the natural means by which all primates interact with their environment [10], and it is a fundamental part of the iterative cycles of perception, evaluation, and reaction that have shaped our evolution and that continue to shape our understanding of, and interaction with, the world around us [11]. Furthermore, as stated above, Calm Technology allows one to focus on their intended action rather than on the tool they are using [1].

This is a completely natural and normal way to interact with the world. In fact, some would argue that it is the way that we do most of our interaction with the world. See, for example, the third chapter in a new book about Peripheral Interaction [12]. This book provides insight into what peripheral interaction might be, and into specific tools developed in order to bring about some semblance of Weiser's Calm. I'd like to refer you specifically to the third chapter, in which an author tries to explain that very little of our interaction with the world around us involves conscious thought; that the vast majority of our information perception and processing has always taken place unconsciously and peripherally. Actually, that author is me. As a result, well, I tend to agree with what he wrote… at least, for now.

Consider the way that you turn the pages on the book you are reading – does it take your full attention? Do you have to switch your full attention away from the content of the book in order to focus all of your efforts on the act of turning the page? For more examples, and deeper discussion, please refer to that excellent volume and to my own chapter. The writing won't be any better than this, but at least you'll find some pretty pictures…

The concept of Calm Interaction is often misunderstood as a means of calming the user, as at The Stanford Calming Technology Lab, and in Rogers' call to abandon the concept in favour of "engaging rather than calming people" [13], as though technology should actively market itself with every use. No one wants their day-to-day technology to be exciting. Sure some of the tools it drives could be exciting, but the underlying technology should be mundane and reliable and so predictable that we consider it dependable; so very unengaging that we don't have to think about it when we use it.

Electricity used to be a frightening new technology, with people afraid to go into buildings that were "wired". At first, they were right to be scared. Wires had a tendency to shock you – sometimes right through the walls, and electric batteries had a tendency to blow up. But the technology became ubiquitous and then it became calm. You can still buy electric devices that will fully engage your attention – in fact you may be using one of them to read this book. I'm using one to write it. But no one wants the underlying use of electricity to be exciting. That would make us uncomfortable.

We don't want to be uncomfortable with the technology that completely surrounds us, we have to be at ease with it, we have to let it rest lightly at the back of our thoughts, at the periphery of our attention. If a light doesn't come on when you use the switch, electricity is so far out of your thoughts, that you will probably test the mechanics of the switch before you think of testing the wiring or the presence of a charge. Really, that's how it should be, we should be at peace with the technology that underlies the tools we use deliberately. Need light? Just turn the switch, and the light comes on. You can even turn on a familiar light without looking, making the adjustment on the periphery of your attention. In fact, can you imagine the marketing of a light switch that doesn't work calmly? I can just see the clickbait headlines:

> She reached for a light and you won't believe what happened next!

As mentioned earlier, "Calm" has also been conflated with the automation of decision processes, as exemplified by Makonin et al. [14] and Olaru et al. [15], and many others, despite the obvious fact that automated decisions remove control from the user rather than simplifying it.

The problem that "Calm" is intended to address is the problem of enabling people to deal with large amounts of information without becoming either overwhelmed by stress or oblivious to the world around them.

"Calm Technology" became a popular buzzword for some years, but it was eventually relegated to the sidelines by the engineers and designers who have built our ubiquitous computerized devices. After all, they ply their trade religiously, in accordance with the articles of faith as they were taught – concern for mechanical and electrical and digital efficiency – and with very little concern at all for whether or not their rituals match up with the parallel but different rituals and articles of faith of their users.

Summary

When an alarm screams for our attention, we anthropomorphise the experience, and reimagine the sound as the voice of someone who is either angry or scared. It behaves like a crying baby in the middle of the night: demanding your attention without explaining why. The alarm screams and screams until someone presses the button or turns the switch or sets the code that soothes it back to sleep.

I'm glad that fire alarms do that – though they could be more informative – but I really don't enjoy being woken up by someone screaming at me…

…by the way, is there a reason you're not reading the chapters?

References

1. Weiser M, Brown JS (1997) The coming age of calm technology. In: Denning PJ, Metcalfe RM (eds) Beyond calculation: the next fifty years of computing. Copernicus, New York, pp 75–85
2. Gibson JJ (2014) The ecological approach to visual perception: classic edition. Psychology Press, New York
3. Norman DA (2013) The design of everyday things: revised and expanded edition. Basic books, New York
4. Weiser M, Brown JS (1996) Designing calm technology. Power Grid J 1(1):75–85
5. Eliot TS (1915) The love song of J. Alfred Prufrock. Poetry 6(3):130–135
6. Lancaster J (2004) Making time: Lillian Moller Gilbreth, a life beyond "Cheaper by the Dozen". UPNE, Lebanon, New Hampshire, USA
7. Frost R (1916) The road not taken, mountain interval. Henry Holt and Company, New York, p 1
8. Weiser M (1991) The computer for the 21st century. Sci Am 265(3):94–104
9. Brown JNA (2012) Expert talk for time machine session: designing calm technology "as Refreshing as Taking a Walk in the Woods". In: 2012 IEEE international conference on Multimedia and Expo. IEEE, p 423
10. Brown JNA (2013) It's as easy as ABC: introducing anthropology-based computing. In: Advances in computational intelligence. Springer, Berlin, pp 1–16
11. Crapse TB, Sommer MA (2008) Corollary discharge across the animal kingdom. Nat Rev Neurosci 9(8):587–600
12. Brown JNA (2016) "…Unseen, Yet Crescive…": the unrecognised history of peripheral interaction. In: Bakker S, Hausen D, Selker T (eds) Peripheral interaction: challenges and opportunities for HCI in the periphery of attention. Human–Computer Interaction Series (In press)

13. Rogers Y (2006) Moving on from Weiser's vision of calm computing: engaging UbiComp experiences. In: UbiComp 2006: ubiquitous computing. Springer, Berlin/Heidelberg, pp 404–421
14. Makonin S, Bartram L, Popowich F (2013) A smarter smart home: case studies of ambient intelligence. IEEE Pervasive Comput 1:58–66
15. Olaru A, Florea AM, Seghrouchni AEF (2013) A context-aware multi-agent system as a middleware for ambient intelligence. Mob Netw Appl 18(3):429–443

Chapter 4
The Evolution of Humans and Technology
Part 1: Humans

"Evolution is a fact amply demonstrated by the fossil record and by contemporary molecular biology. Natural selection is a successful theory devised to explain the fact of evolution."

Carl Sagan, 1977

The Dragons of Eden: Speculations on the Evolution of Human Intelligence

Ha! Who's going to choose the boring one with lots of words and no pictures?

J.N.A. Brown, *Anthropology-Based Computing*, Human–Computer Interaction Series, DOI 10.1007/978-3-319-24421-1_4

Abstract Imagine that you're a proto-prosimian about 65 million years ago. You're about the size of a dormouse and live in the trees. You have a long tail and a pointy nose, but underneath your furry little frame, you have the same basic physical and neurological characteristics of a modern human. What's more, the tiny, furry version of you uses the same kind of physical and mental processes to deal with everyday problems as the version of you currently reading this abstract. According to MacLean's triune brain theory, there are three fundamentally different but interconnected subsystems of the brain, each responsible for a subset of the basic ways that you perceive, process, and respond to the world around you (MacLean 1949).

Spoiler alert
None of those ways is based on a computer's operating system, a viral advertising campaign, or whatever is trending right now on your choice of social media.

Items perceived in any of those three streams can easily become the center of your conscious thoughts, and can just as easily be relegated back to the periphery of your attention. This dynamic environmental focus (DEF) is the key to designing interaction that is truly human-centered. In this chapter, we will briefly examine the natural forces that created the demand for DEF, and demonstrate that you have been using it all of your life.

Evolution, with a Brief Digression to Discuss the Nature of Scientific Theories

"But evolution is just a theory, right? It hasn't been proven."

A friend of mine, a very clever computer scientist, said those words to me while reading through an early draft of the table of contents of this book. I considered the quote from Carl Sagan mentioned at the top of this section, then lifted a pencil from my desk, held it away from us both at shoulder height, and told her the following.

"In the common use of the word theory, it really just means "idea". When someone says "I've got a theory about that", or uses the phrase "conspiracy theory", what they are really saying is that they've come up with a possible explanation for something they don't know for sure. That's not how scientists use the word "theory". We have the same general idea, but we add a little more to it. For a scientist, a theory must be both measurable and falsifiable.

"What that means is that, in order for me to consider something a theory, the idea, the explanation, whatever it is, must:

1. Be something that can be measured – and measured in a consistent way. People working independently have to be able to come up with the same kind of measurement, and;
2. Be something that could possibly be proven false."

I let go of the pencil and it fell to the ground. I picked it up and told her the following story.

> *A few years ago a friend and I were showing a new colleague the beach near our lab in Vilanova i la Geltrù. There for the first time, he pointed at the palm trees and proclaimed them date trees. I pointed out the small yellow berries clustered under the fronds, and explained that I'd heard that there are 15 different species of palms in the region, including one imported from North America for decorative use. We can learn what kind they are from the fruit and from the shape of the fronds, I said, but he wagged his finger and shook his head.*
>
> *He insisted they were date trees, producing dates that we could pick and eat. I pointed out they could be date trees, but that I walked past these particular trees every day, and they were certainly not producing sugar dates. They shed small unripe, inedible berries that the locals did not harvest, but he said that they must produce sweet dates because it is a promise from God that everywhere land meets salt water, man will find date trees for sustenance.*

I dropped the pencil and made a face. As I picked up the pencil, I reminded her that I have family in Newfoundland, an island in the North Atlantic Ocean. It's a big rocky chunk of land completely surrounded by salt water, and I've never seen a palm tree there that wasn't imported. My friend laughed and I dropped the pencil again and this time she picked it up and asked if I was comparing her to the fellow on the beach.

"You're nothing like him. He was certain beyond doubt that he already knew the truth without proof. You are doubtful of my certainty, and say that I have no proof. I'm comparing *you now* to *me then*."

"He was certain that all palm trees that grow near the sea produced sweet dates. I was trying to tell him that his theory was unproven, but he just wanted me to accept his source. It seemed to me that he was unwilling to examine the facts scientifically."

My friend smiled at that, and nodded her head, and she handed me my pencil again, and I held it up and dropped it again to the floor. At her look of exasperation I held up my palms towards her and finished my explanation.

"In science we don't try to prove our theories true, not by citing sources or even through empirical research. In science we can only prove that something is false. When I let go of this pencil, the fact that it falls does not mean that the theory of gravitation is true, but…

"…if just once the pencil were to rise in the air, or float in place, or even just fall more slowly, then it would prove that gravity does not always behave the same way on the same things in the same place. That would mean that our theory of gravitation is wrong.

"Religion knows truth according to faith, with rules that require no proof, or even evidence. Mathematics uses rules and evidence to prove truths. Science uses rules and evidence to disprove theories by measuring things right here in the real world.

We should never claim that a currently-accepted theory has been proven true. At best, it is only working model that we can use to describe some small measurable aspect of the greater, unknown truth.

"Maybe you can try to accept "a *theory* of evolution", like the one that says it happens through natural selection, as a working model. You don't have to have faith in it, just use it for what's it's worth until someone disproves it."

She laughed, and thanked me, and invited me for a coffee as I picked up that poor, abused pencil and set it back on my desk. We left my office and that discussion behind us, but on the way out, I had to add one last detail to the story.... if she would only ask.

She turned back to me as I stepped into the hall. "I thought you said that you were comparing me to *you* in that story...*You* ended up being *right*."

"Me? I make mistakes every day, I told her with a smile. Just because he was wrong doesn't mean I was right. You remember those trees along the beach in Vilanova? Well, I looked it up later. They really were date palms." (Fig. 4.1).

Fig. 4.1 Where the land meets salt water in Vilanova i la Geltrù

Imagine You Are a Little Prosimian, Just About the Size of a House Cat…

About 45 million years ago long-tailed and long-fingered prosimians could look at a single object with both eyes at once, giving a sense of depth perception, and establishing that some things are near and others are further away. In the midst of a rich sensory environment, we had to learn to focus on single tasks without losing our perception of the cascade of environmental input. How would we do that?

About 30 million years later (about 14 or 15 million years ago), we no longer had a tail and the fingers on our feet had become a little shorter than those on our hands. Our faces were flatter, and we had started to spend more time out of the trees and in the tall grasses of what is now Southern Europe. Our cerebral neocortex was now more developed than that of the previously-discussed prosimian, which probably allowed us to better compare possible outcomes of our actions. The question remains, how would we focus on one task while maintaining peripheral awareness?

Approximately 6 or 7 million years later, our ancestors follow the receding warmth and migrate into what will later become Africa. We are bigger now, with a much bigger head and a much bigger brain, but facing the same small problem. We know that this ancestor had delicate, precise, and very powerful fingers, and was as related to modern humans as to chimpanzees and bonobos. But what do we know about how they interacted with their environment?

The truth is that we don't know anything about what happened then. We can only apply inductive reasoning and try to generalize a theory based on the fossil record and the behavior of similar animals today.

Genetically modern humans (GMH) have unusually big and complex upper brains, and so require unusually big skulls. There are a number of interesting theories about the way in which our brains were pressured to grow. Some say that our increased brain size is due to the proliferation of broad-leafed trees and other vegetation during the late Mesozoic Era, which increased the available amount of oxygen in the atmosphere. Others theorize that extra thickness in the cerebral cortex was an evolutionary response to our need for insulation from heatstroke when we moved into a diurnal life on the African savannah.

A skull big enough to house a fully-developed GMH brain cannot fit through GMH pelvic openings, so we are born with a brain that grows and develops over years. GMH are born with a brain only 25 % of adult size. Our closest cousins in the modern world, bonobos and chimpanzees, are born with brains roughly 35 % of adult size. By comparison, the brain of a capuchin or a rhesus monkey is already close to half adult size at birth and their skulls have stopped growing. A GMH brain takes about 8 years to reach full size and then spends about another 8 years (or more) maturing. The result of this is that our young need to be protected for at least 8 years while they develop their mental abilities. This period of learning how to think while learning what to think could be responsible to some degree for the richness of human culture and language. If our brains learn to think while exposed to a particular physical and social environment, wouldn't we naturally develop an understanding of the world, of how things should and must be, based on those environments? If the familiar gives us comfort, couldn't some of that comfort come from the fact that a familiar environment makes it easier for the unusual (and possibly dangerous) to stand out?' Thus, pattern recognition and, more fundamentally, the ability to detect sudden changes in regular patterns becomes an important survival strategy. Let us look even further into the past to imagine how this might have been applied.

Looking 20-million years further back than before, we can see a sort of tree-mouse, a tiny proto-prosimian; our common great-great grand-mama. Her pointy little snout is sniffing at food. Since flowering plants and succulent fruits have not yet spread widely around the world, grandma is less likely to be holding a piece of fruit, and more likely to be holding a nice juicy insect. Since she has not yet inherited eyes that can both look at the same thing at once, her head must be cocked so that one eye can focus on the lovely snack. Her long tail twitches, and grandma thinks about this snack without losing track of everything else going on in the environment.

The proto-prosimian is dealing with the situation in a very human way, processing information in a manner that is probably very similar to the way that her descendants in our earlier examples would have done it. The little proto-prosimian, closer in shape to a modern mouse than to a modern man, is using the natural abilities of brain and body to deal with the problem. The cerebral neocortex, the part of the brain that lays like a wrinkled, six-layered blanket over-top of all the rest, would likely have been very small in the skull of our proto-prosimian protagonist. It would be small, that is, in comparison to modern humans, but vastly bigger in comparison to earlier creatures, if it had existed in their skulls at all. Using three separate parts of the brain simultaneously, the creature is processing input in three different ways. Let's try to imagine it in more detail. (Fig. 4.2)

You are a proto-prosimian sitting in the crook of a branch about 65 million years ago. Your hands have fingers that curve only inwards, and your arms reach only about as far backwards as your peripheral vision can see. At rest, your arms fall to your sides with bent elbows and your hands overlap in front of your chest. I believe that this is your region of focus. Your precise little fingers overlap here and hold things where you can best smell and taste them. It is also the area in which you can most easily focus your eyes on near objects. Of course, this is where you want to hold your food, so that you can really focus on it. At the same time, though, you are aware of your surroundings. Your ears point outwards, shells cupping and adding directional information. Your hair detects wind movement and you sweep your tail back and forth, to add to your chances of early detection of shifting air currents. Our senses work together to form perceptual units out of these data, grouping them according to characteristics like spatial continuity, chronological coincidence and symmetry.

Every now and then you pause, looking away or tipping your head to one side. These interruptions of your routine happen when you have detected something on the periphery of your attention, something that doesn't seem to fit an anticipated pattern and so might become important; something that you might need to consider

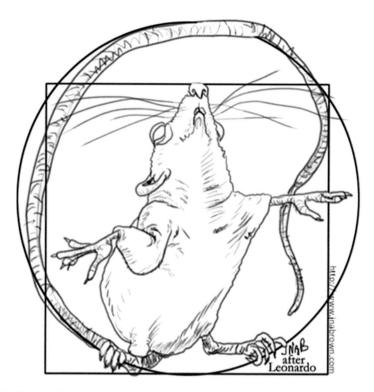

Fig. 4.2 Vitruvian Protoprosimian (which, if nothing else, should at least be a band name)

more deeply. You weigh the importance of interrupting your meal and you either return to eating or drop your hands a little and stop chewing so that you can divert more of your cognitive resources to processing the information.

This is normal behavior.

More than that, this is how we feel comfortable; surrounded by large slow streams of perceptual data, most of which we feel safe to ignore. Though we do not focus our attention on all of these currents of information, we feel their comforting presence around us and we believe that we can access them at any time, shifting our attention, and reassuring ourselves that all is well.

We have processed information this way for the last 65 million years. There have, of course, been situations where something demands immediate attention. Such situations, if they derive naturally, and if we have the opportunity to influence our own chances of survival, must trigger responses as quickly as possible. It is a survival characteristic to be able to respond quickly to stimuli that demand attention, just in case it turns out to be a matter of life or death. Similarly, it is a corresponding survival mechanism to avoid false alarms that might needlessly reduce our resources for dealing with real threats or might even desensitize us to stimuli that will be important later.

Let's talk a little more about these stimuli and our responses to them.

Learning, Adaptation, and Evolution: Circles Within Circles Within a Bar Room Brawl

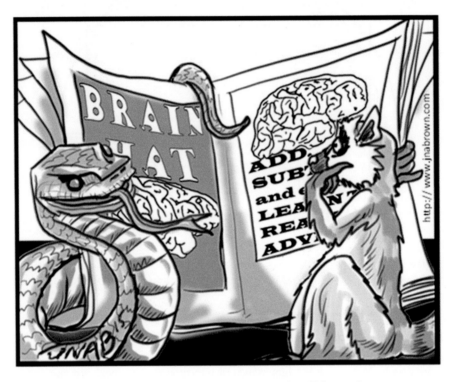

You go ahead and invessst if you want… I'm going to wait and see if they catch on

However it is our brains work (and I'll be proposing one fairly superficial theory and model just a little further on in this book) it is clear that we learn from and adapt to our environment.

As mentioned a few pages ago, we have these giant brains that necessitate a longer-than-usual childhood so that they have time to grow to maturity. While the brain is growing, the human child has an insatiable drive to acquire new data and new means for explanation. She is doing more than learning new things, she is developing theories to explain how these new things relate to the established information she has already acquired.

This fantastic rate of growth is probably the reason that children can learn languages and other skills faster and more deeply than adults. It is probably also the reason behind two things that children do – to the frustration of almost all of the adults around them:

1. They ask "why" incessantly,
   and

2. They store and then regurgitate immense amounts of trivial information about whatever happens to interest them.

The thing is, these are not trivial behaviours. It is true that children will ask for explanations for everything around them until they learn to stop asking. For reasons we will discuss later, it is difficult for children to control their impulses and to separate external facts from internal emotions. As a result of this confounding of data, many children learn restraint based on shame or embarrassment or fear. It is not just that they learn not to ask, they learn that they are wrong to ask, wrong even to wonder at all.

Other children, whose experience is either less emotional or more positive, learn to ask only in the right situations; at the right time or place, or from the right person.

Many children retreat into books or on-line, looking for sources of information that will not belittle their drive to learn or their attempts to make sense of the world. Most find that reassurance in the company of like-minded peers, and build passionately-guarded thought compounds, in which their shared ideas can remain unchallenged, protected from doubt and unbelievers. I believe that an open-ended mental model of attainable knowledge makes it less likely that people will build walls around their opinions and refuse to look further, but I am forced to admit that it seems to be much more comfortable for many people to accept and embrace a strong limit on what they could learn, and to project hostility and ignorance on those who disagree. In Chap. 9 I'll talk more about this emotional, reactive kind of thought and the opinionated, segregated world-view that seems to result from it. For now, let's return to the way that children try to gather data and then try either to fit it into the mental models they have, or to form new mental models that account for the new information.

I remember this process from my own childhood, and I'd like to share one of those stories with you. Looking back, I am proud of my actions, but at the time, it was very embarrassing.

I learned to read at a wedding. Shortly after I turned 5 years old, a wedding took place in our home. My primary job was to be the ring-bearer. My secondary job was to stay out of the way. On the big day, the groom gave me a giant comic book to read, in order to help me with my second job. It was an "80 Page Giant" as they used to call them, full of reprints from the past three decades, the kind that sold for more than twice the usual cover price: 25 whole cents! The comic was World's Finest #170, and all of the stories featured Batman and Superman working together. Taking my second job as seriously as my first, I read the book from cover to cover... sort of. I mean, I wanted to read it, but I didn't know how. I asked a number of usually helpful people to read it to me, but was rebuffed. I sat with the book for hours, turning the pages and wishing the letters made sense. Then I noticed something obvious for the first time. Batman's logo had six letters with his cape behind them and with his face in the middle. Three letters on one side and three letters on the other! B-A-T and M-A-N. I could read! I had already learned how to sing the names of the letters in French, but now I knew how to pronounce five of them in English! ...and I knew how to write three words! B-A-T and M-A-N and B-A-T-M-A-N!! No, wait! Not three – five!! I knew five words, because right there on the cover, right next to Batman's logo was the logo for Superman – and it had the same last three letters! BatMAN and SuperMAN had the same last three letters! So the first four letters in Superman's logo had to spell the word "super".

I went through the comic again and again for the rest of the day, finding every instance of my five words. "Bat" and "Man" and "Batman" and "Super" and "Superman".

Later that day I tried to show my older sister what I had figured out – that I could read now, too! She was furious. I was doing it wrong, and I was stupid, and that's not how to read!

Boy, was I humiliated. I don't think that she and I ever talked about reading again. I still tried to figure out words, and I fell in love with dictionaries, but I stopped trying to talk with other kids about reading. I went to school and learned to read words from start to finish, rather than by looking for familiar pieces, but I still did it my way when no one was watching. It was years before I realized I didn't have to be embarrassed about "reading the wrong way".

So we learn, and we adapt, and we try to improve both at each turn of the wheel. What's more, we do it all in an unpredictable environment; unable to guess the source of the next reward or rebuff.

But we try to prepare for what the future will bring, and we try to base our preparations on what we know. Sometimes, though, what we know is not enough and we have to try new things – not just the probing and curious experimental step forward that is part of the cycle of learning we have already touched on, but a bold step into a new way of doing things.

We Adapt More Than Our Behaviour

When I was a young man, I worked for some time as a free-lance illustrator. I loved the challenge of ever-changing fields and the chance to do a lot of free-hand drawing, but I had a strange rule: I didn't like to use rulers, T-squares, French curves, or other guides. I felt that I had to work free-hand in order to be truly challenged. After all, it's hard work to paint straight lines or smooth curves, and it showed some skill.

It also wasted a lot of time. Working free-lance one tries to be as good as possible in order to earn a shot at more work, but one also learns to be as fast as possible in order to have the time to take on any more work you are offered.

I hung a sign behind the lamp that perched over my drafting table. It read: "EVOLVE: Learn to use tools".

In the years since then I have left that profession and those tools behind me. I haven't sat at a drawing table in years but, after that initial success, I do still use some version of that sign. The original is long since gone, which gave me the easy chance to make a slight change to the text. The one hanging between my monitors now reads:

"ADAPT: Learn to use NEW tools".

Maybe making a sign of your own will help to motivate you to improve your own skills. Mine serves the dual purpose of motivating me acquire new skills, and motivating a fair number of my visitors to make jokes about "old dogs".

Humans have adapted to our tiny little world in a wide variety of ways. I'd really like to talk for a while about human adaptation to life in space. I'd like to, but I don't have the personal experiences to relate to it directly, or the wide body of data that would allow generalizations that you might relate to. I will touch on it in passing, just because it's cool, and because I want to mention one particular problem that needs a solution. After all, I believe that the way to find solutions is to share the problem. I won't go into details here, but at least those of you who are interested will now have someplace to start.

When humans stay in the micro-gravity of near-earth orbit they experience progressive bone loss. We adapt to near weightlessness by shedding bone mass, and that makes us fragile when we come home.

This is a serious problem that must be solved if we are going to build footholds away from our mother planet. Returned astronauts have to go through physical therapy just to be able to walk without pain and risk of injury under Earth-normal gravity. Some details are available to the scientific community thorough formal reports [2–4]. One of the authors on the most recent paper cited there is Canadian astronaut Chris Hadfield. He has also published more personal reports of the psychological and physiological effects of being in space [5]. You may already know the name. Maybe you saw the photos he posted on-line while he was in space, or the many videos in which he demonstrated life on the International Space Station by answering questions from children. If you're lucky, you also saw his two great musical performances – a live broadcast of an original song and an officially-endorsed cover of David Bowie's "Space Oddity". If not, you should really take the time to track at least some of them. I think that seeing a small sample will encourage you to look for more.

I think a partial answer to bone degradation might be deliberate exercises of the small, usually unconsciously-controlled muscles that allow our bones to move in coordinated effort, like the multifidus muscles in the spine or the piriformis, and obturator internus, for example, in the hips. Unfortunately, I just don't have the knowledge to begin to frame a formal investigation of that idea, or even to develop any other insights. Do you? I really believe that it would be worth investigating… …and maybe you'd get to meet Chris Hadfield! If you do, please ask him how he's enjoying his latest retirement.

Let's take a closer look at a different adaptation problem relating to invisible conditions in our environment; one that we are all more likely to have experienced first-hand.

How long can you hold your breath? You can test it right now if you want. I'm willing to wait right here until you've taken a measurement in seconds. In fact, you had might as well take three measurements. If one is significantly different from the others, then you should think about why, make a plan to avoid that problem and try taking three more measurements. I recommend that you wait a half an hour or so before you repeat your set of trials. I don't want to find out later that you passed out while reading this book. It might be good for publicity, but I would worry that you might have hurt yourself.

So, how long can you hold your breath? Write it down.

Now, how long can you hold your breath while walking, rolling, or other light physical activity? Please do not hold your breath during heavy physical activity – that's dangerous!! There is nothing at all impressive about hurting yourself, and holding your breath while you lift weights can cause serious damage. Actually the same is true about holding your breath while trying to force out a reluctant bowel movement. See what I mean? It's really, not impressive at all.

But I digress.

How long can you hold your breath? They say that the current world champion free diver held his breath for nearly 12 min. I used to be able to last just about 3 min, having trained for years to try and match Harry Houdini's claim. Ever since I had pneumonia a few years ago, I can barely last one. That's the bad kind of adaptation – the kind that diminishes us. There will be more about those later.

If you've ever watched the Olympic Games, and statistically, it is likely that you have, then you may already know about the influence of altitude on sports performance. Athletes, who have trained at higher altitudes - even if only for a few days, perform better at high altitudes than those who have not had a chance to adapt to the "thinner air".

In 1953, Sir Edmund Hillary of New Zealand became "the first man to climb Mount Everest". Twenty-five years later, Peter Habeler of Austria and Reinhold Messner of Italy became "the first to summit the same mountain without carrying additional oxygen". The formal medical opinion of the time was that such a task was impossible, and Messner and Habeler described the extreme effort of working so hard at such high altitude, but both men had done a lot of climbing in "thin air" and had learned to adapt.

Now, the story of those two record-breaking climbs is also a story of socio-cultural adaptation. You see, when Hillary made his ascent, he was in the company of another man, one who was hardly acknowledged in the world-wide press and their initial talk of record-breaking feats.

Tenzig Norgay was a Sherpa, one of the indigenous peoples of Tibet. He is now included in all accounts of Hilary's climb, but never received the same honours either at home or abroad. In fact Norgay had climbed Everest seven other times, and had been within 200 m of the summit the year before, with a Swiss team.

Hillary and the leader of the expedition were both knighted by the Queen of England. Hillary said that he and Norgay reached the summit together. Looking back across the years, it is easy to assume that our recent predecessors were not as enlightened as we are today, when it comes to the treatment (or even the acknowledgement) of indigenous peoples.

I will not discuss the treatment of indigenous peoples here, at least not in the detail that it deserves. As a dual citizen of Canada and the United States, I have inherited a terrible tradition of abuse – historical, recent, and on-going. I am not willing to discuss the internal politics of Nepal, but I do not want to miss this opportunity to address an important form of adaptation.

As I am finishing this book, there has been big news in Canada. Seven years ago, the Government of Canada made an "official apology" for the historical treatment of indigenous people, specifically, for their mistreatment in a programme of assimilation through enforced enrolment in residential schools outside of their home communities that ran for more than 120 years. As I write this, the independent body investigating that school system has finished a 6-year investigation and released the summary of its report. Justice Murray Sinclair, chairman of the Truth and Reconciliation Commission of Canada presented the summary, which concludes:

"The Canadian government pursued this policy of cultural genocide because it wished to divest itself of its legal and financial obligations to aboriginal people and gain control over their lands and resources. If every aboriginal person had been 'absorbed into the body politic,' there would be no reserves, no treaties and no aboriginal rights" [6].

I am very proud of the idea that the entire country of Canada will now try to adapt, socially, culturally, politically, and legally, to a new understanding of how we – as a people – treated our brothers and sisters. I hope that we will find a new way of dealing with each other, based on open and logical thinking, rather than the reactive and emotional patterns we have followed in the past. To have those reactions is an unfortunate reality of human thought processes. To use them as the basis of political policy is a terrible embarrassment.

I'll discuss those alternative mental processes in Chaps. 9 and 12. Here I have tried to keep the focus to the idea of adaptation and evolution. We have focussed mainly on physiological adaptation, but I hope you'll agree that the socio-psychological ones are also challenging. In human history, we moved from being nomads with temporary fishing camps and hunting camps, to living in settlements. Our houses became increasingly permanent and we settled in villages and towns and cities.

And we settled into chairs. It is normal to sit all day now, at work or at school, but this is an idea that would have shocked our ancestors all the way back to the proto-prosimians we were looking at back at the beginning of this chapter.

How on earth did we ever come to expect that most everyone should sit all day? It used to be that only specialists could afford to that.

Summary

This chapter was the first of three that have the word "evolution" in the title.

If you believe in evolution for the wrong reasons, then you might just believe that you should really read this chapter (and the next two) – purely out of team spirit, and with no regard for the actual content.

If you don't believe in evolution, then you should really read this chapter (and the next two) just so that, when somebody says that you never even tried to understand evolution, you can answer that you read three whole chapters on the topic, written by a real scientist/evolutionist/atheist, who believes that humans influence climate change and denies that his home country is either in (or particularly close to) the centre of the universe.

...

Actually, if you believe in evolution for the right reasons, then you should read this chapter for a small insight into the beginning of an argument that will grow through the rest of this book. An argument that offers an explanation of the differences between the way we design our computers to give us information and the way that humans normally perceive in our natural and built environments.

The same reasons apply if you don't believe in evolution. Really, though, if you don't believe in evolution, then I think that you should raise chickens. Seriously, I raised chickens in my youth, and my father continued to do so for decades. I learned a lot about the inheritance of ancestral characteristics when talking with chicken farmers, and a lot about the forces of natural selection watching the roosters and hens in the yard. Did you know that there are hundreds of varieties of chickens in the world right now, and that some factory farms only raise and sell first-generation hybrids? This is done so that they can unnaturally select which of the usual breeding characteristics are expressed in the chickens they end up with, without having to worry about whether or not the genes combine well beyond the first generation.

You can learn a lot about evolution from farmers. It's one of the tools that they've been using for thousands of years.

References

1. MacLean PD (1949) Psychosomatic disease and the "Visceral Brain": recent developments bearing on the Papez theory of emotion. Psychosom Med 11(6):338–353
2. Mack PB, Lacuance PA, Vose GP, Vogt FB (1967) Bone demineralization of foot and hand of Gemini-titan IV, V and VII astronauts during orbital flight. Am J Roentgenol 100(3):503–511
3. Iwamoto J, Takeda T, Sato Y (2005) Interventions to prevent bone loss in astronauts during space flight. Keio J Med 54(2):55–59
4. Marshburn TH, Hadfield CA, Sargsyan AE, Garcia K, Ebert D, Dulchavsky SA (2014) New heights in ultrasound: first report of spinal ultrasound from the international space station. J Emerg Med 1(46):61–70
5. Hadfield C (2013) An astronaut's guide to life on earth. Penguin Random House Canada, Toronto
6. Norman A (2015) 'Our strength comes from the land': the hybrid culinary traditions of the six nations of grand river in the early twentieth century. Cuizine. doi:10.7202/1033506ar

Chapter 5
The Evolution of Humans and Technology
Part 2: Technology

*Look, I'm just saying that our model hasn't changed in about 2,000,000 years
and maybe it's time to consider adding some new features...*

Abstract In this chapter we will examine the evolution of tool use. There are three specific ideas that I hope to introduce here. The first is that our tools evolve in parallel to ourselves, each adapting to changes in the other and to social and environmental pressures. Tools are invented and improved by these pressures, and the same pressures move some tools into prominence and others into obsolescence.

We will again discuss Dynamic Environmental Focus (DEF), and how it may have enabled us to use group dynamics to survive in a hostile environment that would have killed more individualistic animals. DEF also plays an unconscious part in our adoption and adaptation of tools. Specifically, in order to become truly useful, a tool must allow the user to shift their attention without accidentally endangering themselves and those around them.

Because evolution is a slow and unconscious process, we are often unaware of the qualities that make the tools we use good or bad – instead we adapt our behaviors to suit them as though they were one of the implacable forces of nature to which we had been adapting for millions of years before we started building tools (Fig. 5.1). We feel an unspoken pressure to preserve the tools and tool-based behaviours of our ancestors. I call this Cross-Generational Habit. I will spend a little time discussing it in the third section of this chapter.

Before we get to those ideas though, in order to truly understand tool use, we have to look backwards a little ways.

Toolmaking and Our Pre-human Ancestors: Setting the Scene

The use of tools by our pre-human ancestors is generally believed to have begun in the Olduvai Gorge some 1.9 million years ago, but I believe that we've been using tools for a lot longer than that. Chimps and monkeys use tools, and so do some birds. I have even seen video of fish using a man-made tool to feed themselves. That might not count as being a "tool-user", but it makes me wonder what they might be doing that I haven't seen. Besides, if you have to make a tool in order to be counted as using it, then I guess I'm not really a "computer user".

Anyway, we know that other animals use tools, but that they don't do so in the same way that we do. Experts will tell you that the difference is a difference of degree [1], much like the purported differences between our spoken languages and the nattering of some of our closest relatives [2].

I have this idea that our social behaviour during the growth of our giant brains gave us insights that turned nattering into language, and fear into multi-tasking, and task-sharing into the chance to specialize in tool development.

These are just ideas. I can't even call them hypotheses because I can't imagine a scientifically-valid way to test them. I see parallels in other species, and I think I see more of it among those that are closer to having shared culture and language, but there are too many variables to control. These ideas stay ideas.

I don't know of anything I could measure in order to disprove them. This means that, as a scientist, I can only propose them as ideas for you to consider. Well, I could follow in the footsteps of other scientists before me and write speculative fiction about the ideas, or even found a religion based on them. Both of those things have happened, and I'm told that in one particular instance, the latter was born in a discussion of how poorly the former paid.

Fig. 5.1 We tend to forget that our common tools were ever uncommon, and that we ever had to adapt to them. The English word "Hello" used to be synonymous with "Hey", just like it is in German, and was considered a rude way to answer the phone. Alexandre Graham Bell preferred the phrase: "Ahoy-hoy"

For now, I'll hold off on the religion, and limit myself to offering you a small sample of a fiction, just enough to illustrate my ideas. I did that earlier in this chapter, talking about prosimians and proto-prosimians, and I hope you'll bear with me as we do it again.

"Return with us now, to those thrilling days of yesteryear…"

> *You live in a tree, and in a crowd. Your crowd spreads out during the day, maybe seeking sunlight and warmth, or shade and free-moving air. Always you watch, and smell, and listen to, and touch your siblings. They are extensions of your sensory system, and they protect you from harm. You natter incessantly, comforted by the constant feedback of non-distress sounds, and you participate as well as you can, because exclusion would mean solitude and, here in the trees, solitude means death.*
>
> *So, if one screams, repeat it and if one flees, join the stampede. If one becomes suddenly silent, then be very, very afraid. Natter in calm and soothing tones, and be a contributing member of the community.*
>
> *Night is terrifying; one long horror. It is not that the danger is unseen. You can smell it and you know that it can smell you. The only questions are whether it will come to eat you tonight, and whether you will be among those who manage to escape?*
>
> *Climb into the sleeping pile. If you chance to be in the middle, then you can relax. You don't need to spread your attention so thin now, you can count on your siblings to provide the alarm. They'll let you know when you should focus your attention outwards again. Until then you can do something solitary creatures cannot; you can focus all of those senses locally. Use them to hunt for nits on your sister's back. If you do a good job, then she will be more willing to trust you with her back in the future, and you will be able to trust her with yours.*

This situational, trust-based ability to switch back and forth between streams of information received and processed by different sensory systems seems to me to be unique. As mentioned earlier, I call it Dynamic Environmental Focus (DEF), and I believe it is only possible in creatures whose conscious and unconscious thoughts compete for control. I believe that the situation I've just described to you may have been one of the stimuli that sparked the co-development of different cerebral abilities in our ancestors and their association with different regions of the brain. It may have, or it may not. In either case, it is an interesting idea. I will discuss the idea of a multi-stage brain, including my own model and a few others, in Chap. 9. Another interesting idea is that the same DEF put us in a position to turn nattering into language.

> *The nattering surrounds you and is comforting. It seems to repeat the message that there is nothing to fear, nothing to fear. Sometimes you think that you hear more in it. Your Auntie is offering to pick nits, or your Grandmother is saying that she is thirsty and thinks that you should all go to the pond. Sometimes your cousin makes a noise, just a little noise, that seems to hold more information, that seems to say that she knows what you dreamed last night, and that is somehow even more comforting than the rest of the blanket of sound. You wrap yourself in that blanket, and you rest. Maybe tomorrow the message will come again…*
> *…maybe you will think of a way to answer.*

In the middle of the pile, there is comfort and the luxury of rest. On the outside there is fear and the responsibility of vigilance. In the very centre there might be a space for something different. Could there be a few in the very centre of the pile who cannot reach anyone to groom? Would they have to be more soothing then in their nattering? Would they have to find other things to do with their hands, and with their brains?

If you do not need to guard or groom, then how should you spend your curiosity and your energy? Might this be the space in which our ancestors were creative? Was this the studio where non-urgent communication could develop? Was it the workshop where animalistic tools could get the focussed attention that would enable our ancestors to develop them into something more?

We know that they were making stone tools a few million years later, but wooden tools wouldn't have survived. We believe that, unlike the cases of tool-making among chimps and birds and many other animals, these early stone tools were made by specialists.

Toolmaking and Toolmakers: The Story of the Knappers

When I started writing this book in 2014, the second section of this chapter was going to read quite differently. I've left the first section as it was, but I'm introducing some new information here. As mentioned in the first paragraph of this chapter, it is well-understood that the stone age, the beginning of the use of deliberate stone tools, started about 1.9 million years ago.

Sometime between 1960 and 1963, Mary and Louis Leakey, and their son Jonathan, found a series of fossils amidst the earliest evidence of stone tool-making in Olduvai Gorge, in Tanzania. In 1964, a team of experts judged these remains to be more developed than the australopithecines previously found in the region because their prognathic jaws held smaller teeth and rested under larger braincases. It was decided that the more evolved creatures were a new, earlier species of man, a man who first used tools. This great-grandmother to us all was named "handy man" or Homo habilis [3].

For the record, when I say "man" here, I mean "creature from the genus Homo, which includes you and me (regardless of gender), and all of our parents and grandparents all the way back to "Jonny's Child" the nickname they gave to sample OH7.

For as long as I have been aware of archeology, and the Leakey family, and Olduvai Gorge, ever since my father held me on his knee and told me stories about the ancient bones and stone tools that gave us clues about our earliest ancestors, I have known that location and that rough date, and the idea that it must have been humans who were using those tools.

This is no longer the accepted theory.

On the 21st of May, 2015, an article appeared in the 521st volume of Nature, that changed all of that. Sonia Harmand and a team of 20 collaborators published compelling evidence that the manufacture of stone tools was going on about 700,000 years earlier than had previously been believed [4].

This news is the result of new fieldwork, as opposed to the result of going through old finds. Their discovery in West Turkana, Kenya, is a 3.3 million year old tool-making site they have catalogued as Lomekwi 3. More than that, the fossils reveal that the stones were worked with different strategies that reveal a deliberate under-standing of the structural properties of the rocks they were using. On top of that, the Lomekwian tool makers predate the Oldowan knappers from Tanzania, which means that the archeological record now goes back seven thousand centuries further than it did last year.

This challenges our prideful assumptions regarding the pivotal role of man (humans, the genus Homo) in the manufacture of stone tools. Remember, 50 years ago, the experts agreed that these early stone tools must have been made by an earlier-than-previously-known species of man.

Now we are forced to either push our genus back even further in time, or to accept that tools were made and used by our pre-human ancestors.

That is cool! Seriously, you may think that a bow-tie or a fez is cool – and they are both demonstrably cool – but this is a beautiful opportunity to test our thinking. Will we be scientific about it, or dogmatic?

You see, this discovery and its revelations, reminds us of two things that are really important for true scientific thinking:

1. That knowledge is dynamic, not static,
    and;
2. That our attempts to classify knowledge will always be oversimplified.

We are limited creatures, able to perceive only the smallest fraction of our sur-roundings, and it is the nature of the universe to contain a greater breadth and depth of knowledge than we can grasp. Our theories and models are just iterative tools intended to grow and adapt and change as we slowly expand our understanding.

So, will we adapt our tools, or will we protect them from a world that challenges their usefulness?

What are the repercussions if we refuse to adapt our tools, if we cling to our old ideas in defiance of the evidence before us, and in defiance of our previously-stated intent to be scientific?

What would you do?

What will you do?

Who, me? What is my reaction to this news? How do I feel about the challenge to the science that I literally learned on my father's knee?

I feel excited! I feel happy that the world of knowledge is expanding. What's more, I know that my father would have felt the same. He was a polymath and a progressive; an avid follower of advances in all of the sciences and arts, with a sin-cere interest in learning as much as he could and a deep-rooted ability to give up old biases in the face of new knowledge.

In that, as in many other things, he was my role model. Our tradition is a tradition of looking forward, of adaptation; of standing with your feet grounded in measurable reality, with your hands, and eyes, and efforts focussed on accomplishing the tasks before you, and with your thoughts questing into the unknown.

I encourage you to do the same.

But I'll understand if it is easier to change some ideas than others. Sometimes it is not the traditions were are aware of that we hold most closely, but the ones that we don't even realize are there.

Toolmaking and Tradition: Sometimes We can't See Over the Workbenches and Gravestones of Our Ancestors

I have given a couple of talks to the international design community on an Anthropological theory of mine. If that seems strange to you, I've also introduced the idea at conferences full of engineers and computer scientists whose specializations ranged from multimedia data retrieval to artificial neural networks. I call this theory Cross-Generational Habit.

Every time I talk about Calm Technology with computer scientists, I mean every-single-time, there is always at least one person who pipes up with some comment equivalent to:

But I like my computer just the way it is!

Of course you do, I reply, patting them on the shoulder, now sit down and shut up while the rest of us try to evolve.

Well, okay, I don't really say that, but boy is it tempting!

Some people would be most content if the world were to mold itself to their fluid, self-serving, and completely unreliable memories of an entirely fictitious mental construct they think of as the "good old days". The "good old days" are often associated with childhood, or the teenage years, but they never really existed. They are a construct of the emotional and illogical part of your brain, used specifically to try and convince the rational part of your brain that there is some external evidence for whatever fictitious, prejudicial, and illogical argument it is trying to make.

There's a commonly understood experience among North Americans. The idea is that you're sitting in one of the archetypal restaurants that offer free refills of coffee. Please don't interrupt my story with a comment about the terrible quality of coffee in a North American restaurant! I don't want to hear how much better it is in Austria or Spain or Italy, or in Bagdad or Damascus or Bahrain… and this certainly isn't the moment to discuss how much better it is to drink a lovely cup of tea with warm milk, or with lemon, or steeped slowly with a dash of roasted and ground rice. Please, just try to fit your mind around this example. I promise that if we should meet in person, I will be happy to try a cup of the warm or cold drink that you think is the best. For now, let's get back to North America, and to the lukewarm, watery, and bitter beverage that we love.

So, you're working on a "bottomless" coffee, and you've been drinking it for a while. It has taken a few cups, but you've finally achieved the perfect balance of coffee and cream and sugar: it is the right temperature and has the right flavour, and you are going to savour it now. Now it will taste the way that you like your coffee to taste. Now it is ideal. That is, of course, the very moment that a passing waitress "tops you up", pouring fresh coffee into your perfect creation, and upsetting its balance.

Well, that's how some people feel about changes in society, or television schedules, or the crowd on the street, or technology. In fact, that's how most people feel about most changes to most of those things. Technology just happens to be one them.

We have a strong compulsion to trust the things we know, and to distrust the ones we don't know. Strangely, we don't like to admit this to ourselves. The result is a reliance on what I call Cross-Generational Habit, doing things the way our great-great grandparents did, without having the decency to thank them, or even to be aware of it. Consider the way you fasten your shoes to your feet, or the position and orientation of steering wheels in cars. Please allow me to explain.

In Chap. 4 of his book Orthodoxy, G.K. Chesterton wrote that

> Tradition means giving a vote to the most obscure of all classes, our ancestors. It is democracy of the dead [5] (Fig. 5.2).

I don't agree with the conclusions he draws in his

> explanation, not of whether the Christian Faith can be believed, but of how he personally has come to believe it.

I do, however, respect his thinking and his turn of phrase.

> The writer regards it as amounting to a convincing creed. But if it is not that it is at least a repeated and surprising coincidence.

Fig. 5.2 Because, with many, many things, it is much easier not to decide for yourself

It is interesting and informative that the lifelong Christian finds it possible to say that his faith would have to be either the result of "a convincing creed" or of "surprising coincidence". I would sooner say that it might have been the result of an underlying and unnoticed adherence to tradition.

> Tradition refuses to submit to the small and arrogant oligarchy of those who merely happen to be walking about. All democrats object to men being disqualified by the accident of birth; tradition objects to their being disqualified by the accident of death.

As clever as the idea is, I would take it further.

We know that shoes have been around since the last ice age. That's the earliest evidence we have of footwear; pieces of skin wrapped up over the foot and then tied in place. In time this changed from being a tool that everyone built for themselves to being a tool built by specialists. Instead of a temporary item that would be replaced either with the change of seasons or as needed, footwear became long-lasting. Cured and polished and brushed it could be used for years or even for a lifetime. In one of life's lovely turns, the footwear industry has become absurdly commercial, with a marketing model based on constant and incessant replacement.

Are there better ways to attach protection to your foot? Sure there are, but they just never become as popular as what we all know. Maybe when 3D printing becomes ubiquitous, we will start to print our own, perfect fit, one-piece shoes that just naturally embrace each foot in a gentle hug.

A surprising amount of the technology around us could be better-designed and better-used; could be, but won't be, because we use it unthinkingly, as though it is a natural part of our immutable and unchangeable environment. Weiser warned that, if we were not careful, we would come to see our computers the same way. By then, it would be too late to make real changes to how we interact with our computerized technology. Not sure what I mean? Consider why electric lights either sit on tables or hang from fixtures on walls or the ceiling. It is due to the fact that the first household electric wires ran where the gas pipes had been, and those in turn had originally led to sconces and stands that were previously used for candles and torches. Wouldn't life be nicer if you didn't have to squint at the bright lights every time you raised your gaze indoors? Wouldn't it be nicer not to have to choose between pools of shadow and pools of light? Is it hard to imagine an alternative of indirect lighting and general atmospheric illumination? We have the technology for it, but most people can't perceive it as something of value. It is too different from what they know.

Let's take a look together at another example of cross-generational habit.

Why do cars have steering wheels? The idea is pretty ridiculous if you really think about how bizarre they are. Let's take a look at them together, okay?

Now, imagine driving along in your car. This means that you're moving much faster than you can run, and you're doing it in a shell that weighs much more than anything you have ever or could ever carry. Sounds like something that shouldn't worry you at all, right? Okay, your street is approaching and it's time to redirect the mass of the bulky metal and plastic shell you're sitting in. So how do you do it? It's just like turning when you're running right? You just sort of lean to one side and take a little more weight on that foot – maybe bend that knee a little more – and, voilà, you've turned. No, it's not like running at all. You can't do it instinctually.

You turn by pointing the front wheels of the car to the place you want to go, right? Well, no; it's more abstract than that.

First of all, turning those wheels means that they are now using some of their momentum to go sideways, and they are taking the front of the car with them. That means that the front of the car is now moving forward more slowly. The back of the car, on the other hand, is still moving forward at the same speed it was using before. When the front slows down in a forward direction, and speeds up in a sideways direction, it's as though it is using judo on the back of the car. The back swings sideways and, hopefully, gets pulled into the new path. I say hopefully because, if you were going too fast, or if your tires got either too much traction or too little, then your car will either "spin out" or roll. Unlike judo players, your car is not able to roll safely until the momentum is spent and then land upright with no ill effects. The faster you are going, the more likely you are to wipe out. This is why many people slow down before turning… and why you should, too.

Secondly, if you just point the wheels where you want to go, then you cut through turns. This takes you through obstacles rather than around them. We all know someone who cuts through their turns like this. If your family and friends all drive, and you don't know which one is the driver who cuts through turns, it may just be you.

So how do you avoid cutting through turns? You turn by pointing the wheels into a curving path that can slowly become a path towards the place you want to go. That means another level of abstraction, and that means the problem is even further removed from the simple task of turning while you run. You have to make those wheels turn in a non-intuitive way.

Imagine holding a steering wheel right now. How much do you turn it to turn the car? What's the relationship between the degree of turning one and the degree of turning the other? It isn't a direct relationship, right? Not if you have power steering. That's not even the weirdest part. The weirdest thing is the position of the wheel itself. There are wheels beneath you and a little forward of where you are sitting. They are also located off to either side of you, a different distance in each direction. You are trying to turn wheels that you can't see, on an axis that you can only imagine, by rotating a wheel that is offset from them in three dimensions and at least one axis of rotation.

So why do we use steering wheels? Some of the earliest cars used rudders and other steering mechanisms. One theory I quite like is that the angled steering wheel, as abstract it is, and as dangerously as it is placed compared to the driver's fragile body, allows us to position our hands as though we were holding the reins of a horse. That would have been *the* well-established and generally-accepted interface for "driving" at the time.

So the wheel would have given the car's control system a tactile familiarity to the control system early drivers would have found much more instinctual.

Hmm… maybe by that logic, the next generation of cars should be steered either by game controllers or by a sliding touchscreen app. I just hope it's stable; you really don't want this system to crash.

Clearly, any designer or programmer (or artist or writer or surgeon, etc....) – will show the influence of her culture in he work. This is true of one's personal or professional culture. Auto manufacturers may have a "company image" that they adhere to, but there is also the general cross-cultural image of what a car should be. And it is not just technology that is shaped by our perspectives. The work of Cultural Anthropologists can be distinguished from the work of Social Anthropologists by anyone who knows a little about their history.

What might not be so easy to understand is that there are other forces at play as well. You might choose to wear a jacket of a particular colour because of personal taste, or because it reflects your chosen affiliation – with a street gang, a football team, a business, or even an academic institution. For a practical example of this behaviour, take a look at the streets of any town in The Netherlands on Königstag, the National holiday in celebration of the sitting head of the royal family or consider what happens to the Chicago River each year on the Saturday nearest March 17th.

These actions might be hard to understand, but we all feel some impulse to "belong", to be a part of some larger group. This compulsion is well-understood and well-documented.

Cross-Generational Habit might appear to be a similar compulsion, but it seems to me to run a little deeper than that.

We are all products of our environment, and that environment includes tools. Most of the time, most of us cannot focus on the plasticity and flexibility and fluid temporality of the most ingrained tools that surround us. Instead, we accept them as fundamental to our world.

That makes life easier in some way, in that it provides another layer of solid, permanence in the frighteningly-unknowable world around us.

I believe that every one of us spends at least a little time outside of the "comfort zone", and some seem to live there. Leonardo da Vinci saw the world differently than most, watching birds fly and imagining technology that could never be built with the tools and materials of his time – parachutes and self-driving carts, and flying machines. Nicolai Tesla would get complete and holistic visions of finished projects, down to the most minute detail, that could perform functions previously unimagined – like power transmitters, and nearly every aspect of the modern circuit board.

Those are two people who inspire me in my creative efforts, and I believe that they may inspire you. I strongly encourage you to read what you can find on them – remembering all the while that many opinions should be gathered, and none should be followed blindly. The best might be if you can actually see the machinery they designed, whether a prototype, a reconstruction, or a schematic.

I'm not saying that you should try to live in face of the limitless horizons seen by Leonardo and Tesla, I'm just pointing out that if you want to be able to look that far away, you may have to take notice of the established structures either obstructing or framing your view.

Summary

Q: What do Homo habilis and proto-prosimians have in common with Leonardo da Vinci and G.K. Chesterton?

A: They are all mentioned in this chapter. So is Nicolai Tesla but – as usual – he is not credited as much as he should be.

References

1. Ottoni EB (2015) Tool use traditions in nonhuman primates: the case of tufted capuchin monkeys. Hum Ethol Bull 30(1):22–40
2. Burling R (2005) The talking ape: how language evolved. Oxford University Press, Oxford
3. Leakey LSB, Tobias PV, Napier JR (1964) A new species of the genus Homo from Olduvai Gorge. Nature 202:7–9
4. Harmand S, Lewis JE, Feibel CS, Lepre CJ, Prat S, Lenoble A, Boës X, Quinn RL, Brenet M, Arroyo A, Taylor N, Clément S, Daver G, Brugal J-P, Leakey L, Mortlock RA, Wright JD, Lokorodi S, Kirwa C, Kent DV, Roche H (2015) 3.3-million-year-old stone tools from Lomekwi 3, West Turkana, Kenya. Nature 521(7552):310–315
5. Chesterton GK (1939) Orthodoxy. Sheed & Ward, London

Chapter 6
The Evolution of Humans and Technology
Part 3: Computers

Abstract Having examined the evolution of humans and tools in general, in this chapter we will look at the "evolution" of the computer. The reader is asked to remember that, while human evolution has happened on a scale of tens of millions of years, and tool evolution has happened on a timeline that is only one tenth as long, modern computers have only existed for a few decades. To put it simply, they have not had enough time to evolve to suit us and we have not had enough time to evolve to suit them.

© Springer International Publishing Switzerland 2016
J.N.A. Brown, *Anthropology-Based Computing*, Human–Computer
Interaction Series, DOI 10.1007/978-3-319-24421-1_6

This means that we are still in the earliest stages of co-adaption with this new tool. To use a tool-based analogy, we have not yet figured out how to put a handle on this hand axe. Because of that, we are still cutting our fingers and working inefficiently. By looking at computers in this evolutionary context, we not only recognize that they are still in a very primitive state, we also open the door to the possibility of consciously and deliberately advancing them quickly through evolutionary stages that would otherwise require many human generations.

Who knows, maybe – as it was with the hand axe – adding a handle for safety will also increase performance and range of use?

Let's start by looking at the first person who seriously proposed that having computers would shape the way humans think. After all, his proposal ended up shaping the way we interact with almost all of our computers, tablets, and smartphones today.

As We May Think

Vannevar Bush was a mathematician and engineer who worked on analog computers; an inventor who was granted 49 patents for inventions such as the Differential Analyzer. He was the first dean of engineering at MIT, then the president of the Carnegie Institution, and then the director of the U.S. Office of Scientific Research and Development. During the Second World War, he was in charge of coordinating the military application of the work of approximately 6,000 scientists with an annual budget of approximately $500 billion dollars. This was the beginning of "Big Science" and it enabled the development of the atom bomb, and of microwave-based radar. This was the beginning of what would become the modern military-industrial complex (MIC) (Fig. 6.1).

At the bequest of President Roosevelt, he wrote a report explaining how the same scientific coordination that had helped to win the war could, in peacetime, be turned to peaceful pursuits. Less than 9 months later, Roosevelt had died and the report was delivered to President Truman. Called "Science: The Endless Frontier" [1], the report recommended the formation of an independent National Research Foundation, which would coordinate the disbursement of government funds to universities for research in the hard sciences. Bush argued that all of this scientific focus should be maintained, but that control should be independent of the military and of politicians, and that it should not be tied to the demands of immediate economic growth. He wanted the same concerted scientific effort turned on a new target – to make the previously unimagined amounts of knowledge available and useful.

This vision of scientists driving science was rejected by Truman, and scientific funding continued to be largely disbursed by the MIC. Bush later wrote a very popular book on the subject, "Modern Arms and Free Men" [2], calling for politicians to take control of scientific research and to run it through research centres and universities for the public good, rather than leaving it under the control of profiteers and the military. One can easily imagine that this was the beginning of the end of his

Fig. 6.1 We interact with our computer via a typewriter and a television set. Changing that to a flat screen television and a touchscreen keypad does not change the nature of the interaction

political influence. For a time, he had been a hero to the government, to the scientific community, to the military, and to the public at large.

At the height of that fame, in 1945, the Atlantic Monthly published a monograph by Bush entitled "As We May Think" [3]. In this article, Vannevar Bush described the Memex, a special and entirely theoretical desk of the future. This desk would be able to receive, store, display, edit and delete information from around the world.

His description may well be the reason that the developers of the first commercial GUIs used the analogy of the desktop. That analogy is central to our most-used computerized devices – the laptop and the smartphone. Of course, that was never his intent. I believe that Bush was trying to talk about a very important matter to the public interest, not to make predictions about future interfaces for interactions between humans and machines.

You see, the thing is that, when Bush proposed this possible future technology, the technology itself wasn't the focus of his proposal. Bush was saying that this access to huge amounts of data would affect our cognitive processing, changing us "as we may think". It is all right there in the monograph, but most of the people who cite this famous paper seem not to have read it. As a result, we have not followed his example, but have slipped into the pattern of developing new technology without worrying at all about how the use of it might affect human thought.

Not sure that technology affects how you think? Consider the following.

Until very recently, writing to someone usually meant waiting days, weeks or even months for a response, and talking with someone usually meant being in close proximity. That was how we communicated throughout all of human history, but now we carry with us tools that let us stay in constant immediate contact with almost anyone, almost anywhere in the world.

Now, I can just imagine a reader – not you of course, you are clever and friendly and will buy copies of this book for all of your friends. There is the reader I imagine- there, shaking his head and complaining that modern communication isn't immediate, because there are, you know, lags sometimes. "Sometimes, he whines, my messages take, like, forever!" I can also imagine Twenty First Century complaints about coverage, whether they are first world ("They made me turn off my phone at the IMAX!") or third world (the refugee camp is blocking cell phone signals because of a terror alert).

However valid those complaints may be – and I am sure that they are equally valid according to some twisted perspective – please try to imagine a world in which phones were tethered to the wall, and were shared between entire families or even entire residences, streets, neighbourhoods, or communities.

Personal portable phones have changed the way we think about distances and relationships, and even how we think about the world. They are the most common and most personal computerized technology that we own, and the technology that underlies their components changes faster than we can keep track of it.

It is our further misfortune that the ubiquitous manifestations of that technology are tools that focus our attention on a computer interface regardless of the nature of the task we are trying to perform. Our focus here is how to change that interface so that we can intuitively focus on the task at hand, instead of the tool we are using.

Maslow's Hammer and the Development of Computers

One of the key issues that has prompted my desire to write this book is my belief that scientific thinking is the best tool that humans have ever developed. The big deal about science is that it is a totally unintuitive way of thinking, that has been developed and refined to be even more unintuitive.

In science, you want to carefully measure what you do – for the very simple and clear reason that you want to make sure that anyone else who understands how to be precise can try to repeat exactly what you did. You do this, not in the hope that they will all agree with you, but in the hope that they will prove you wrong!

In science, being proven wrong is a victory for humanity. It means that knowledge is advancing. Now, that's being proven wrong, not being called wrong, or being called stupid, or ignorant, or sacrilegious. In mathematics you can prove a truth, in science, you cannot. The best we can do in science is to disprove something, under precisely measured conditions.

You start by imagining some viable explanation for some measurable event. Then, you figure out which variables are involved, and how to control them so that you can test as few as possible at any one time. But here's the hard part: your question has to be one that could be measurably proven wrong.

Not "How high is up?", or "How high is the sky?", or even "How high is that very particular cloud over there?". Those are all fine questions, and the last one could be answered using the scientific method. But the kind of question I've been talking about has to be disprovable. Not "What is one plus one?", but "What is one apple plus another apple?". Until you specify that you are talking about real, measurable apples, the question is purely theoretical.

A scientific publication might seem to outsiders to be bragging, but it should be the opposite. Scientific findings should be published modestly, asking your peers to check your work in the sincere hope that some or all of them are smarter than you are, or more skilled than you are, or have information you do not, and the further hope that they can find any mistakes you might have missed. We publish so that the entire community can test our work in order to determine if there is a flaw in our process, or if our findings really are a step forward for all of us.

You see, our brains lie to us about nearly everything that we think we are experiencing. That's a bold claim, and a strange one, but it is true. The scientific method is a formal way of trying to control how much your brain can lie to you – through both self-control and help from your peers.

Now, I know that some of you have been taught that science is something else, something esoteric, and highly-guarded. Something shared only with a few, and based on expert knowledge of arcane subject matter. Something that experts can tell you about, but that is much too complex for "normal people" to understand.

I'm sorry, but that's religion, not science.

The true beauty of science is that, once you learn how to run formal tests, how to measure things carefully and without bias. then *anyone* can do it. Do you have doubts about your work? Good! You should! Share your efforts and share your doubts, and the community will help.

That's another one of the reasons for this book, to build up that community with people who can think scientifically, but who have not been immersed in the indoctrination of academic training in science or engineering. We need more people who think like scientists, but who stand outside of our cliques, watching and celebrating and criticising our work.

Far too many of the scientists I know and have worked with do not think scientifically about their own field. We are bound, as users of the scientific method, to doubt and question our own work. We should believe that our ideas and ideologies, and our tools and technologies, are all temporary. We are not building temples intended to last forever, but temporary shelters that should be redesigned and rebuilt continuously in an unending evolution, to better suit our dynamic and limitless universe.

Instead, some scientists fall into the much easier pattern of thinking about their knowledge religiously. This means that they start to believe that, even if their own ideas might only be temporary constructions, the foundations on which their ideas have been built must certainly be made of stone, and set upon unyielding bedrock.

The French have a great term for this bias based on one's field of study or of work. The term "déformation professionelle" describes the distortion of reality caused by our professional perspective. For a beautifully-written discussion of this idea, I strongly recommend you read a post in Psychology Today, written by David McRaney [4]. If reading is not a tool you use easily, McRaney discusses the post on his podcast "You Are Not So Smart" [5]. Both the podcast and the post are based on McRaney's experiences at the Being Human 2012 conference in San Francisco.

Really, McRaney has written the example of "déformation professionelle" that I wish I had written, referencing a number of our shared heroes, each with their own beautiful biases:

> If you are a biologist, bodies are gene-replicating devices. If you are a physicist, the brain is made of atoms formed in a star. If you are an astronomer, the Earth is a pale blue dot. [4]

Engineers and computer scientists, like the rest of us, see the world through this distorted lens. You may have heard it called the "Golden Hammer" or "Maslow's Hammer", based on a quotation from his book "The Psychology of Science: A Reconnaissance":

> I suppose it is tempting, if the only tool you have is a hammer, to treat everything as if it were a nail. [6]

This has been the danger of the Era of Ubiquitous Computing: so many specialists in so many fields have come to believe that computer technology is their Golden Hammer.

How shall we improve this device (whatever device and for whatever purpose)? Why, by adding a processor, of course! From then on, every improvement can be carried out as an easily quantifiable improvement, according to the professional bias of computer scientists and engineers.

Improving laptops or smartphones or automobile dashboards then becomes a question of improving processing speed and battery weight and other technical issues, with little or no concern given to whether or not the laptop or the phone or the dashboard would benefit from a radical redesign based on new knowledge and new perspectives.

This is my corollary to Maslow's Hammer:

> If you could just make every problem look like a nail, then you might be justified in using your hammer to try an solve them

Consider how this has applied to the development of computers. In the 1950s, the mantra of the computer scientist was, "if we make this problem simple enough, if we can reduce it to a question that can be answered by a series of binary decisions – no matter how many it might take – then a machine can solve it."

Making processors faster and smaller meant being able to apply the computer to more complex problems. Almost every advance in software and hardware since then has been designed to improve the working ability of the computer. The measurability of these improvements, combined with profit-minded technological dissemination, led to the ubiquitous application of computers.

If you take a tool intended specifically for one job, and you start using it for every job, you will soon end up with a whole lot of jobs that are re-designed to suit the tool.

Fig. 6.2 Is the internal computer a benefit to you or to the sales department?

Have you ever had the experience of taking the perfect photo, one where the timing was just right, and everyone was laughing, or the cat was looking at you with sincere concern for your well-being, or the sasquatch had stopped and agreed to a selfie?

Okay, maybe not that perfect.

But have you ever had the experience of taking a photo, and catching the very moment that you wanted, and then looking at your camera to see how it came out – only to find that the picture wasn't taken? Instead there's a message there from your camera's onboard computer, telling you that some setting has to be adjusted, or that it wants to know if you might consider changing a setting because then it would work better under these conditions, and allow you to make better use of the available technology in order to have a better photo of…

…that perfect moment that has now passed (Fig. 6.2).

Why do you need a computer in your stove? In your watch? In your television? Does it really improve the experience of using these tools, or is it just something that we could be told is an improvement?

Consider how that example would work if we replace the computer processor with a hammer? I know it seems silly, this style of thinking is supposed to reveal that an idea is good or bad by reducing it to an absurd level. So, if every home appliance you bought had to have a hammer, wouldn't that seem a little unnecessary? Even if you could see advantages to hammering the laundry with tiny little scrubbers that eliminate the need for detergent or water, for example, or hammering the dishes with a blanket of nanohammers that clean off detritus to the cellular level – again without using any detergent or water. Would you not sometimes wonder at night, as you lay in bed with a mattress of tiny hammers massaging your aching back, if maybe there was another way to look at some of these problems?

No? What if there was continual marketing pressure to replace the little mechanisms that drive the hammers back and forth with faster, more agile mechanisms? If you had the option of updating those drivers, would you? And when the drivers got to be better than the machine around them, would you feel the need to invest in the new technology, even though the old one is still working to the standards you used to find very impressive?

If we begin to make our tools with the intent that they must have a computer in them, then aren't we building in obsolescence?

In the next subchapter, we will discuss this problem with a focus on two particular instances of professional bias in computer science: the abusive relationship we have with most of our computerized technology, and the danger that we are getting used to it.

ERROR 404: And Not-So-Smart Technology

Let's start the final discussion in this chapter by looking at the fact that a computer can ask me for help in a language I don't speak, unconcerned with whether or not I understand what it means.

Let me take a few steps back, and approach that problem again.

Of course we accommodate our tools, you don't insist on holding a hammer in your teeth, if you have any other options, and we and our tools adapt to each other as we evolve. Besides that, computers are really complex and we might have to adapt to them more than to other tools. I mean, if you have more room and need more force, then you hold your hammer further back along the handle. If you're trying to be precise, or gentle, then you hold the hammer very close to the head and make small movements. A computer is more complex than a hammer, true, but I would like to be able to adjust how much of my body must be used to interact with it... it always seems to come down to typing if there is a keyboard, to caressing a screen if there is not.

The interface with any of my hammers is actually much more flexible than the interface with any of my computers, even though it cannot change in form at all, and even though it is based on a model that has been around for centuries.

In fact, I believe that that is why the hammer's interface is so intuitively flexible; it had already gone through generations of user-testing before I was born. Almost as importantly, these were not user tests run by committees, intended to increase marketability. If you want to see how that kind of user testing has impacted on hammers, take a look at all of the different hammers for sale in any big hardware store. There are a lot of varieties created specifically for subsections of the broad range of applications to which one might put a hammer, but there are also lot of variations that exist just to sell hammers.

I seems to me that the big difference is that hammers have spent centuries being two-part tools. There was the hammer head that had to be made by a specialist with special abilities, and then there was the simple wooden handle – the Human-Hammer Interaction interface that allows a user to apply a hammer head to a nail.

When I was a boy, everyone I worked with on the farm knew how to replace the handle on a hammer, and thought nothing of doing it. In a few minutes of carving, you could produce a serviceable hammer handle, tack it into place, and get back to work – provided you were wearing gloves.

The handle would get better with sanding and smoothing and, to some degree, that would happen over time. The first handle I made was almost perfectly straight – not because of any skill on my part, but because of a lack of thought. My mental image of the handle was a simple one, and the pile of scrapwood I used happened to contain a reasonably-long piece that was straight. My father pointed out the value of having a curve to the handle. Later that day we examined his small finishing hammer, and his ballpeen and sledge, and his rubber mallet and his rock hammer. Then we looked at the handles on the hammers we had been using to drive nails. We found a nice piece of round firewood that had a natural curve that suited my hand, and we whittled it down and sanded it, and set it in place with shims.

Not many of our modern tools get that kind of customization. Maybe it is experiences like that that keep me from being satisfied with the many deplorably low standards in Human-Computer Interaction.

If you consider it abstractly, the purpose of a good hammer handle is to give us the greatest possible range and quality of service while making the least possible demand. In the hands of an experienced user, it shouldn't break and it shouldn't slip and it should allow you to modify the way that you use it according to any conscious or unconscious needs you may express.

When was the last time you felt that way about a computer interface?

Let me take a moment to discuss one common Human-Computer Interaction that is a total failure in terms of both input and output.

Have you ever seen the on-screen message: "ERROR 404"? If you use the internet, you've likely seen it more than once. Maybe you've sublimated the experience, pushed it out of your thoughts the same way we avoid worrying about the small inconveniences we cannot avoid. Maybe you haven't and it bothers you as much as it does me.

Error 404 is one of those messages that comes up sometimes when you're trying to do something, one of those messages that really tells you one thing but does another. In this case, the other thing is does is to stop you in your tracks with no ability to go ahead with what you were doing, and without any reasonable explanation.

Imagine walking down the street. You're on your way to meet friends or to go shopping or to go to work; whatever it is you're on your way to do, it is your business and your thoughts are occupied with anticipation. Suddenly a huge person is standing in front of you, arms crossed, blocking your path.

Now imagine the giant is wearing a sign over their head with the words "ERROR 404" written on it (Fig. 6.3).

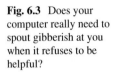

Fig. 6.3 Does your
computer really need to
spout gibberish at you
when it refuses to be
helpful?

The giant makes no other attempt to communicate. You can't tell who might be behind the sign or what they might want. You can't even tell if they can see you – until you try to walk around them. No matter what you try to do to go around they step into your path. Not hostile, or not openly so, they simply will not let you do whatever it was you were trying to do.

When you try to explain that you just want to go on your way, they speak for the first time.

"Okay"

You agree, and turn slightly to go around them, and they move to block your path again.

You soon learn that their single word is not really an agreement, and that capitulating does not let you continue on your way. Your only choice is to turn around and go somewhere else. Hopefully, you have the time and patience to make that choice.

It would certainly worry you if someone behaved that way on the street; blocking your progress, refusing to answer your questions, stubbornly offering you only "Error 404" and "Okay".

Now, I can just imagine that some of you reading this are already trying to justify the inanity of "Error 404".

Maybe you just think it's not a big deal – "you just wait and try again later or go somewhere else!" Maybe you know a little something about html protocols and you've been waiting for years for the chance to show it off. Then, you might be pointing out the 4xx status codes are designed to quickly communicate types of "client error", ranging from improper syntax (Error 400 – Bad Request) to the inability of a server to meet a request (Error 417 – Expectation Failed). Error 404 just means that the server could not find anything that matches a requested URL.

Now if you happen to think that it's okay for these error codes to just appear without an explanation, then I'd like to refer you to the list and descriptions at www.w3.org, the site of the World Wide Web Consortium.

In the published guidelines for these codes, it says specifically that Error 404 does not reveal whether the error condition is permanent, so Error 410 "should be used" if the server has certainty that the target resource is gone forever and has left no forwarding address.

> This status code [404] is commonly used when the server does not wish to reveal exactly why the request has been refused, or when no other response is applicable.

The guidelines also say that the notice "SHOULD include… an explanation of the error situation, and whether it is a temporary or permanent condition" and that this "SHOULD" be displayed to the user.

So you see, even the people who oversee these codes acknowledge that they can be used inconsiderately, but that they "SHOULD" not be…

…and yet they are. 40 years ago, when you had to take your computer problems to an expert, it was a good idea to know which error codes came up. This would help them know where to look. It was also important to keep the messages short, because memory was scarce. Neither of those is true today. A new "Not Found" message could include speech and a musical score, original animation, and scrolling text in multiple, customizable languages.

True, some people and companies have taken to putting pretty pictures on their 404 screens, or even written jokes, but that shouldn't be at the expense of an apology, an explanation, and clear directions for how to carry on about your business.

This is why Weiser said that we would need "calm technology". Not because of the limitations of the hardware or software, but because of the limitations of the people making them. That is what makes computers seem impolite, and that is what makes using computers frustrating. And if you think one computer can frustrate you, imagine what it would feel like to live surrounded by them; surrounded by a thousand little frustrations that might come up at any time when a system won't let you do what you want, when you want to do it.

Now, it wouldn't be very polite of me to criticize without offering an alternative, would it?

The alternative is considerate kindness. The alternative is to design each interaction as though the person who is going to experience it is a human, equal in their right to decent treatment. It sounds facile, but I believe that this mental model is fundamentally important. This is what Weiser was warning us about when he said that technical advances in ubiquitous computing would have to be evaluated by Anthropologists and Psychologists. It shouldn't just be a question of whether or not technology is well put-together or attractive, it should be a question of whether or not it is the kind of technology you'd bring home to mother.

As I said in a talk at the Pecha Kucha evening that ended Vienna Design Week in 2012 [7]:

I don't want a "smart" home. I don't! I don't think anyone wants a "smart" home. What we really want, deep inside, contrary to the name, is we want a home that makes us feel a sense of wonder. Don't we? We want a home that likes us. I don't care if it's smarter than I am, I want it to make me feel good.

The same is true of a smartphone, and of a smart car, and of any technology that's been deliberately designed for my use. I wouldn't use a hammer that had design elements that made me feel badly about myself or about my skills, or about the experience of hammering.

Since we deliberately build every facet of these devices, why not build them with the very specific goal of creating a good experience? Not at the cost of working well, but as an intrinsic condition of what we mean when we say that a tool works well.

Even smart homes can become better than just "smart". Gerhard Leitner of the Alpen-Adria Universität-Klagenfurt (Klagenfurt University) in Austria has a solution. His long-term application of smart home technology to the personal homes of rural senior citizens in the state of Carinthia have made him a household name in the right circles [8].

Dr Leitner suggests that it is not enough for the technology to be customized or to be inexpensive or to be useable, all of which were provided by he and his associate Anton Fercher, for years [9]. Dr Leitner's recommendation is that homes should evolve to the next stage, the stage that one should aspire to once one has achieved intelligence. Dr Leitner calls for the concept of the smarthome to be replaced by the concept of the Wise Home [10].

A smart home can turn off your lights at the same time every night, according to a preset calendar or detection of the sun. A wise home knows not to do it while you are in the room.

Leitner and Fercher studied these functions in 20 real homes around the state of Carinthia for 4 years [10, 11]. If this is possible in something with as many overlapping and contradictory technologies as a normal house retrofitted with new technology, then how could it possibly be too hard to take the same approach with one of those component technologies?

If you think that's too much trouble, that computer scientists and engineers should not and would not let their work be driven by non-technical motivations, then I invite you to reconsider the role that salesmen play in controlling which technology is available to the public, and whether it is designed to be used, or to make money.

The availability of technological advances to the general public is definitely motivated by the corporate and individual demand for profit.

Wouldn't it be nicer to be motivated by real human needs?

Summary

If you did not read this chapter, then you do not know the exact date and time at which the computers will overthrow all human life.

That is as it should be.

Carry on.

References

1. Bush V (1945) Science: the endless frontier. Trans Kans Acad Sci 48(3):231–264
2. Bush V (1950) Modern arms and free men: a discussion of the role of science in preserving democracy. Simon & Schuster, New York
3. Bush V (1945) As we may think. Atl Mon 176:101–108
4. Maslow A (1966) The psychology of science: a reconnaissance. Harper & Row, New York
5. McRaney D (2012) Maslow's Hammer are we entering a new phase in anthropology? On-line article at "Psychology Today". https://www.psychologytoday.com/blog/you-are-not-so-smart/201203/maslows-hammer
6. McRaney D (2012) Maslow's Hammer episode of the "You Are Not So Smart" podcast. http://youarenotsosmart.com/2014/06/23/yanss-podcast-26-maslows-hammer/
7. Brown JNA (n.d.) Designing calm technology "…as refreshing as taking a walk in the woods". Plenary lecture in the "Time Machine" session, IEEE International Conference on Multimedia and Expo (ICME2012), in Melbourne, 2012. Video available on-line: http://videolectures.net/icme2012_brown_calm_technology/?q=calm
8. Leitner G, Fercher AJ, Felfernig A, Hitz M (2012 Jul) Reducing the entry threshold of AAL systems: preliminary results from casa vecchia. In: Proceedings of the 13th international conference on computers helping people with special needs-volume part I. Springer, pp 709–715
9. Leitner G, Mitrea O, Fercher AJ (2013) Towards an acceptance model for AAL. In: Human factors in computing and informatics. Springer, Berlin/Heidelberg, pp 672–679
10. Leitner G (2015) The future home is wise, not smart: a human-centric perspective on next generation domestic technologies. Springer, Cham
11. Leitner G, Felfernig A, Fercher AJ, Hitz M (2014) Disseminating ambient assisted living in rural areas. Sensors 14(8):13496–13531

Chapter 7
Computer-Centered Computing: What Are "Human Factors" and Why Should We Care?

Now where's that warranty?

Abstract Have you heard the old joke about the fellow who finds another chap searching for his lost car key under a single street lamp on a dark night? He offers to help and gets down on his hands and knees on one edge of the circle of light, but after a half an hour feels like he's not having any luck.

"Are you sure you dropped it here?" he asks and the other fellow answers:

"Here? I didn't drop it here. I dropped it about a hundred and thirty paces back, over on the other side of the street."

© Springer International Publishing Switzerland 2016
J.N.A. Brown, *Anthropology-Based Computing*, Human–Computer
Interaction Series, DOI 10.1007/978-3-319-24421-1_7

Upset at having wasted his time, our hero asks why they've been searching on the wrong side of the road, and gets the following reply.

"Don't be stupid! There's no light over there. We'd never find my key in the dark."

With that in mind, let's consider a simple task, say, reading a sentence in a book.

I'm going to presume that you've just read that last sentence, and use it for my example. Now, if we were to try and express the task of reading that last sentence mathematically, there would be many factors involved. To reduce them to a useable example, and for the sake of expediency, we'll ignore all of the factors that went into how you came to be reading that sentence, and just work from there.

Could you see the book and the words in it well enough to read them? Is there enough light, or maybe too much? Are the letters expressed clearly enough to be read, or do they seem blurry and out of focus? Should they be more sharply defined, or presented in greater contrast to their background? Maybe they should just be bigger? Maybe they should be written in a different language, presented in a different medium, or available at a different time or place.

The Human Factors

In mathematics, the factors of a number are all of the other numbers that act together to make it up. In this way, 1, 2, 3, and 4 are one set of factors of 24, because $24 = 1 \times 2 \times 3 \times 4$.

Mathematical factors are pretty straightforward. What are the factors of taking a walk, or of driving a car? As a first approach, we can see that some of the factors must be environmental (weather and geomorphology will have an effect on one's ability to drive or to walk) and some must be technological (the nature of a built path or road is a strong factor in one's ability to follow it, as are the engine, the surface of the tires, and the fit of one's shoes). These factors are all in the domain of specialist engineers and technicians.

But we must also allow that some of the factors are human. How well can the traveler see? Has the traveler learned to drive – or to walk, for that matter? It becomes more complex when we factor in emotional states, as Einstein reasoned in his famous illustration of the relative nature of time. Adding more people to the equation means considering their individual skills, values and emotions, and also demands a consideration of their interactions.

It is easier for engineers to quantify technical and environmental factors than human factors. Because of this, human factors are considered a peripheral specialist domain and are largely ignored by other engineers during the development of either simple or complex systems. Despite their relegation to the sidelines during the design and development stages, they are often the focus of investigations when a complex system fails. Why do such investigations routinely blame individuals? For that matter, if the failure was due to human error, was it in the use of the technology, or in the design of it?

Over the next three chapters we'll look at this general concept of human factors as opposed to technological and environmental factors. In Chaps. 8 and 9 we will delve more deeply into the applied biomechanics of physical ergonomics and the applied psychophysiology and neurology of psychological ergonomics, but first, let's spend a chapter talking about how Human Factors are applied.

Look, I'm not denying that it's getting warmer, I'm just saying I don't believe that it's caused by frogs

What are the Human Factors that are shaping your experience of reading this chapter? Do you need corrective lenses, or the chance to focus with one eye at a time? Maybe you need the text to be further away from your eyes, or closer?

Do you recognize the alphabet? Do you recognize the words? Can you attach meaning to them at all, and if so, can you do so with them in this combination?

Maybe you are too hot or too cold to focus on reading, or there is wind blowing in your eyes and blurring your vision? Maybe the words are bouncing and you cannot focus on them and trying has upset your stomach? Maybe you and the words are both bouncing in unison, and trying to read has strained your neck muscles?

Maybe there is something in your culture or in your personal understanding of the world that prevents you from reading here and now.

Maybe there's a distracting noise in the background, or the person beside you keeps farting and you don't know whether to be disgusted or laugh out loud. Maybe the person behind you keeps kicking your chair.

Maybe you're too tired to read, or something has caused your eyes to be less functional? Maybe you could read but you are overcome by anger or sadness and cannot focus? Maybe your lack of focus is based on boredom – this example is getting to be rather long-winded. Maybe that is an excuse you use to hide the fact that you have emotional defects that prevent you from reading, or maybe you are drunk, or drugged, or just plain stupid.

Maybe you feel that this book has just insulted you, and now you don't want to read it anymore.

Any and all of these factors could affect your ability to perform the task of reading this chapter. In fact, the best-designed machine in the world for text display, running the best software in the world for text display, on a customized operating system that is working at 100 % efficiency could still fail to provide you with text that you can read, due to any one, or any combination, of the human-centered reasons listed above.

Those are the human factors, and they are largely ignored by the engineers, technologists, and computer scientists who have built most of the tools we use every day: machines and tools made up of components they have studied, for use by humans, whose components they have not studied at all. Unfortunately, they prefer to do their work in the circle of light they know, rather than venturing into the darkness to find the key.

Even that wouldn't be so bad, if that were the end of it: I begrudge no one their fears. But even if they want to confine themselves to the circles of light where they feel at home, they should allow some of us to explore the darkness.

Humane Factors

Officer, there is no doubt whatsoever that the cause of death is human error! My report clearly shows that there is nothing wrong with this rock!

Back in the first decade of this millennium, I was hired as the Human Factors specialist for Safety Intelligence in the civil aviation branch of Canada's Ministry of Transportation. One of the first things that happened to me after settling into my office in Ottawa is that I was sent to Las Vegas to attend a course that had been arranged by the woman I'd replaced.

The course was an introduction to a very popular method of accident investigation. The creators of the method were teaching the course and certifying the participants in the use of their very popular software. I won't mention the names of the people or products, because the story I'm about to tell does not shine a nice light on any of us. Like the other stories in this book, this one is true to the best of my recollection, but it is only my version of a series of events that happened a long time ago. If anyone is offended by this story, I ask that they please consider all of the parts they dislike to be figments of my poor memory. The story is told without malice or intent to harm. It is told as an example of how perspective often misleads human factors investigations.

So there we all were, 20 or 30 human factors specialists from around the world, sitting in neat rows and watching presentations being put on by 2 collegial gentlemen. The course went well, but I should admit before I go any further that I did not then, and do not now, subscribe to any of the theories that espouse simplification and categorization as necessary to accident investigation. The truth is that I believe that the system being presented that day is very good for finding scapegoats, and very bad for finding preventable contributing causes. In other words, I think their system is based on a false concept of how their work should be done.

That said, I think they've done it well. If your intent is to build a strong evidence-based case for blaming someone for an accident, then I could recommend their system and their software… so long as you don't care whether or not the individual you identify should actually be blamed for anything more than one in a series of mistakes, most of which were likely made far away from her in both space and time.

Accident investigation is supposed to be about finding out how an accident happened, with the goal of learning from it and generating remedial actions that will either prevent that particular type of accident from ever happening again, or further limit both the conditions under which it is unavoidable, and the impact it will have when it does occur. Too often, especially in private corporations and in the military, the purpose of accident investigation seems to be to find out who you can blame for what happened, so that political and financial liability can be managed with minimal impact on the entity that employs you.

The men running our course were former military who now made their living as consultants to private industry. So their perspective may well have been doubly-reinforced. All the same, I would not have disagreed with them and made a public scene among my peers, if not for the fact that they did something that I found particularly offensive during the course.

Towards the end of the course, one of the instructors offered up an example from their current caseload, and provided details about a fatal accident that was still under investigation at the time. They walked us through the entire event, even though that allowed a number of people in the class to loudly proclaim that they knew which accident it was. That is a real professional "faut pas", but it's not why I spoke up. The instructors even had the gall to walk us through to a conclusion that was patently false, blaming the one person who died for the entire incident and absolving the two corporations that violated their own rules and procedures to make the accident possible. I ignored that, too.

The thing I couldn't ignore was the message they gave us along with their pronouncement of the dead man's guilt.

Let me tell you a condensed version of what they told us. An experienced mechanic had been gruesomely killed in front of a great many witnesses while trying to figure out why an engine wasn't responding properly. The accident was, of course, his death, and they explained at great length how their system allowed them to pinpoint the personal problems that had caused the error in judgement that resulted in his death.

They didn't address the fact that the whole thing happened in front of witnesses, except to offer brief commentary on the potentially catastrophic civil suit that could be put against both the airline and the airport. The location of the accident was the key to the whole thing.

You see, the airline, faced with having to run tests on the engine, should have emptied the plane of passengers and sent it off to a service hanger. They should have, but that would have seriously delayed their flight and required them to deal with the expenses of taking a plane off-line and finding a replacement – not just for that flight, but for all of the other flights that plane was due to make before its next servicing.

The airport, faced with an airliner that needs this kind of service is supposed to require the plane to move away from the passenger area, and into an area dedicated to testing and repairs, like the previously-mentioned service hanger. Insisting on that protocol being followed would have forced the airline to make the more expensive decision.

Instead, the decision was made to call in a contractor who could hurry through testing and repairs. It was this hurrying that made it necessary for a man near retirement to do the job, with only a new trainee to help him, and it was this hurrying that had the plane sitting next to an occupied plane and in front of the big windows of a boarding area, when the error was made and the man died.

If the plane had moved, no passengers would have seen the accident. More importantly, if the plane had moved, the immense time pressure would have been entirely removed, and the entire operation could have been carried out by the book. In fact, the man who died would probably never have touched the plane that killed him that day.

So when the instructors joked about how easy it was to isolate the person responsible, using their privately licensed software, I had to point out that the software was only making it easier for them to justify the assignment of undeserved blame to a victim, and the absolution of their corporate client.

I passed the test and got my certification, but the instructors and a number of my fellow students did not think kindly of me. Some of the other students told me privately that I was right…

…that I was stupid to think the system would ever change, but that I was right.

Maybe I was being stupid, and maybe I was just being optimistic. Certainly, I was still holding on to this notion that scientifically-minded people share their ideas in order to test them; that a scientist would welcome valid criticism of hypotheses and theories, and even of methods and conclusions.

The problem was that it's not just pilots and mechanics and conductors and drivers who make Human Factors-based errors in judgement.

Investigators do, too.

What Are Factors and Which Ones Are Human?

As mentioned earlier, in mathematics the factors of a number are all of the other numbers that act together to make it up. In this way, 1, 2, 3, and 4 are one set of factors of 24, because $24 = 1 \times 2 \times 3 \times 4$. In the same way 4 and 6 are another set of factors of 24, whether or not we include the number 1. In fact, the number 1 is a factor of every number because its presence has no effect on the other members of the set. We'll come back to this in a little while.

Aside from being an art unto itself, we can use mathematics to model ideas that reflect our understanding of some aspect of the real world, and so test those ideas theoretically. This is what an engineer is doing when she calculates the range of potential joint strain on the buttress of a bridge in order to determine the material factors that will allow it to be made and used safely. It is mathematics that tell us the gradient to use on the upper and lower surfaces of a plane's wing, so that the wing can pull the plane up into the sky. Applied mathematical models do a fine job of holding up bridges and planes and they hold up in many other areas as well. The only problem is that – by their nature – models are simplifications. We have to consider whether the factors in our model represent every important factor in the real-world system.

For many years, the aviation industry resisted the idea of even considering human factors in the modelling of flight. Captain and crew were expected "simply" to perform without making any errors [4]. I hope that we have reached a point in our general popular knowledge now, from which we can look back at that idea and recognize it as a ridiculous example of false pride. You see, humans make mistakes. Not some humans, but all humans. It is in our nature to have physical and psychological limitations, and to fail if we try to surpass them. It is also in our nature to fail, occasionally, even when we are performing a familiar task in a familiar setting.

I'm sorry, what's that? You say you know someone who never fails at familiar tasks? That it is just a question of developing a high level of skill with the tool in question, or that it is just a question of performing 10,000 h of practice? That's an interesting theory. When was the last time this acquaintance bit their tongue? Was it due to a lack of familiarity or to a lack of practice?

This conscious acknowledgement of our propensity to fail is crucial to designing and executing tasks so that they can be completed safely. We must try to understand the human factors that may contribute to the safe completion of the task at hand, or to the failure.

Let's return to the examples of taking a walk or driving a car. As mentioned earlier, we can immediately see that some of the factors must be environmental. For example, 1 m of snow on the ground would have an effect on one's ability to drive or to walk, as would a steep downwards gradient. Along similar lines, the surface texture of a built path or road is a strong factor in one's ability to follow it, and so are other technological factors. One might consider every aspect of the tool being used, whether it is a car, a truck, or a pair of boots. Each of these factors is the domain of specialist engineers and technicians working for corporations, whose concern is the steady, marketable impression of improvement over time.

These factors contribute to the experience of walking or of driving in very fundamental ways but, can we really consider the either experience without giving some thought to the person or persons who will be doing it?

Some human factors are fundamentally physiological. How well can the traveler see? Do her legs function well enough for her to drive, or to walk at all? If so, has she learned to drive - or to walk, for that matter? The factors quickly become extremely diverse, without losing any importance. Is she mentally prepared to travel safely, or is she too agitated, too pre-occupied, or too tired. The complexity increases when we factor in one or more additional fellow travelers. Not only must we ask each of those earlier questions again, we must also consider the effect each person will have on every other person. Again, this is not a simple matter of saying the people "get along".

How will each traveler affect the experience of the others individually, as sub-groups, and as an overall group?

There are well established metrics for measuring the friction of a road surface, and there are well-established standards for determining the range of safe and un-safe grades or slopes or turns. There are even international metrics and standards for measuring skill at driving, and for providing both static and dynamic safety information to travelers.

But what is the metric for measuring how well two people will get along? Does it change based on the type of task each is performing, or based on whether the two are in a larger group?

How does being tired affect your skill as a driver? How about the presence of two friends, does that affect your performance? Exactly how does the effect differ if the two of them love each other, or hate each other? These human factors are not clearly defined. This means that they do not have a direct measure, which means that they are not easily quantifiable, and that means that they are not easy to formally incorporate into any practical model of the factors that contribute to driving.

Are we ready to admit that our model of driving doesn't represent enough of the real world problem? What about all of our other models?

What Is and What Could Be in Human Factors: What If Safety Were More Important than Profit?

We have discussed Maslow's Hammer and the idea of "déformation professionelle", so let's apply them to the question of why Human Factors investigations routinely blame individuals.

Could it be that their tools measure human failure better than they measure other failures?

Even if the error was human, was the failure in the use of the technology when and where the incident happened, or was the human error made by the designer of the technology, or by the manager who sets or enforces policy about how it should be used?

Have you ever read any of Richard Feynman's autobiographies? In the first one, "Surely you're Joking, Mr Feynman", the Nobel laureate shares stories from different periods of his life, including his time on the committee investigating the cause of the explosion of the US Space shuttle "Challenger" in 1991 [1]. I won't spoil the story here, but the book is easy to find – just ask your local librarian. Yes, yes you can just search for it on-line instead... ...but I think you're missing a great opportunity if you pass up the chance to discuss science books with a knowledgeable librarian.

Now, if you hate the idea of hunting down a story that I could just summarize here, then... well, then you'll probably also hate my next suggestion, and the one after that, too. I suggest that you stop and reflect for a little while on all of this hatred. It used to be a much stronger word than it is now. I suggest that you put some thought into whether or not you could use the word "dislike" instead.

But I digress. I hate it when that happens. Let's take a look at one of the basic tools of the trade of Human Factors.

The idea of human factors seems to me to be fairly straightforward. I hope that, if you have read the earlier parts of this chapter, you might agree with that opinion. I find it interesting that, during my tenure as a Human Factors Specialist, I dealt with so many people who were convinced that the whole concept was hard to understand.

I mean, so near as I could tell, most of them were human. I think that puts you at a natural advantage... or at least that it should give you a good starting point.

Well, I did meet one person who clearly thought the field was even simpler than I do. She was the political appointee whose job was to decide if I would be allowed to publish or present any information to the public. Her HF training had been a one- or two-weekend seminar. What's more, she didn't feel the need to apply any of the information she might have gained during that training. Her job was just to enforce the policy of the government at the time, which was that the only science worth reporting is science that directly supports some government policy.

Really, that happened, in Canada, in the Twenty-First Century. I won't go into detail about it here and now, but will encourage you to look it up on your own. You

Fig. 7.1 The human-centered relationships reflected in the SHELL model

don't have to look for it among conspiracy theorists or anything like that. You can check the archives of any of the major Canadian news services.

What I will say about it before leaving it behind until the end of this book, is that the policy seems to me to neatly reflect a very normal form of human behaviour – the kind of self-delusion that we are able to use to convince ourselves that terrible, illogical decisions are actually rational and justifiable. I'll discuss that mechanism in Chap. 9. For now, let's discuss one of the tools that shape the way that Human Factors specialists try and solve their problems in my old field of aviation.

The SHEL model was first proposed by Edwards, in 1972 [2]. It was an attempt to simply represent the fundamental concepts of human factors so that others could apply them. In order to explain the model, we will refer to the modified SHELL model as it was illustrated by Hawkins in 1975 [3]. There are five images presented in Fig. 7.1. The first is the SHELL model itself with its five components. The next four images are intended to illustrate four possible relationships between the central component and the four on the periphery.

Let's go through them in turn.

The basic model shows five tiles with rough, irregular edges. The central tile is labelled "L" for "Liveware" or living creature. This is the human at the center of the task. That human has to interface with four general things. Software (S), Hardware (H), the Environment (E), and more Liveware (L) such as co-workers, management, clients, etc…

The borders of the tiles are rough and irregular in order to represent the rough and irregular interactions that take place in the real world. We see these relationships modelled in the four smaller images. Starting in the top row, next to the larger model, we see that the relationship between the central human and the software they must use. To the right we see the relationship that the user has with their hardware. Bottom left shows the relationship between human and the environment in which the work is being done, and the final image models the relationship between the

Fig. 7.2 My modification of the SHELL model, in which each individual factor is assumed to be human-centered, unless it is considered in one of the four other direct relationships

central human and other humans. Some have argued for the addition of a C for culture, but I believe that the way that L interacts with everything else is fundamentally based in their culture, so the C must be assumed to be a part of each L.

I have always found this model to be too simplistic. Each human on the job must have a similar network of connections, and so must each of the other tiles. Hardware and software must be compatible, so there should be some connection between the two. A poor or missing connection would be very important and it would be a clearly measurable and improvable problem. Just the kind of thing that a model should reveal. Hardware that suits some environments does not suit others, there should be a link there as well. When I was working in Human Factors for Civil Aviation, I proposed a series of more complex models that were intended to better reflect that depth of interrelationships.

My final attempt was a pyramid. The letters are the same, but the peripheral tiles are differently-shaped. If they are each triangular, points outwards from the center, then they could be folded up into a pyramid in which software is also connected to hardware, and hardware is also connected to the environment. Software and environment are both connected to the outside liveware (Fig. 7.2).

I was happy with that for a little while, because it illustrated all of the relationships intended in the original model, but also served to make all of the connections more clear. What's more, it moved the user from the center of the situation to being the basis of the model. I thought that nicely reflected the idea that user who is central to an investigation is not always the center of our focus but, as shown in the pyramid, should be the basis of our work. The truth is that the complex interrelationships between multiple people and multiple devices would be better represented with something more akin to a rhombic triacontahedron (30-sided object) in which the shape of all component surfaces reflected their function and relative importance to the group.

In the end, it proved too complex for me to make a single geometric model that reflected everything I wanted it to do. What's more, it was overwhelming to start talking about geometry when trying to explain the importance of human factors. Most of the people I was working with hadn't given a thought to theoretical geometry since high school. If they applied it practically (in terms of their work in flying or maintaining planes), they did so without thinking of it as geometry. I did carry the pyramid with me, though, and I'd hand it to the people with whom I was discussing problems, just so they could see that any issue with any element came back to the person, and any action by the person would be reflected in one or more of those elements.

It was fun, but I thought that there had to be a better way to talk about how humans interact with their environment and the other things in it. I wanted to show that categorizing the elements with which we interact was not the important thing. This always made up too big a part of discussions when people tried to apply the SHELL model.

XERES: "Well, does our problem with the air conditioning get sorted under E for environment or under H for hardware?"

JERRY: "You're asking about fitting the problem with the air conditioning into a SHELL model?"

XERES: "Yes, yes I am. In fact the air conditioning is supposed to be monitored by a central computerized system, so maybe the problem should be under S."

JERRY: "Actually, the real problem with the air conditioning is you, Xeres! You're picking at the manual controls three or four times every day! So, yeah, we could file it under the second L, or you could just stop mucking about!"

Just so you know, the above is not an accurate transcript of a real conversation I heard during my days as a specialist, but there were far too many times that people were trying to make the facts suit the model, rather than trying to use the model to address the facts.

This led me to develop a very different model. Figure 7.3 is my model of General Human Interaction (GHI) in which one's thoughts, one's immediate environment, and the world at large are categorized as either restricted (inside a square) or unrestricted (inside a circle). The three differently-sized pairs of squares and circles were intended to represent one's interaction with the world at large, with one's work environment, and with the same kind of conflict between one's own deliberate and task-minded thoughts, and one's more emotional and impulsive reactions. While I found the model useful, it was hard to make it seems practical to people who were less concerned with why something went wrong than with fixing it. That level of practicality keeps planes taking off on time. Finding the underlying factors behind recurrent problems and learning to prevent them, that's what keeps those same planes in the air.

I came back to this model in developing Anthropology-Based Computing. You'll see that it looks quite different when we find it again in Chap. 10.

Fig. 7.3 A model of General Human Interaction (GHI) in which one 's interactions with the world at large, with one's immediate environment, and even one's thought are forced to adapt to externally-determined restrictions (inside a *square*) or are allowed to occur intuitively and in a manner that seems natural (inside a *circle*)

I want to leave you with an explanation of two standard approaches to investigating HF-related issues in aviation. James Reason [5, 6] explained the dichotomy of as follows. The human approach "…views these unsafe acts as arising primarily from aberrant mental processes such as forgetfulness, inattention, poor motivation, carelessness, negligence, and recklessness", while a system approach, is based on the belief that "…though we cannot change the human condition, we can change the conditions under which humans work."

I used to agree with that statement whole-heartedly, but now I have come to believe that changing work conditions to suit workers is a very basic first step. I think that the next step is to learn how to adapt our tools so that it becomes reflexive and intuitive for the worker to do their job accurately and without the risk of undiscovered failure.

To do so would require a better understanding of how the body and mind really, naturally, work.

Summary

Well, there *was* a craft you could make with scissors and glue, and I think the cartoons were funny…

References

1. Feynman RP, Leighton R, Hutchings E (1985) "Surely you're joking, Mr. Feynman!": adventures of a curious character. W.W. Norton, New York
2. Edwards E (1972) Man and machine: systems for safety In: Proceedings of the BALPA, Technical symposium, London
3. Hawkins F (1976) Some ergonomic aspects of cockpit panel design for airline aircraft. Shell Aviat News 437(438)
4. ICAO Circular 216-AN31 (also called Human factors Digest No 1), republished as CAP 719 in 2002
5. Reason J (1990) Human error. Cambridge University Press, Cambridge, UK
6. Reason J (2000) Human error: models and management. BMJ 320(7237):768–770

Chapter 8
Ergonomics and Biomechanics: The Surprisingly Simple Science of Using Your Body

Ouch

Abstract "Guns don't kill people; people kill people."

You may have heard this argument before. Even though you may have a strong emotional reaction to this phrase, associating it with Michael Moore's excellent film "Bowling for Columbine", or with strongly-held beliefs of one sort or the other, I am going to discuss it here. In fact, it is because of the strong emotional reactions that it inspires that this phrase is an illustration of how our brains often react when we believe they are thinking.

It is especially likely that you've heard this phrase if you're from any of the areas where the National Rifle Association tries to wrangle public opinion and control the laws that might hurt the short-term profitability of the US Firearms industry. Long before the NRA came to Canada officially; their propaganda was washing over the Southern border and soaking into some Canadian minds. Consider the following more stereotypically Canadian example:

"Axes don't cut trees; people cut trees."

No one actually believes that the tool goes out on its own to do the job without any human present. That's an absurd idea and, when you are arguing against someone who is right, it helps if you can make it seem that their idea is absurd. This is why the argument for gun control is always turned into either an argument against human rights, or an argument that guns kill all on their own. I hope the example of the axe can help you to see that this is deliberate manipulation of your opinion.

Axes or guns, in both cases it is really a question of the responsibility that underlies ownership of the tool. That boils down to a decision on whether the tool is useful and safe, and a separate decision on whether or not it is suitable for the job. Let's continue with the example of the axe.

It is true that people cut trees. It is also true that they use axes to cut trees, because axes are more efficient for that job than hammers, teaspoons, tampons, and swimming fins. Unlike those other tools, the axe in our example was invented, marketed, sold, and bought for the purpose of converting a living tree into a pile of wood. It will be replaced in that purpose when a more efficient tool becomes culturally acceptable. An amorphous public understanding of relative safety keeps us from using lasers to cut down trees, but has allowed us to replace axes with chainsaws.

Chainsaws are quite useful, even though they are much more narrowly-focussed than the once-ubiquitous axe. They are not really safe at all, except in comparison to how dangerous they used to be... ...but they are very well-marketed.

The same is true for guns. They are marketed as tools that increase personal and domestic safety. The truth is that there is very little evidence linking guns to increased safety, and a lot of evidence that they are directly related to an increase in risk-taking, injury, and death.

But, boy, are they marketed well!

Introduction

Good marketing causes you to react emotionally to a product. In this way, the part of your brain that will consider the issue logically will never participate in the decision to buy. The right kind of campaign reinforces this lack of consideration by playing on the same parts of our thought processes which, as discussed previously, allow our unconscious mind to convince our conscious mind of all kinds of other lies. This is why people react emotionally when defending "the right to bear arms", despite the fact that the arguments pertaining to gun control aren't about that issue, and aren't emotional.

"Guns don't kill people; marketing that propagates ignorance and fear kills people."

Now that I've offended a fair portion of the North Americans reading this book, let's look at less controversial tools that are still being marketed as though they are safer than they really are: computer peripherals.

I'm not suggesting that computer peripherals cut down trees when no one is looking, nor am I suggesting that they are used in killing people – though that statement might actually be more difficult to defend.

What I'm saying is that mouses and keyboards, the ringtones and alarms that signal incoming phone calls or text messages, all of these have been directly related to human injury and even death, but we buy them and use them anyway.

I believe that part of the reason for that is ignorance, and part of the reason for that is cross-generational habit. Another reason that we buy these devices is that they are marketed to appeal to our emotions, not our rational brains.

Some of that marketing is the sort I've just referred to regarding guns, axes, and chainsaws. Another type of marketing, one that is especially popular in the marketing of technology, is the misappropriation of scientific terminology.

In particular, let's look at the misappropriation of the word "Ergonomic".

Ergonomics can describe a wide range of work-related factors. In Chap. 9, we will discuss some of the neurophysiological, cerebral, and psychological factors that make up part of the field of Psychological Ergonomics. This chapter will discuss Physical Ergonomics, and will present simplified pictures of neurophysiology and of the underlying biomechanics that can be used to describe the musculoskeletal workings of our bodies. Really, it should be fairly straightforward.

The Biomechanics of Having an Endoskeleton

Biomechanics is the science of using the methods of mechanics, as they are expressed in Physics, and applied in Engineering, to study biological systems. This can be done at the microscopic, cellular level or at the macroscopic level of a musculoskeletal system. In my work to date I have focussed on the latter. That is what we will do here.

If you want to really learn about biomechanics, then you should read a good book on the topic, or take a course, or even a degree. That's what I did, and I would happily recommend the same to anyone who'd care to ask (Fig. 8.1).

Here in this book, I'm just going to give a few pretty simple examples of biomechanics in order to explain a bit about the body, a bit about ergonomics and a bit about how we use models in science.

You see, the body is an incredibly complex machine. There are thousands of separate chemical reactions going on in your body right now. Most of that is being performed unconsciously as a part of the myriad metabolic tasks that keep you

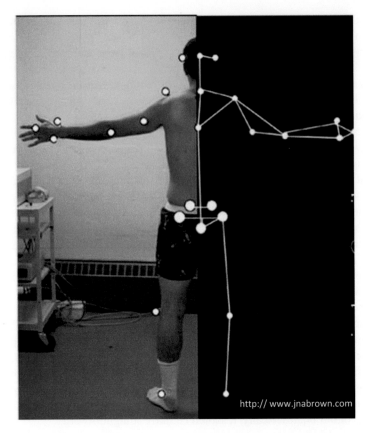

Fig. 8.1 An illustration of the full-body bilateral model of both the kinematics (movements) and kinetics (forces) involved in lifting that I developed while working under Dr Wayne Albert in the Human Performance Lab and the Institute of Biomedical Engineering at the University of New Brunswick. This illustration shows the internal computer model, and the corresponding markers used to identify the skeletal landmarks on the body of a participant

alive. If we wanted to look deeply into any aspect of these processes, we could focus on something like the transportation of oxygen in blood, and spend the rest of our lives studying nothing else. We would never have time to finish, or even to catch up with what has already been written.

In order to make use of some small, measurable subsection of this knowledge, we have to have a rational framework, or mental model, that ties it together in a way that is at once abstract enough to be measurable, and detailed enough to reflect real life.

For example, people can describe the way a nerve sends a signal to a muscle using either an electrical model or a chemical model. The actual thing that happens inside the nerve cells is a combination of both. As I've mentioned before, models are simplifications. That's why we use them. In mechanics it is common to use simple models and to make them more complex only when we need them to be more complex. If I were to try and explain the mechanics of the knee to someone with little or no interest in mechanics, then we would probably come to a very quick agreement that the knee is a lot like the limited hinges that allow a door to swing open and closed.. That is, the knee can bend forward and back within a limited range, but it can't bend side to side or twist. At least, it shouldn't do either of those last two things in the course of normal use, and if it does, that is a sign of damage.

A knee is much more complex than that, even if all you are looking at is the shape of the separate bones where they rub against one another.

If you start to consider the muscles, then you have to switch to a model that is complex enough to account for the fact that the four muscles in the quadriceps group at the front of the thigh each connect to different spots both before and after running down the femur, and that the same is true for the three hamstring muscles at the back of the thigh, and for the gastrocnemius that stretches up from the back of the calf to assist the others in changing the angle of your knee joint.

If you want to study the mechanics of these specific muscles – say in order to help a physiotherapist figure out the best angle of inclination for a remedial training programme, or in order to help a prosthetist design or mount a functional artificial leg – then you'll need to use some pretty precise models.

On the other hand, if you just want to capture the movements of Andy Sirkis so that you can map them on to computer animation models of either Golum or King Kong, you can probably get away with a fairly simple model of each knee. Then again, that model of the knee will have to be designed as part of a chain of models so that the actor's full body can be captured and translated onto a more or less complex model inside the computer. While the first model is mapped to the actor, the second is mapped to the animated character.

Before becoming a scientist I spent a little time designing, building, and using those kind of models as rigging for animated 3D characters. It was a lot of fun, and it helped me a lot when I studied biomechanics. Our pairs of models (one to capture, and one to apply) served a different purpose, but they were still required to meet the same kind of parameters: to be as simple as possible in order to provide the necessary detail. Allow me to switch from knee to shoulder in order to illustrate the importance of that.

The human shoulder is an extremely complex system. That's where the glenohumeral joint at the top of the arm connects with to two very mobile bones; the clavicle and scapula. You can see my redrawing of that joint, based on an original drawing in Grey's Anatomy [1], in Fig. 8.2. While many, many models have been attempted [2], they generally fall into one of three types.

The first of the three models in Fig. 8.3 is a simple hinge joint with 1 Degree of Freedom (1DOF). This means that it can only rotate around a single axis. In more practical terms, this could account for one's ability to swing one's arms forward and back, as though dancing the twist, or to flap them up and down, as though dancing the funky chicken. A simple hinge model would not allow for both of those dances, or for a more complex arm movements, as though one were dancing the robot.

The second model in the series offers 3 Degrees of Freedom (3DOF). The limited hinge from the first model has become a spheroidal or "ball and socket" joint,

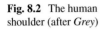

Fig. 8.2 The human
shoulder (after *Grey*)

http:// www.jnabrown.com

which is a fairly accurate representation of the gleno-humeral joint, but ignores the other parts of the shoulder. This would allow you to dance the YMCA, so long as you didn't shrug while forming the letters.

The final model illustrated in Fig. 8.4 offers five degrees of freedom (5DF). It takes the same gleno-humeral spheroid, but puts it on the end of a chain of two other spheroids. This would allow you to shrug in indifference to all of my dance references, or would allow you to jive, to do the wa-watusi, or to wave your arms about in Gangnam style.

So, if you were trying to generate models of the shoulder you can see the advantages offered by the increasing levels of complexity, right? Well, then it is time to point out that sometimes a simpler model works better.

Years ago I was hired to work at a company developing motion capture systems. One of their difficulties was in trying to come up with a workable model of the human shoulder and arm; one that could be captured using their patented system and translated onto models for a wide variety of purposes. They had tried for years to develop models that always turned out to be either too complex for their system or too simple to represent real arm motion. I simplified the process by telling them that we didn't have to capture any movement or static postures in the shoulder or arm at all, just the rib cage and the wrist. My new "I don't care how many degrees of freedom" model (WTFDF) was based on knowing the difference in location and rotation between the sensor on your wrist and the sensor on your torso. Their sensors could be easily fastened in those two places, so their system could calculate that. The it was just a matter of explaining to their engineer/programmer that a human body of a specific size could only put those two points of reference into those

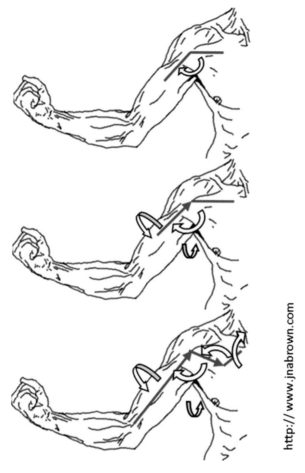

Fig. 8.3 Common shoulder models; single hinge joint, spheroidal joint, and series of two hinges and a spheroid

two places in one possible way. So our capture model for the shoulder and arm only had two points (Fig. 8.4).

The relative coordinates of those two points were applied to the wrist and torso on our internal computer model. Knowing those two sets of relative rotational and positional coordinates put the character on the screen into the right pose automatically. The model itself calculated how much to rotate its own shoulder and elbow in order to match the captured input.

As mentioned earlier, most of the use we make of our body is done unconsciously. This includes breathing and the incredibly complex balancing act that allows us to stand still or hold a finger in the air. These tasks involve the unconscious, reflexive cooperation of dozens or hundreds of muscles. If we had to control each one deliberately, either task would be incredibly challenging. Still, that is how

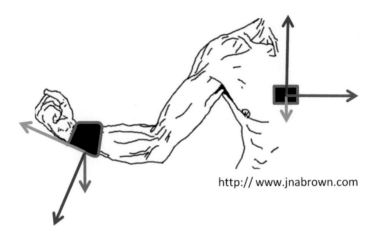

http://www.jnabrown.com

Fig. 8.4 My "I don't care how many DOF" model of the entire shoulder in which the difference between the two points tells us exactly the pose that your arm must be in

we learn to stand and to walk and to run, or to reach and to grasp and to use. We learn to do these things as babies, or re-learn them in remedial therapy, slowly and deliberately repeating our attempts until all or some of the individual actions become routine and can be initiated and modified subconsciously. We'll talk more about that in the next chapter. For now, let's take a look at how we measure the performance of these tasks and routines once we have taken our bodies to work.

Studying the Workings of the Body at Work

Ergonomics is a scientific focus on understanding how work is done how it could be done, and what effect those styles of doing might have on the person or groups of people doing them. The term was coined by Wojciech Bogumił Jastrzębowski in 1857, combining the Greek words for "work" (ergon) and "principle" or "law" (nomos) [3–6]. Many professionals consider Ergonomics to be a synonym for Human Factors, while others see distinctions that are not universally accepted. I have heard that the Human Factors Association of Canada changed their name to the Association of Canadian Ergonomists just so that the acronyms would match in French and English. I've heard that, but it may be apocryphal. Even if the association felt that the titles were interchangeable, that that seems to me to suit the profession. If the distinction between the two terms sometimes seems protean, well, that is a quality that goes far in describing the tasks an ergonomist might undertake or the realms that she might explore.

As with Biomechanics, Ergonomics is a wide field with a vast range of specializations. My mentor in the field was Professor Wayne J. Albert, a generalist who specializes in calculating lower back strain [7], but has published in a wide range of fields [8]. Wayne taught me a lot more than ergonomics and I strongly encourage you read his papers and attend his lectures. If you ever have the chance, I hope you can sit down with him for a chat over a cup of coffee. Doing so changed my life.

I have met other Ergonomists who are generalists [9] and others who tend to focus more in one area, such as specializing in the biomechanical factors involved in sitting at work [10], or who specialize in the repetitive strain to hands and wrists during fish processing [11]. Three colleagues who trained in the original UNB Human Performance Laboratory back when I was there built their respective careers around the study of low back strain among massage therapists [12], the study of additional postural strain when handling equipment on board a ship or floating platform [13], and the study of neck strain in air force pilots wearing helmets with incorporated enhanced vision [14]. Still, these were all examples of Physical Ergonomics. Others branches include Cognitive Ergonomics and Organizational Ergonomics, in which professionals might specialize in colour perception, in lighting, in the social and psychological pressures of workplace seating arrangements, and more.

Physical Ergonomics has improved the usability of simple tools and of complex machinery. The word usability is key. That means that it improves some or all of the factors that allow humans to safely and effectively put a device to the use for which it is intended. That balance is what really makes the science important. Trying to improve safety, for example, without considering how effective the tool is, would result in replacing hammers with pillows. You might never again drive a nail, but you will certainly not be able to flatten your thumb.

Similar nonsense results in considering only effectiveness, in complete ignorance of safety. Like fishing with dynamite, this would replace the same hammer with a nail gun. Oh it is possible to use a nail gun without injuring yourself or anyone else, but only because of the addition of safety features after the fact. In fact, even with safety features in place, nail guns remain quite dangerous. Though they are used by only a small subsection of the construction industry, nail guns are associated with more injuries requiring hospitalisation than any other tool in that field [15].

Even though nail guns are loud and dangerous (read: cool), I would like to use this space to continue to establish a basic understanding of the concept of ergonomics. For more about nail guns, the impatient reader can skip ahead to Chap. 13.

So, how do we balance usability and safety?

One common approach is to focus the design of tools and processes around the person who is going to be using them, rather than around cross-generational habit, mechanical or electrical standards, or corporate policy. This is called a Human-Centered approach. As the reader might judge from a comparison of that phrase with the title of my book, I am a fan of that idea, but do not believe that it goes far enough.

In my opinion, most of the "human-centered" work that I have encountered still focusses too much on available tools and traditional settings. In other words, it tends to consider the human, but not as more important than the material limitations involved in getting the work done.

Ergonomics is the science of work, and so it makes sense that there should be capital factors in the equation, and corporate factors, but we shouldn't confuse them with *human* factors.

Standing in an assembly line can never be human-centered, and neither can sitting at a desk for 9 h. Those are not human-centered tasks. Actually, they are tasks that, by their very design, are bad for human health.

This is true of using a computer mouse, or a keypad, and it is true of the way our phones call our attention to incoming messages. In Chaps. 13, 14, 15, 16, 17, 18 and 19, we'll take a look at the specifics of how those particular things (and others) are not ergonomic, and I'll share some practical advice on how to make them more human-centered and how to measure the results of your own interventions so that you can see them empirically for yourself and share them with others.

I'm not saying that corporate-centered design means that we should throw our wooden shoes into the workings of the machines, or that we should stand on our desks and quote poetry. I'm just saying that I would like people to stop trying to sell me on the idea that their particular product – whether it is a job or a tool or an organizational philosophy – is human-centered when it is profit-centered, or that it is ergonomic when all they've done is to provide padded carpeting along the sides of the assembly line.

Misappropriation of the Word Ergonomics

Let's take a quick look at a tool that you have probably used before, one that is marketed directly and indirectly, that is sold around the world, and that is probably in almost every office and home that has a steady and regular supply of electricity: the computer mouse.

The people who built the first computer mouse never intended for it to be used for more than a few minutes at a time, over the course of a working day. They simply did not consider, in their design, what it might do to the human body to try and use the mouse for the majority of one's waking hours.

They built the prototype by hollowing out a chunk of wood and installing two wheels set at right angles to each other. There was a mechanism for measuring how much each wheel turned, either forward or back, and an algorithm to turn those numbers into two-dimensional paths. No rotation in either wheel means that the mouse is sitting still. Positive rotation in only one of the wheels means that the mouse is moving straight to the side or straight forward. Both wheels rotating means that the mouse is moving but not straight to the side or straight back and forth. The rate of turning in each wheel describes that path.

It's been about 50 years since the mouse was invented, and it's been about 30 years since it became a common tool in almost everyone's home and in almost everyone's office. Using a mouse makes you twist your arm and then move it in weird repetitive patterns, and injuries related to that activity are part of why – after a hundred years of obscurity – the word Ergonomic has now become quite popular.

Medical practitioners and the general public noted an increase in repetitive strain injuries related to computer use, and ergonomists responded by studying the problem and making recommendations to improve both the way we use the mouse, and the way it is designed. There were a few improvements made to the design of the computer mouse, but for the most part, industry seemed to realize that it is easier to use the word "ergonomic", then it is to apply ergonomic principles to re-designing your products.

I say this because there have been dozens upon dozens of superficial mouse redesigns, and I have seen them for sale, labelled "ergonomic" in big pretty letters, but no one has stopped to ask why we are still controlling our computers by rubbing a block of wood around on our desk.

This material is easier to grip, and this outer shell is angled by 5°, and that mouse is smaller and the other one is bigger, but they're all designed to imitate the functions of a prototype that was made 50 years ago. We modify that design and call the modifications "ergonomic", but real ergonomics would call for the device to be redesigned in order to actually suit the way that humans can best perform small, precise, Two-Dimensional movements. I presented my own alternative about a dozen years ago. You can read about it in detail by looking up an old paper [16]. For a detailed discussion of the computer mouse problem, and for a simple behavioural solution that you can apply and test on your own, please see Chap. 13.

So, if we all have bodies, and if we accept that our bodies have certain practical limitations (like how much we should use our arm once we've twisted it into a weird position, or the endurance of small muscles, or the natural range of focus for our eyes, or the fact that reflexes sometimes make us do things we shouldn't do near heavy machinery) then why don't we design all of our tools and activities to accommodate that? Wouldn't that be better ergonomics, and more human-centered?

Well, I believe that we used to – back when we all built our own tools, and even when we had a variety of choices of manufacturers to choose from. I believe that that choice was killed by reactive, short-term, profit-driven focus that led to giant companies competing with one another – not to provide a range of services in response to the needs and wants of the buying public, but to provide a limited range of goods in response to the needs and wants of short-term profiteers.

Remember the story I told earlier about making hammer handles? That used to be normal – that the tools you used would reflect your preferences... not by bearing the same brand logo as your favourite sports franchise, or by dint of having been sold by the chain that sponsors your nightly distractions. It used to be that we adapted our tools to ourselves and to our manner of working. The process of adaptation leading to evolution that I discussed in Chap. 5 falls apart when we use tools that we can't or don't modify.

It may be that something else falls apart, too.

Maybe modern tools are so polished and finished and sealed and complete; so complex and fragile and so-very-easily-replaceable, that we don't even think about repairing them.

What does that do to us, psychologically? What does it do to the dynamic process of human evolution if we learn helplessness in face of our tools? In the next chapter of this book, we will discuss this issue in greater detail. Let me preview that by saying that dogs that learn helplessness give up when faced with problems; failing to see workarounds and alternatives that they would otherwise have used and even learned to anticipate and seek out [17].

Humans, according to the studies, are the same way [18]. We learn situationally-specific helplessness, and it stays with us for the rest of our lives [19]. Does this mean that we are several generations along in an unsupervised experiment on learned helplessness? Are we like the dogs in the shuttlebox, laying on the floor and accepting the painful stimuli that reinforce our growing subconscious acceptance of our own inability to make or repair or improve the tools and processes we use every day?

It's a frightening thought.

Fortunately, there is an alternative. Scientists tell us that people who have learned helplessness can unlearn it [20, 21]. Again, for more on that, turn to the next chapter.

The last section of this book is all about taking control of the tools you use every day. If you'd like, you could consider that a chance to jumpstart the flagging evolution of human tool use, to "hack" the system that is making you better at consuming tools than at making them.

And if you can take your time, and measure your innovations, and test them empirically and in a repeatable manner, and if you can avoid buying into the lies from marketers or from your own internal self-delusions, then that would be ergonomics!

If you share your developments and let like-minded people criticize them and re-test them, and improve upon them, the that would be science!

How do you avoid the negative propaganda from your own mind? Well, it helps to start by knowing that it is there. The next chapter is an attempt to provide you with some insights into the conflicted workings of your mind, and a few of the ways in which we delude ourselves.

Summary

Meh, it was probably nothing important. I wouldn't worry about it if I were you... What are the odds anyone would put anything from this chapter on the exam?

What's that? You don't have any exams on this book? You mean you just bought it without being told to? Wow...

Thanks very much. I hope that you're enjoying it and that you'll take the time to contact me and tell me what you think.

If you're not enjoying it at all and you don't want to be bothered to write and tell me so, well then please consider buying up all of the copies available at the shop where you bought yours. That way, you'll be helping the world by making certain that no one else gets to read it...

...until my giddy publishers see the numbers and put out a second printing.

No, really, please punish my terrible book by buying it all up. I've heard that it has worked well in the past, and I promise that it would certainly teach me an important lesson.

References

1. Gray H (1918) Anatomy of the human body, 20th edn. Lea & Febiger, New York
2. Bolsterlee B, Veeger DH, Chadwick EK (2013) Clinical applications of musculoskeletal modelling for the shoulder and upper limb. Med Biol Eng Comput 51(9):953–963
3. Jastrzebowski WB (1857) An outline of ergonomics or the science of work based upon the truths drawn from the science of nature, part I. Nat Ind 29:227–231
4. Jastrzebowski WB (1857) An outline of ergonomics or the science of work based upon the truths drawn from the science of nature, part II. Nat Ind 87(3):236–244
5. Jastrzebowski WB (1857) An outline of ergonomics or the science of work based upon the truths drawn from the science of nature, part III. Nat Ind 31:244–251
6. Jastrzebowski WB (1857) An outline of ergonomics or the science of work based upon the truths drawn from the science of nature, part IV. Nat Ind 32:253–258
7. Wrigley AT, Albert WJ, Deluzio KJ, Stevenson JM (2005) Differentiating lifting technique between those who develop low back pain and those who do not. Clin Biomech 20(3):254–263
8. Albert WJ, Miller DI (2010) Takeoff characteristics of single and double axel figure skating jumps. JAB 12(1):72–87
9. Rickards J, Putnam C (2012) A pre-intervention benefit-cost methodology to justify investments in workplace health. Int J Work Health Manag 5(3):210–219
10. Black N, Fortin AP, Handrigan GA (2015) Postural and perception variations when using manually adjustable and programmable sit–stand workstations in an emergency call center. IIE Trans Occup Ergon Hum Factors 3(2):1–12
11. Kuruganti U, Albert WJ (2013) Ergonomic risks in fish processing workers in Atlantic Canada. Occup Ergon 11(1):11–19
12. Albert WJ, Duncan C, Currie-Jackson N, Gaudet V, Callaghan JP (2006) Biomechanical assessment of massage therapists. Occup Ergon 6(1):1–11
13. Duncan CA, MacKinnon SN, Albert WJ (2012) The effects of moving environments on thoracolumbar kinematics and foot center of pressure when performing lifting and lowering tasks. J Appl Biomech 28(2):111–119
14. Harrison MF, Coffey B, Albert WJ, Fischer SL (2015) Night vision goggle-induced neck pain in military helicopter aircrew: a literature review. Aerosp Med Hum Perform 86(1):46–55
15. Lipscomb HJ, Nolan J, Patterson D (2015) Musculoskeletal concerns do not justify failure to use safer sequential trigger to prevent acute nail gun injuries. Am J Ind Med 58(4):422–427
16. Brown JNA, Albert WJ, Croll J (2007) A new input device: comparison to three commercially available mouses. Ergonomics 50(2):208–227
17. Overmier JB, Seligman ME (1967) Effects of inescapable shock upon subsequent escape and avoidance responding. J Comp Physiol Psychol 63(1):28
18. Seligman ME, Maier SF (1967) Failure to escape traumatic shock. J Exp Psychol 74(1):1
19. Young LD, Allin JR JM (1986) Persistence of learned helplessness in humans. J Gen Psychol 113(1):81–88
20. Thornton JW, Powell GD (1974) Immunization to and alleviation of learned helplessness in man. Am J Psychol 87(3):351–367
21. Mikulincer M (2013) Human learned helplessness: a coping perspective. Springer Science & Business Media, Berlin

Chapter 9
Psychology and Neurology: The Surprisingly Simple Science of Using Your Brain

Abstract For some reason, we spend our lives in s state of perpetually renewed surprise, startled by the world around us and by how our bodies have responded to it.

It's the reflex arc, working on different levels, firing off responses long before the mind has a moment to think. This is fine for jumping out of the path of a moving car, but sometimes the confusion of stimuli cause us to jump in the wrong direction.

© Springer International Publishing Switzerland 2016
J.N.A. Brown, *Anthropology-Based Computing*, Human–Computer
Interaction Series, DOI 10.1007/978-3-319-24421-1_9

Besides that, these arcs – or cycles of sensing, processing, and reacting – they don't only work at the level of reflexes. They are also going on in the mind. This is how we learn everything we know, from walking to writing and from reaching to religion. Trial, detection of the results, consideration of the results, and retrial: it's just a slightly deeper version of the same reflex arc.

But what if I were to tell you that our mental reflex arc had a short cut; a way to let us save our lives first, and then think about it afterwards? "Better to apologize than wait for permission", right? And what if I were to tell you that this short cut, and the process of thinking about it afterwards, is at the heart of some of the worst things we do to ourselves and to others?

Would you like to know how to fix it?

Before we can discuss it, let's take a quick look at a working model of the nervous system and of the brain. Like all models, they are functional simplifications, tools we can use even though they fail to perfectly reflect the depth and range of how the systems really work. I encourage you to learn more in the future, but I hope that this chapter will give you a new perspective or even a starting point.

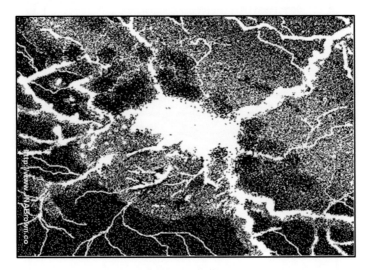

Have you ever noticed that, under an electron microscope, nerve cells look like the Flying Spaghetti Monster (mybtbhna)? No? Maybe you should pray about it and then look again

Iterative Cycles, the Structure of Feedback-Control Systems and a Trifurcate Model of Reaction

When a gentle breeze cools your skin, the small hairs there stand up and your skin becomes covered with little bumps. This is an almost immediate reaction. Specialized cells in your skin detect the temperature change and a signal is sent to cause a pilomotor reaction. This doesn't involve any conscious or unconscious thought. It doesn't make any use of your brain at all (Fig. 9.1).

This kind of unconscious interaction between our bodies and stimuli from the outside world is going on all the time. There are a great many muscles and nerves involved in standing still – proprioceptors that allow us to know which forces are acting against our joints and in which way, so that we can make the small, unconscious, but vitally important adjustments to our posture that keep us from falling down.

A case of a single stimulus leading to a complex response is when you kick out as the doctor "tests your reflexes" by hitting you below the kneecap with a little rubber hammer or the edge of her hand. What she's actually doing there is stimulating your patellar nerve, causing an immediate unconscious response that makes your leg straighten. At the same time, there is another related reaction that also takes place, one that is just a little bit more complex. You see, when your quadriceps femoris muscle group contracts (those are the muscles in the middle of the front of your thigh that makes your leg straighten out into a kick), there is also a signal sent

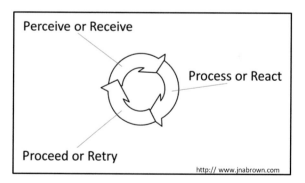

Perceive or Receive

Process or React

Proceed or Retry

http://www.jnabrown.com

Fig. 9.1 A simple model of an iterative feedback loop

Fig. 9.2 Iterative feedback loops feeding back into one another in a hierarchy

to the opposing muscle at the back of your thigh. The hamstrings (the semitendinosus, semimembranosus and biceps femoris) have to relax or else they will prevent the leg from straightening.

If you combine your mental picture of the second example (the complex interactions that let us stand still) with the second part of your mental picture from the third example (the part where one muscle group is triggered to relax so that the other one can be triggered to contract), then you should be able to imagine what it takes for us to walk or run. This involves a huge number of these reflex arcs working in unison (Fig. 9.2).

Repeating through many iterations, the different cycles of stimulus and response from the proprioceptors and muscles around your toes and ankles, and knees and hips, have to coordinate with the ones from your spine and shoulders and arms. This coordination takes place in the cerebellum or "hind brain" – so called because it sticks out behind your spinal cord instead of in front. One can imagine that complex motor patterns work like the simple iterative cycle we saw earlier. We compare an expected cycle to the cycle that actually happened, and that allows us to detect that something unexpected has happened. As perception takes place at the beginning of the next cycle, we can detect how an unexpected change has caused us to deviate, and we can make corrections. This is the point where stumbling may lead to a fall. Sometimes, the accidental movement has improved our chance to make the next coordinated move, sometimes it has decreased our chance so badly that we fall, initiating an entirely different set of coordinated reflexes... if we're lucky (Fig. 9.3).

Years ago, when I was studying Aikido several times a week, we practised falling and being thrown forwards and backwards and to the side. I had practiced in a similar manner as a child, working through the breakfalls and rolls of Judo. Aikido, though, was different. My teachers in both arts emphasized precision, and gentle behaviour, and self-control. In both arts we practiced until the movements became

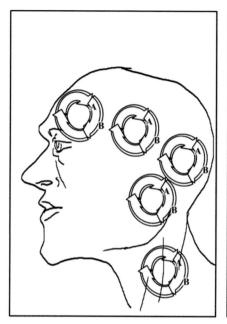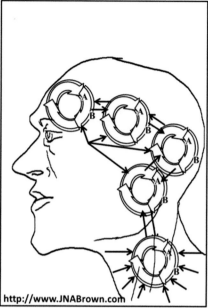

http://www.JNABrown.com

Fig. 9.3 Five different sets of feedback loops, representing the five different levels at which that happens: below the brain, at the medulla oblongata, the cerebellum, at the reactive parts of the brain, and at the reflective parts

what we called reflexes. I'm told that a better term would be "muscle memory" and I think now, that it is a learned coordination pattern. One of these patterns came back to me years later. I was working as the assistant coach in a fencing club at a small university, and I had joined the coach and some students in warming up by playing a game of pick-up basketball. It had been more than 15 years since I had played the game, and I soon saw that all of my old coordination patterns for basketball were gone. I couldn't dribble, pass, or shoot with the facility I once had. Trying to cut around a pick, I caught my toe on an outstretched foot, lost the ball and went crashing towards the ground. I tried to relax into the kind of graceful shoulder roll that I had performed so easily a decade earlier. The little finger on my right hand pointed in a long curve towards the floor ahead of me, and my chin tucked itself to my chest. I rolled along my arm and across my shoulders and came to my feet on the other side of the defender. I saw the ball coming up from the floor and caught it with two hands.

"That's it for me", I said! I passed the ball to one of the other players, lumbered over to a bench and sat down.

After warming up, a couple of people came over to where I was sitting. One joked that I was "too ninja for them" and another said that they weren't used to "kung fu basketball" and they were glad I had decided to sit out. They wanted to know if I could teach them how to roll like that, and I realised that they hadn't

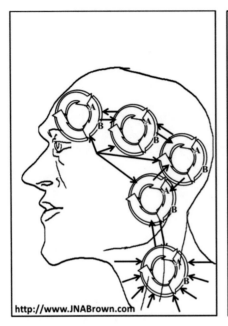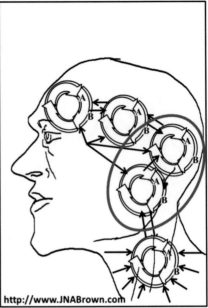

Fig. 9.4 In the second image, the information going from the cerebellum to the medulla oblongata is distorted. The message to the limbic region is still intact, so you feel that everything is all right until you perceive the failure of your efforts

noticed what really happened; the detail that I left out of the description above. When I was relaxing into the breakfall, when my finger was stretching out and leading my arm into position, the coordination pattern was not quite as thorough or accurate as it would have been in the past.

As illustrated in Fig. 9.4, the signals from my cerebellum to my spinal cord, the ones that should have initiated my old, familiar patterns of coordination, had become distorted either at the source or in transmission. At the same time, the signals from my cerebellum to the rest of my brain were still functioning normally – so I expected that the breakfall was working. I was wrong. Around the time my leading fingertip touched the floor, so did my leading knee.

I don't know how I managed to do the breakfall, and I couldn't remember catching the ball, because I was entirely occupied with the shooting pain in my leg. I had stopped, not because I was "too ninja" but because I was embarrassed at having demonstrated in one fell swoop that I had forgotten both basketball and how to fall safely.

The two takeaways from this story are:

1. That the patterns of coordination that allow the reflexes to work together can be forgotten, or fall out of immediate recall, or at least that there can be some systemic decay in the coordination between the cerebellum, the nervous system and the musculoskeletal system, and

2. That the execution of these patterns is extremely fast – much faster than the conscious thought with which they are observed.

I believe that this is the sort of pattern that has to be learned again if a brain injury causes someone to lose their ability to walk, even though they can still perform all of the individual component actions. Of course, I could be wrong; it wouldn't be the first time today.

Speaking of being wrong, I want to share with you a model of the brain before we move on to the next topic; a model of the brain that is generally regarded as inaccurate. I believe that it is more than accurate enough for our purposes and that, in combination with the idea of iterative cycles we've just been discussing, it provides a good explanation for most of the things we misunderstand about how we perceive the world around us, and even how we think.

The Triune Brain: Separating the Conscious, the Unconscious, and the Reflexive

The Dragons of Eden is a Pulitzer prize-winning popular science book by the great Carl Sagan [1]. In it, he refers to the brain as being a construct that happened in three fundamental stages, each reflective of a major step in evolution, and each reflected in the development of every individual human brain that takes place during gestation. This idea was formally proposed by Paul MacLean in 1954 [2] and became widely accept by the general public after the publication of his book: "The triune brain in evolution: role in paleocerebral functions", in 1990 [3].

MacLean called his model the Triune brain, and proposed that the basic system of reflexes, the system of emotional responses, and the system of cognitive thought, each took place in different physical structures. In 1949, he distinguished between the cognitive and emotional regions:

> …though our intellectual functions are carried on in the newest and most highly developed part of the brain, our affective behaviour continues to be dominated by a relatively crude and primitive system. This situation provides a clue to understanding the difference between what we "feel" and what we "know." [4]

MacLean called these two regions the Paleomammalian Complex and the Neomammalian Complex, with each name intended to evoke the evolutionary stage at which that part of the brain developed. He attributed reflexes to an older region he called the Reptilian Complex. Let's discuss all three of them in turn.

The Reptilian Complex

MacLean categorized the most primitive part of the brain as reptilian. Physiologically, this meant the basal ganglia, to which contemporary science attributed "instinctual behaviours".

The Paleomammalian Complex

Far higher up MacLean's version of the evolutionary ladder, he placed his second brain region at the beginning of mammalian evolution and named it accordingly. Physiologically, he included the septum, amygdala, hypothalamus, hippocampus and the cingulate cortex, areas (thought at the time to be responsible for emotion and for the motivation involved parental behaviour). At first, in 1949, MacLean referred to this as the "Visceral Brain". Later, perhaps in response to Turner's olphactory-centered term for the region ("rhinencephalon"), MacLean retrieved the term used by Broca and referred to the complex as the "Limbic Region" [5].

The Neomammalian Complex

Located at the pinnacle of evolution, MacLean identified the attributes of language, abstraction, planning, and perception as being present in only the most modern mammals, especially in humans.

In the last few decades, MacLean's model has been heavily criticized as an oversimplification and, more importantly, as inaccurate. I will not address the issue of oversimplification, because simplification of complex ideas is the very purpose of a model. I encourage simplification and the other steps in the building of representative models, and I wonder who should be allowed to say that it is too extreme. It served the purpose of allowing the general public to see the evidence of evolution in our own bodies, and to experience some grasp of the emerging field of brain science… …and not just the general public. Modifications of MacLean's model are still taught in universities around the world. Hopefully, the modified models reflect new knowledge and still retain the simplicity and intuitive clarity of MacLean's use of evolutionary progression. In fact, in Part II, I'll be sharing my own modification of MacLean's model. I hope you'll let me know whether you think I've oversimplified the matter, too, and whether or not my model has already followed MacLean's in vectoring away from the path of current advances in neurology and brain science.

For example, we have learned in recent years that the functions MacLean attributed to his three evolutionary stages actually predate all three of his categories. His Reptilian attributes exist also in fish, and other creatures that vectored away from the path millions of years before the appearance of reptiles. If you like the mental model of an evolutionary tree, then consider that reptiles are one large limb of the tree, and mammals are another. If you follow the limbs out to branches and twigs, there you will find the wide variety of modern reptiles and modern mammals. If you see me waving, please say hello before continuing on your journey.

If you follow the same twigs and branches and limbs in the opposite direction, to before they grew apart, there you will find creatures with whom we share common ancestors. Now you have to go pretty far back to find a common ancestor between mammals and reptiles, and that's what MacLean was saying. The "reptilian complex" is part of our brain that has been around a lot longer than humans. He wasn't wrong in that opinion, he just didn't go far enough back. I try to remedy this in my model by using a different section of the brain to represent the earliest evolutionary stages at which nerve cell ganglioblasts became complex enough to be called brains. But that's for later. For now, let's climb back up into the high reaches of the tree, and look again at the limb full of mammals.

MacLean located the origins of our emotional and familial reactions at the base of that branch. In fact, though – or at least according to our current knowledge – the physiological structures of MacLean's Paleomammailan Complex are also present in birds, lizards, and other creatures that existed before mammals, and so are the familial relationships.

Finally, some form of neocortex is now believed to have been present in the earliest mammals, not only the most recent among us. To put the point to rest, even birds have a brain structure that allows them to learn, to make decisions, and to use tools. The fact that their birdbrained (sorry) version of the neocortex doesn't have six full layers of nerve cells strikes me as a very minor nit to pick. That kind of human-centric bias would have been better served in the early days of science than in the modern age of big data. We used to be happy to declare things fundamentally different from one another based on measurable attributes. We are learning that such generalization is always inaccurate, which brings us back to my earlier comment about oversimplification. Our models are always simplifications – which is one of the many reasons that we must always remember that our models are not perfect reflections of reality. Simplify as part of the categorization that allows for formal measurement and study. Use those categories to test your hypotheses, sure! Publish them and share them like a good scientist should, of course! You can even print them out if you want, on the surface of a fine silk handkerchief, and fold it in twelve secret ways, and carry it always in the pocket nearest your heart… but don't take it out and wave it around in public as though it means something more than it does.

Trying to insist that one's own precious model is more accurate than reality smacks a little too much to me of being one of "The Sneetches on the Beaches" [6].

Does this mean that MacLean's model is no longer of use to us? I hope not because, as I mentioned earlier, I will try to make good use of it – with some fairly substantial modifications – in Part II. How can I justify using an out of date three-stage model of the human brain? I base my choice on the fact that observation has shown us strong evidence of trifurcate decision trees in human behaviour. Let me tell you about a few of them and show you how my new Triune Brain model helps to explain some of our common cognitive biases.

The New Triune Brain and Trifurcate Decision Trees

You are walking along a mountain trail.

No, I'm not trying to hypnotize you; I'm trying to share another illustrative example.

You are walking along a mountain trail that winds along the edge of a cliff. To your right, densely-packed trees are crowded on a steep slope. A dense undergrowth ends at the edge of your path. To your left, a sheer drop to sharp and jagged rocks far, far below.

Of a sudden, a snake slides into your path and you, someone who is not very used to or comfortable around snakes, react in three similar but different ways.

The part of your brain that reads, does arithmetic, and thinks logically immediately starts thinking about what kind of snake that might be? Did the guidebook say anything about snakes?

Another part of your brain, the part that's good at pattern recognition notices how it's moving – whether it is passing by or attacking, whether it is slow or fast, and the fact that it has rings of three different colours all long its body.

The first part of the brain is interrupted in its thoughts about the guidebook, with the news about the rings. It knows the colours of the rings are important, or is it the order in which they run? It starts trying to recall what these particular rings might mean, according to a comic strip you read a long time ago. There was a poem, how did it go?

"Red, black, and yellow will kill a fellow" – was that it?

"Red touches yellow, bite kills a fellow" – maybe… "Red touches black, hit the road, Jack"? That doesn't seem right…

Unfortunately, the first part of the brain never gets to finish its search. You see, while it was thinking, and while the much faster second part of the brain was analyzing the movement and recognizing that the snake had a pattern of colours, an even faster part of the brain was also at work.

The third part of the brain, the part that encompasses complex and coordinated reflexes, like how to run without tripping, or how to catch a baseball, or how to sign your name, that part of the brain has executed two fairly complex patterns. These complex patterns involve activating and coordinating a number of consciously- and unconsciously-controlled muscles. Since that part of the brain is much faster than the others, these two actions still manage to interrupt the thinking going on in the two other parts of the brain.

What are those two actions?

The first is that you try to scream – probably an inarticulate noise or some word close to the surface of your thoughts, like: "AAAAH SNAAAAKE!!"

You try, but you only get as far as "AAAH SNAA-" before you are cut off. Your second action, you see, was a big jump away from the snake which, by unfortunate coincidence, took you over the cliff.

So you never got a chance to finish what you were screaming or what you were thinking. Just before your brain could figure out that the snake is a harmless coral snake, it was dashed to pieces against those sharp and jagged rocks that had been waiting far, far below ever since the first paragraph of the story.

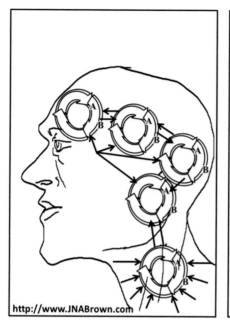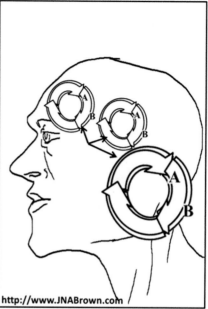

Fig. 9.5 The New Triune Brain, representing a simple version of human refection, reaction, and reflex

This trifurcate model, as shown in Fig. 9.5, explains the story of the snake, and what happens when you lose your temper. It also explains change blindness, delusions of grandeur, and knowing we don't need to ask for any directions, dammit!

The reflective feedback loop can go on for seconds or for minutes. If you can focus your concentration like Einstein could, then that cycle could go on for much longer, maybe for days or weeks. This loop is initiated by intellectual triggers, or on call from the "older" parts of the brain.

The reactive feedback loop, the one we will relate to the limbic region in the middle of the brain performs its actions within tenths of a second. These are unconscious reactions based on the recognition of patterns and triggers of the memory. I think it is possible that our fast pattern-based reactions are often confounded with emotion because of the proximity of the two regions.

The reflexive feedback loop, the one encompassing the cerebellum, the medulla oblongata, and all of the other reflexes of the spinal cord and body, those all happen with a hundredth of a second.

The result is that, if the stimuli is sent to all three regions, then their reaction times will still be out of synch – with reflexes happening before either of the others. We've all experienced that, even if we haven't jumped off of a cliff to avoid a snake.

Have you ever found yourself thinking "Why did I say that?" after blurting out something you had meant to keep secret?

Have you ever found yourself eating another potato chip after having deliberately closed the bag because you had decided to stop?

Have you ever set aside some work that you have to finish, so that you could watch just one more funny video of cats training their humans, or compilation of epic fails, or Russian dashcam of an impossibly stupid driving accident?

The limbic part of your brain, the middle part, anticipates and recognizes patterns, and really likes getting that right. It triggers the release of pleasure-inducing hormones as a reward, which make you feel good and skillful and clever. This nice feeling of accomplishment is very easy to achieve when you are only anticipating the consequences that are named in the title of the video.

"'Skateboard Fails', eh? I bet that guy is going to fall off- YES! Oh, I saw that coming!! I bet this next guy can't ride that rail all the way down th – OHO!"

And you feel clever, and you feel good, and you laugh in a mix of schadenfreude and some other feelings you don't really understand, and it is very hard to turn away from that and go back to the less predictable, less rewarding, real world.

So, if we all have brains, and we all know that they are not only fully conscious, and we all know that these unconscious reward systems will sabotage our ability to work, then why don't we design all of our tools and activities to accommodate that?

Well, some of us do.

No, I'm not talking about some semi-secret religious order that wants you to believe that they can teach you to control the world, and I'm not talking about some fully-secret martial arts school that will train you with the power to cloud the minds of men.

Advertising agencies do it all the time. That's why they try to build emotional relationships with their projects. They don't want you to think intellectually about buying a car you can't afford, or about putting something truly horrible into your digestive track. They want you to react emotionally, quickly, in a way that undercuts all rational thought.

That's also why some movie trailers now unveil the entire plot. They are deliberately trying to "spoil" the film. "Spoiling" a surprise used to mean ruining it. Now it just means to give away information that will be released later. The companies involved have learned that the major demographic for some types of film would rather know what's coming before they get to the theatre. In some ways, that makes them the perfect audience. They will happily watch a film several times, because part of their enjoyment comes from knowing what will happen next [7].

The big culprit, though, is the video game industry. The world would be a much better place if game designers turned their skills to education or world peace, instead of just manipulating your pleasure centres during game play. That sounds facetious, but the creation of emotionally-rewarding cycles is a fundamental part of game design. The challenge must increase just enough to be demanding. If it increases in too big a step, players will look for something more immediately rewarding.

Have you seen some of the truly insipid games being played now? They give you the constant promise of reward, and pay you for your time with stimuli rather than anything that is actually useful. This is how slot machines were optimised, and it is why people will play all day, even though they know intellectually that the odds are and always will be against them. The lights flash and the bells ring, and your reactive brain will keep you there until you run out of chips. Your reflective brain has no choice in the matter. It may struggle for a while, reminding you that you have to be elsewhere or that you should hold back enough money to have cab fare. It will likely just stop trying eventually, and let itself be bathed in the reward hormones that the Casino has been designed to trigger.

On-line games do the same. When you could only play once a day or once a week, a game had to be substantially rewarding in order to be justifiable. Games that you can play all of the time never have to be intellectually justified. They are designed to only be of interest to your reactive brain.

If you are human, and most of you reading this probably are, and if you play insipid on-line games, and most of you reading this probably do, then you are probably already justifying your endless, meaningless gameplay.

That's just self-delusion, friend. You're letting the irrational part of your brain try to rationalize bad decisions. It's the same self-serving reaction that allows people to deny evidence in preference of faith, like a smoker trying to justify paying billionaires to poison her children, or a drunk trying to explain that it's just a short drive home.

Those justifications are just emotional reactions, patterns of reactive thought and behaviour that are so automated that we are unaware that we follow them, and so illogical that they can seriously impede our lives. In 1967, Martin Seligman and Steven Maier reported the accidental discovery of what they called "learned helplessness" [8]. You know those experiments in classical psychology where you build an association in unrelated things – like Pavlov training his dogs to salivate at the sound of a bell by building an association between the ringing and the arrival of food. Well, Seligman and Maier theorized that they should be able to pre-train dogs, in advance of that classical training, and that the result should be that those dogs would then learn faster than dogs that were not pre-trained.

They were not, however, using rewards like food for their training. They were using electric shocks. Yes, psychologists used to do that. The innate cruelty of some branches of science, as expressed in their experimental design, often seems to me well beyond coincidence and casual schadenfreude, and clearly sadistic. On the other hand, we learn from it. Sometimes the theories are supported by experimentation and sometimes they are not. Sometimes, when they are not, we learn something interesting, and informative, and very surprising.

The pre-training involved exposing dogs to an electric shock, but sounding a noise first. The idea was that they would learn to associate the noise with the shock. Later the dogs were put in a shuttlebox (a sort of a big cage divided in two by a wall that the dogs could jump over – thus "shuttling" from one side to the other).

Here's how a shuttlebox would be used. When the floor on one side of the shuttle box was electrified, dogs would eventually learn to jump over the low wall and onto the side that was not electrified. In another example of classical conditioning, the experimenters would get the dogs to associate a noise with the shock, and then if the dogs would learn to jump over the low wall when the noise came. It usually worked well, with dogs learning to wait near the wall as soon as they were put into the box. They had apparently learned that these floors sometimes hurt you.

The dogs who had been pre-trained to associate that same nose with electric shocks actually performed worse than the untrained dogs. They had not just learned to associate the noise with pain – they had learned that that pain was unavoidable; they had learned that they were helpless to do anything except wait for the pain to stop.

When the noise sounded the other dogs would escape, but the dogs that had learned helplessness in the prior training would just lie on the floor and accept the abuse [9].

Now, it is accepted in psychology that this reaction, this learned helplessness also occurs in humans. It said to be why some smokers believe they will never be able to quit, and why some people in abusive relationships don't leave. It is not that the person involved lacks intelligence, it is that they have learned to react on a different level, one that doesn't involve conscious and deliberate thought.

We all know people who persist in making terrible self-defeating choices that are clearly illogical. I believe that these decisions are being made in a different processing system inside the brain. Please consider my model of the new triune brain in Fig. 9.5. I believe that they have learned a complex coordinated pattern of reactive behaviours that happens automatically in the limbic or visceral part of the brain – much the same way that a complex coordinated pattern of reflexive behaviours (like riding a bike, or running, or knitting) can be learned in the internal feedback loops in the reflexive brain.

What's more, I propose that we can take deliberate control of training and retraining these systems and that we can design technology to use those different processing systems to benefit all humans.

Summary

The Story of the Angel and the Ape (Excerpt)

One day, God took the brain of a clear-thinking and rather clever Angel and set it like a hat on top of the brain of a particularly nervous and self-important Ape, and forced them to share a single body, which God made look like a new creature all together.

Why would God do that? It's hard to say… Who can know the thoughts of God?

To make matters worse, God gave Ape's brain full control of the body. God told Angel, "You can try to control what you do, but you will have to convince Ape to let you have control before your interface with the body will work".

The body wet itself.

I think it was just a coincidence, because Ape really hadn't been listening, but Angel took it as a sign. You get used to signs after spending any amount of time dealing with God.

Angel retained his ability to enjoy the finer things, like sunshine, and laughter, and time with friends, even poetry and mathematics and art and the pure joy of learning something new.

But Ape not only had control of the body, the brain below also had a very strong influence on the brain above. So sometimes sunshine and laughter became overwhelming for the Angel, who would be completely overpowered by Ape's rich emotional reactions. Angel would also be overwhelmed by Ape's spontaneous and illogical thoughts, and by Ape's pervasive fears and pleasures. Speaking of which, sometimes Ape's idea of how to behave with friends made Angel wince, and he often found himself having to try and apologize after having done something embarrassing.

But that was not the worst thing about this new arrangement. The worst was the way in which Angel's other pleasures were affected. The joy of maths and of poetry and of art and of learning all became selective. Angel liked just to sit still sometimes, and Ape preferred to chase things. If Angel couldn't convince Ape to sit still, Ape would always find something to hate or something to lust after or some way in which to take offense. Ape always wanted to be entertained on the most visceral level, and there was nothing that Angel could do to stop that. Angel had to go to extreme lengths to convince Ape not to indulge every urge and appetite, and it was almost impossible to study anything at all. All of this internal fighting was exhausting… …rewarding when it worked, but too hard to keep at it very often or for very long.

Mostly, Angel had no real choice but to sit back and watch what Ape got up to. It would be Angel's job to find a way to try and survive any trouble Ape either found or created, and Ape would always make it sound as though that solution had been in the plan all along.

In fact, Ape did that with all of Angel's memories, twisting them around until they suited Ape's world view. Angel had to try very hard to remember that he was prone to making mistakes, and that he wasn't good at everything, and even that he might not always have a good plan before he starts to speak or act. Strangely, in the midst of all of this ridiculous overconfidence and egocentrism, Angel's thoughts were always awash with Ape's fears and uncertainties.

Angel was faced with a tough decision: to struggle incessantly, trying to maintain perspective and reasonable self-control, or to surrender to Ape's emotional and unpredictable whims.

That's about it for this story. There's really not much else to say, except maybe that it turned out that God did this to more than one Angel and more than one Ape,

and that they bred true,

and that their descendants include me,

and that their descendants include you.

(*Excerpt from John NA Brown's unpublished collection of short stories,* "*Fairytales for the 21st Century*")

References

1. Sagan C (1977) The Dragons of Eden: speculations on the evolution of human intelligence. Random House, New York, 263 p
2. MacLean PD (1952) Some psychiatric implications of physiological studies on frontotemporal portion of limbic system (visceral brain). Electroencephalogr Clin Neurophysiol 4(4):407–418
3. MacLean PD (1990) The triune brain in evolution: role in paleocerebral functions. Springer Science & Business Media, Berlin
4. MacLean PD (1949) Psychosomatic disease and the "Visceral Brain": recent developments bearing on the Papez theory of emotion. Psychosom Med 11(6):338–353
5. Broca P (1865) Sur le siège de la faculté du langage articulé. Bull Soc Anthropol Paris 6(1):377–393
6. Seuss D (1961) The sneetches and other stories. Random House, New York
7. Giedd JN (2012) The digital revolution and adolescent brain evolution. J Adolesc Health: Off Publ Soc Adolesc Med 51(2):101
8. Seligman ME, Maier SF (1967) Failure to escape traumatic shock. J Exp Psychol 74(1):1
9. Overmier JB, Seligman ME (1967) Effects of inescapable shock upon subsequent escape and avoidance responding. J Comp Physiol Psychol 63(1):28

Part II
Anthropology-Based Computing: Bringing It All Together, for the First Time

Putting the Human Back in Human-Computer Interaction Is as Easy as ABC

"Ran out of letters, eh? That's okay, I don't think anyone will notice..."

Introduction

"You have to stop saying things like that!"

He was pointing at me from across the table, wagging his finger like in a cartoon. The others sitting with us, the rest of our research team, suddenly grew those blank expressions that people can grow when they don't want to be pulled into either side of an argument, and he continued.

"You always do that! You just say some idea as though it's true, without doing any research to test it! That's not science! You have to test your ideas before you can claim they're true!"

We were on a research retreat at a ski hotel in the Austrian Alps. I'd just returned to Austria after a year in Catalunya, and I was in the middle of presenting my research goals for the coming year. Suddenly, it didn't seem to be going very well.

Two years earlier, I'd come to Europe to join a consortium of five universities in the first cohort of the Erasmus Mundus Joint Doctoral Programme in Interactive and Cognitive Environments. I had applied with the hopes of being able to specialize in Human-Computer Interaction, and to focus on developing my replacement for the computer mouse and my idea to use weak haptic signals to trigger rich emotional responses [1]. During the interviews, it had become clear that I would more likely be working either on social robotics with a primary base in Barcelona, or on something more human-centered and affective based in Eindhoven. When the invitation finally came, my position was based out of Klagenfurt in southern Austria. My work there went well during my first year and now, after a subsequent year in Spain, I was back. My work was starting to be recognized internationally. I'd been invited to give a plenary lecture at a conference in Australia, and other lectures across Australia and Europe, including the IEEE Region 8 anniversary celebrations in Malta, the Digital Inspirations lecture series hosted by Telefonica in Barcelona, and even a keynote lecture at the IWANN conference on artificial neural networks in Tenerife. To put it mildly, I was feeling pretty good about my ideas and my work on them so far.

In that meeting room in Austria, I had just finished proposing the theory that I had developed over all of that time touring and speaking with experts around the world. I suggested that it might be possible to use the brain's natural filtration system as the basis for designing alarms and alerts. The example I used was ringtones on a phone, and I was suggesting that it should be possible to design a ringtone that could be heard and understood only by one person in a loud and crowded room. That it might even be possible that the ringing of the phone would inform the intended recipient of who was calling, without interrupting whatever work they were doing at the time.

This was when my colleague had pushed back his chair and raised his voice.

"You can't just say any idea that comes into your head, and then decide to base your thesis on it! Your work needs to be based on established theories not fantasies!"

Red in his face now, he waited for an answer, and red in my face, I tried to think of what to say. Everyone else at the table was trying not to notice the conflagration, except for the fellow to my colleague's left. This man, more senior but not the boss, holds a MSc in Psychology and a PhD in Computer Science. He turned slightly to face the finger-wagger, lightly cleared his throat to get everyone's attention, and then spoke softly.

"This idea that John wants to use is called the Cocktail Party Effect. It has been well understood in Psychology for more than 50 years."

There was silence around the table for a moment, and the finger-wagger pulled his chair back up to the table, and he grunted a little and shrugged, and then our boss told me to continue my presentation.

In the end, my proposed plans were not approved for inclusion in the programme.

In this section, I will present the underlying theory and the models of interaction that led me to use the cocktail party effect in designing new means of interaction for humans to use with simple or complex tools including computers and computerized devices and environments.

At the end of the section, I'll talk a bit about the way I applied these theories to my PhD work, and about the use I made of the Cocktail Party Effect in my first postdoctoral project 2 years later in Portugal [2].

References

1. Brown JNA (2015) "Once More, With Feeling": using haptics to preserve tactile memories. Int J Hum Comput Interact 31(1):65–71
2. Brown JNA, Oliveira J, Bakker S (2015) I am calm: towards a psychoneurological evaluation of ABC ringtones. Interact Des Architect 26:55–69

Chapter 10
It's as Easy as ABC

Nattering has been going on for a long, long time…

Abstract In this chapter I will discuss the natural way that humans interact with their environment, and the theory that this natural interaction has developed over millions of years of evolution. Our proto-prosimian ancestors developed the ability to simultaneously perceive, process, and respond to multiple streams of information, filtering out the vital from the unimportant. We still perform this filtering, but ringtones and text alerts are deliberately designed to bypass our filters. What does it mean when your phone always gets your attention? It means you can be distracted while driving a bus or a plane, or while walking in the street. That's one problem, but it gets worse. Not only are you suddenly, fully distracted every time your phone goes "beep" or "boop" (or someone else's phone does so) but you really cannot perceive just how distracted you are and how much it interferes with your ability to focus on other tasks… …even tasks that might be critical.

The Idea of Anthropology-Based Computing

Anthropology-Based Computing is the application of the fundamentals of Anthropology in order to remake traditional Human-Computer Interaction into a science that is truly based on humans, instead of the motley series of brilliant innovations, glorified mistakes, and obscure Cross-Generational Habits that comprise the computer-centered HCI that we practice today.

Currently, a single human uses dozens of computers, or maybe hundreds or even thousands, if one includes the machines that are used by many individuals, such as the servers run by Google or by Wikipedia; the network that helps you find a flight, or; the one that supports the television weather forecaster in his nightly performance. This is, of course, in addition to the computers or computerized systems shared at work, at home and during the transition between the two. One should also include in the list any and all personal systems being used either deliberately or without any conscious awareness. After all, being consciously unaware of a pervasive technology is a sign of being well-adjusted. Less than a century ago, having electricity in the walls was a fantastic idea that could not be ignored. Fifty years ago, the same was true of using a computer. The only factor in that equation that changes from generation to generation is the technology we learn to ignore.

Earlier, we asked the question of how our ancestors might have thought about the problems and pleasures of their daily lives and we had to admit that we do not and cannot know the answer. All we could do is to conjecture about it based on what we do know of modern humans and of the other modern animals that may be similar to our ancestors.

We may not know what they did, but we do know what they didn't do – what they could not possibly have done. Not one of our remote ancestors could possibly have approached the problem facing them by thinking like a computer.

If we are going to consider the issue of Human-Computer Interaction in any kind of a meaningful way, then we must remember that humans come from stock that spent millions of years not thinking like computers. This is the basic fact that Weiser was trying to communicate when he stressed that the ubiquitous presence of computers in our lives would make it absolutely necessary to change the way we work with them.

The goals of ABC are to explain why Weiser was right to say that HCI must be changed when computers become ubiquitous, and to show how that might be done.

If alarms and alerts annoy you when they come from a smartphone at a nearby workstation, park bench or seat in a movie theatre, how much more would they annoy you if you were living inside the phone? The smart environment of the near future will surround us with computerized recommender systems, ambient information systems, and distributed interfaces and displays. No one expected that the widespread dissemination of electronic mail systems would lead to incessant interruption or that text messaging functions on portable phones would mean that we would be in constant low-fidelity communication throughout the waking day. How will incessant communication expand when every wall, window and door of our homes is automated? How will our "time to be more fully human" diminish when every device in and around our lives is always on the verge of demanding that we stop everything and reply to the technological equivalent of a newborn baby's inchoate and inarticulate demands for attention?

Previous Models

Imagine a tennis court with one side painted entirely in bright red, and the other, entirely in blue. The two players are wearing full body paint of the very same colours and using equipment that matches. The ball is a novel sort that glows very softly, and that changes colours as it crosses the net.

Almost everything on one side is always the same colour, and you are the player wearing blue. The only thing on your side of the net that is not blue is your glasses. They look blue from the outside but on the inside they are red, and their particular shade of red matches the shade of everything on the other side of the net.

You stand ready to play, holding your blue racket in your blue hands, and they all look dark grey to you, through your red glasses. You look forward and you can see the net, but squinting into the field of bright red light shining on the bright red void on the other side of the net, you see nothing.

Suddenly the ball is there, crossing the net, becoming a colour you can see as grey, and it is within reach. You hit it back easily, but now what? Will the return be as easy, or will it arrive from a different angle, at a different height or speed?

You hear the *thok!* of the ball being hit, and try to anticipate, but all you can do is wait until the ball becomes visible and trust that your unseen opposite number also wants to play, and that her strategy is to keep the game going rather than to humiliate you.

The game would be easier if the court were narrower, or if the ball moved more slowly, or if you could take off your goggles and look at what's happening on the other side of the net.

But you stand in the middle of the back end of the court, anticipating, and reacting, and trying to keep it simple and easy. If the game is going well, then in time you convince yourself that it is because of your skills, and you stop doubting the system, and the obvious flaws in the design of the system disappear, and you decide that anyone could play this game – if they were just as clever as you. If the game is going badly, then you learn helplessness and convince yourself that the game is just like that, and you cannot play it -even though you are certain that others can – and you learn to hate the game, and yourself, and you wait for it to end.

Why am I telling you this story when I'm supposed to be talking about models of HCI? Because telling you this story is a way of talking about models of HCI. My ABC model of HCI is based on my triune model of the brain which advances the well-understood concept that humans take in and react to information rationally, reactively, and reflexively, and proposes that input and output devices could be developed to do the same. You might say the model, though, was built on a tennis court. In fact, that tennis court was built on top of a series of other tennis courts that date back to 1991. To see what was there before all of these tennis courts were built, we'll have to go all the way back to 1984.

That's when Donald Norman proposed a seven-step model of human interaction he called the Human Action Cycle [1]. His seven steps take place in three stages: Goal Formation, Execution, and Evaluation. Though the steps and stages are different, the astute reader will recognize some aspects of the iterative feedback cycles discussed in Chap. 9. Variations and modifications of Norman's model have been generated by numerous authors in order to illustrate the interaction between humans and computerized systems.

In going on to those other models, let's consider the way they are laid out. Norman's cycle gave way to a very different layout, one that looks less like an iterative feedback cycle and more like a tennis court, with the human on one side and the computer on the other. Separating them is an interface.

When I began my doctoral studies I was presented with Abowd and Beale's adaptation of Norman's action cycle that shows the single incoming and outgoing actions on both the "human" and "machine" sides of an "interface" [2]. Information is translated four times; towards the barrier and then away from it, on each side. A user's task is translated into input through articulation. The input is then translated again by a performance so that it can be understood by the system. The response from the system is translated into a presentation for output which is subject to observation by the user. It was explained to me that these translations are the focus of this model, in order to enable formal analysis of interface-based issues.

To me it seemed clear that the focus of this model was not the translations but the obstacle that made them necessary. Abowd and Beale's "interface" sits like a barrier between the computer and the human trying to use it. Human and machine lob and return volleys back and forth over the net, unable to perceive the player or the action on the other side (Fig. 10.1).

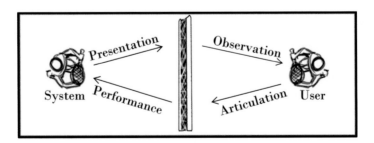

Fig. 10.1 Abowd and Beale's translation-based model, translated onto a tennis court. When the ball crosses the net towards the System, it is "input". The other direction is "output"

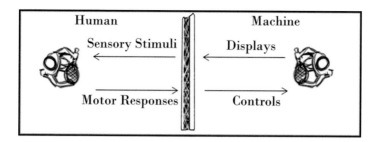

Fig. 10.2 Mackenzie's model on the tennis court. The human uses information processing and decision making while the machine uses a machine state

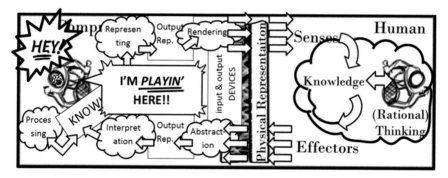

Fig. 10.3 Coomans and Achten's model of interaction, expanding the interface and breaking down the processes on a crowded tennis court

Mackenzie [3] has the players switch sides. The human's "motor responses" now exert actions on the computer's "controls", and the computer's "displays" feed into the human's "sensory stimulae" (Fig. 10.2).

At APCHI, in 1998, the players switched sides again when Coomans and Achten introduced a model that illustrates the processes between each action, labeling them with such descriptive terms as "thinking", "representing", "rendering", and "abstraction" [4]. Through naming, this model gives some implicit value to the differences between human and computer, telling us that the computer uses "processing" on "knowledge in internal digital representation", while the human conducts "rational thinking" using "knowledge" in an "internal mental representation". Despite these improvements, the tennis court – however crowded (Fig. 10.3) – remains focussed on getting the balls back and forth over the net.

All of these lovely models of interaction continued the tradition of the tennis court and, in time, I followed suit. My own tennis court model was presented as part of my thesis (Fig. 10.4). You can see that it is nothing like the model of General Human Interaction that I had been working on earlier, and that I shared with you at the end of Chap. 7 (Fig. 7.3).

The ABC model, a modification of the Coonans and Achten model, illustrates the means by which multitasking and peripheral interaction take place, thus pointing

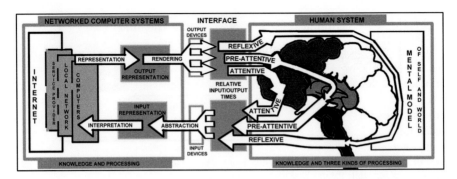

Fig. 10.4 My own tennis-court-style model of HCI based on ABC (Please note that there are three separate processing systems on the human side)

towards the HCI modifications necessary to enable Calm Technology [5]. Based on the theory of "Anthropology-Based Computing" (ABC), this model included the "attentive", "pre-attentive", and "reflexive" information sensing and processing that take place in different parts of the brain and at different speeds [6]. Since then, I have re-named the different levels, in part to avoid confusion with the separate realm of study of attention, in part to provide a closer tie to the usage of the words in normal spoken English, and in part for the simple joy of alliteration. What was "Attentive" is now "Reflective", and "Pre-Attentive" has become "Reactive". "Reflexive" has stayed the same. This model, by any other name, illustrates the natural multi-processing aspect of human interaction with the world and suggests the possibility of deliberately-parallel input and output devices that would focus on one or the other of these sensing and processing modalities [7–11].

The key problem that I have with all of these tennis court-style models is that they center – both literally and figuratively – on the interface rather than on the human. The human is relegated to the periphery, where she sits and waits for the chance to react to a message from the imperceptible realm of computers on the other side of the net.

To continue with the analogy, what does it look like when your attempt to interact fails? You've hit a ball over the net and you are waiting for a return, and waiting… and you don't know if you should try again right away or wait a little longer. You don't know if you should do something differently, because what you just did usually works… Instead of acting, you are relegated to the role of waiting to react… and the ghost of learned helplessness is heckling you from the crowd.

As a counterpoint, but staying with the same analogy, what does it look like when a phone rings?

That's an unanticipated serve that is suddenly on your side of the net. Hurry! Respond! Hurry! React! No time for thought, the serve triggers a reaction in you that interrupts your ongoing conversations or work or play, and you leap to answer the serve. You mustn't miss it…

…unless you have already learned to ignore this kind of serve. That happens sometimes with serves and with phone calls. Sometimes you just let it ring, accepting the annoyance of being hit repeatedly with the ball because you have made the decision to ignore the game for a little while.

Maybe you have even learned not to be stressed by the barrage, but what about the others around you? The serves you are failing to answer are annoying the people around you, and they don't have the choice of returning the serves you are ignoring. They just have to tolerate it, and accept that they have no control over the things that are bothering them. Maybe soon the ghost of learned helplessness will be heckling them, too.

In open resistance to that ghost, I continue to modify my tools, and recommend that you do the same. The next section of this chapter will focus on the latest modification of this model.

BRAINS

The ABC Model of Interaction uses Brown's Representation of Anthropogenic Interaction in Natural Settings (BRAINS) (Fig. 10.5). This incorporates three parallel streams of interaction with the world, each of which has its own cycles of

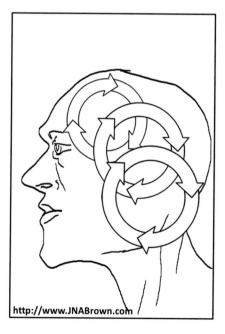

Fig. 10.5 The BRAINS model, ranking our parallel processors according to awareness (height) and dominance (overlapping)

perception, processing, and reaction. Following the examples of MacLean's Triune Brain [12], and Miyata and Norman's bifurcated "approximate theory" in support of multiple activities [13], I relate these three streams to stages in brain evolution and development.

Let's go through them in turn.

1. Reflexive – This incorporates simple reflexes (like when your skin responds to a touch), as well as reflexes that are coordinated in the spinal cord (co-activation and inhibition that allows you to balance the use of all of the muscles in your upper leg so that they don't work against one another when you kick a football), and also those coordinated in the cerebellum (riding a bicycle, or knitting).

This is the fastest of the streams, and using it consumes the least of the body's energy.

In balance, the use of this system is involuntary, unintentional, unwitting, and unmindful. This system is used for reactions that are either too common or too fast to be done consciously. This includes the parts of your brain and nervous system that pull your hand away from a flame, jerk your knee under a doctor's rubber mallet, and keep your body balanced when you are standing still.

Physiologically, this system is related to the cerebellum, medulla oblongata, spinal cord, and nerves (simple reflex arcs and coordinated reflex arcs).

Embryonically, these are the earliest parts of the system to develop, and they are in use starting in utero.

Evolutionarily, this is the part of the nervous system we share with our most distant cousins like starfish, worms, beetles, etc....

Conceptually, this is related to real reflexes (like a knee jerk), and not the "knee-jerk reactions" that people often speak of as reflexes. You don't get angry with opposing political views or argue with someone about global warming because of reflexes. Those are reactions and they take place in the next system we will discuss.

2. Reactive – Unlike reflexes, there is some sort of thinking that goes on in the reactive system. It is the fastest and least expensive type of thinking, so it is good for speed and bad for long-term planning. It is involuntary, unintentional, impulsive and, like reflexes, unmindful.

This is the part of your brain that knows to start reading a new page at the top left corner, and that feels little confused when the page is not laid out that way.

Physiologically, this stream is related to the amygdalic region of the brain which hosts emotional reactions, complex pattern recognition, some aspects of facial recognition and a lot of other types of information processing that are faster than conscious thought.

Embryonically, this is the second part of the brain to develop in utero, and it is in use, to varying degrees, from shortly after birth.

Evolutionarily, this is the part of the brain that we share with more distant cousins like dogs and cats, and sheep and pigs, etc....

Conceptually, this type of processing is related to Freud's "unconscious", and it includes all of your emotional reactions, "gut feelings", "intuition", faith, and irrational thought. This is where you feel either above average or useless; where self-deception takes place, and where we convince ourselves of self-serving false memories. It is also the place where we do the sort of complex pattern recognition that unthinkingly guides you when changing course to match the changing flow of traffic on a sidewalk, crowded staircase, or highway.

I propose that this is where most of our decisions are made, especially the decisions we feel very strongly about and refuse to reflect upon. Rational doubt and reflection take place in the level of processing we will discuss next.

3. Reflective – This is the kind of thinking that is slow and expensive in terms of the body's resources; possibly very slow and very expensive. This kind of thought is voluntary, intentional, deliberate, mindful, and reasonable.

It is the part of your brain thinking about this sentence, as opposed to the part tapping your foot or the one thinking about lunch.

Physiologically this kind of thought is related to the neocortex and it incorporates logical thought, reading, arithmetic and many different processing systems.

Embryonically, this is the last part of the brain to bud, and it doesn't finish developing or come fully into use until the early 20s.

Evolutionarily, this is the most recent addition to the brain, shared with close relatives like other great apes.

Conceptually, this kind of thought is related to Freud's "conscious", and to the "mindfulness" you might learn in a seminar on meditation. It is reflection, and ratiocination, cogitation, logical reasoning, etc....

This last is the place where the scientific method forces us to work. You will still react with the other systems while trying to be scientific, but you can learn to control those reactions and proceed mindfully and with a rational acceptance of your own fallibility.

I'd like to finish this discussion of my BRAINS model, by offering you another, more visceral, analogy for the three types of processing.

MacLean proposed that his three systems became part of the human brain in turns over millennia, and he named them for three types of ancestors, from three different evolutionary eras. He called the most primitive part of his model the reptilian brain, then leapt forward in time to label the next two sections the paleo-mammalian and the neo-mammalian.

The last two illustrations in this chapter are two new ideas. The first (Fig. 10.6) is my attempt at a better attribution of the evolutionary stages at which we gained the ability to interact with our world according to Reflex (Fig. 10.6a) Reaction (Fig. 10.6b), and Reflection (Fig. 10.6c). The final illustration of this chapter is a new model of the way that humans interact, whether with computers, or other humans, or hammers, or any other, tool, system or environment, or any combination thereof (Fig. 10.7).

So interaction works like this:

The analogies of the starfish, tree-mouse and ivory tower provide the inspiration for an interesting model of human interaction. In the same way that Dawkins suggested that "The Selfish Gene" is protected in a pool of the primordial ocean in

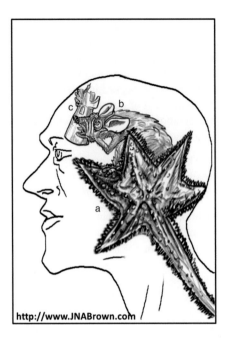

Fig. 10.6 Reflexes like a echinoderms (**a**), emotions like protoprosimian (**b**), and conscious thought in an ivory tower (**c**)

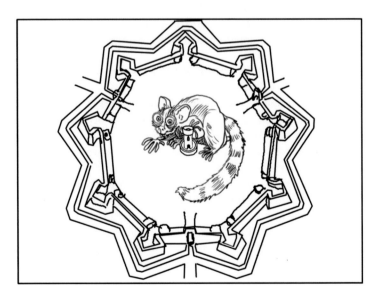

Fig. 10.7 Most stimuli are dealt with at the reflexive level and never reach our thoughts. The stimuli that do penetrate that barrier trigger the reactions of the protoprosimian who is not likely to waste the time or energy involved in seeking advice from the intellect that sits alone in its ivory tower. Remember that the intellect knows only what is shared in the whispers or screams of the protoprosimian

which it evolved [14], so it is with our conscious selves. We sit in an ivory tower, removed from the world, protected from the realities that might inhibit us from moving outward from our nests. The tower is set inside a star-shaped fortress, and the grounds are guarded by the embodiment of the fearful but curious great grand-parents who first learned to think.

Our peripheral nervous system perceives most input and responds either directly or with coordination through the spinal cord, medulla oblongata, or cerebellum. That's the starfish that perceives, responds with reflexes, and allows a very small amount of filtered and reconstructed information to pass inwards for further pro-cessing. The starfish is always busy with a thousand things but, unless it is fully occupied in an unusually challenging situation, it does pass a small amount of infor-mation to the protoprosimian.

The subconscious, visceral, or limbic portions of our brain receive some infor-mation that has filtered through the first wall and some that has been reconstructed by the processes of the first wall. We are now in the region symbolized by the pro-toprosimian, who roams around perceiving the filtered information, reconstructing it according to models in place, and then reacting. Reaction includes reconstructing that data again, responding according to ingrained habits and unreasoning shortcuts, and also sharing some information with the person sitting alone in their ivory tower.

The Ivory tower is the most interior of our thoughts. In my earlier models, I put this region in front of and above the other regions, in keeping with the cross-generational habits inherited from MacLean, and Norman, and Freud. Now I see that it is really the region most removed from the world outside. The only informa-tion that reaches that region is information that has been filtered and reconstructed at least twice already. The person sitting alone in the ivory tower may or may not be paying attention. She relies entirely on the other systems for her most of her infor-mation and for most of her rewards. The result is that she can spend a lot of her time sleeping, relying on the other two systems to keep everything working smoothly, avoid danger, and entertain her.

I just want to point out that I am using the term Ivory tower in the sense of Charles-Augustin Sainte-Beuve's use of the phrase in "Pensées d'Aout" [15], meaning a place of isolated intellectualism that is sheltered from the real world. I know it's also used in "The Song of Solomon", but I'm not (currently) describing anybody's neck.

We'll discuss practical applications of this model of HCI in the next two chapters, and see how you can make immediate use of it improve your relationship with your digital devices in the last section of the book.

Summary

Really? You're thinking of skipping in this chapter? This is the chapter that the book is named after. I mean, at *least* read *this* one!

Of course, if you do try to read it, and you haven't read the others, then you probably won't understand every part of it. I mean, you likely *could* figure it all out if you were to put some effort into it, but if we've already established that you're not putting a whole lot of effort into reading this book, then…

…maybe just grab a bag of something crunchy and a bottle of something sweet, pop on the TV, and see if there's an old episode of some show you've already seen. You can watch what you already know, and consume familiar-tasting poisons, and leave the real thinking to someone who wants to be more human than angleworm.

If you do make the choice to live like that, – without thinking hard about things- then, until you decide to grow up, do us all a favour and stop expressing your opinions on complex issues like vaccination and the economy, and the immigration of refugees. Actually, please also stop expressing your opinion on simple issues like feminism and evolution, or whether there are separate human races.

Just buy lots of insurance and pay your taxes, and stay out of the way of people who choose to think with the part of the brain that's harder to use. We may come and join you on the couch from time to time, because everyone likes to relax and take the occasional break, and we all get pleasure from cycling through predictable patterns but, while we're there, let's keep the conversation light. Tell me, what's new with the millionaires you follow?

You probably feel like you have a lot more to say, but until you take the time to really think deeply about your opinion, why should anyone else?

References

1. Norman DA (1984) Stages and levels in human-machine interaction. Int J Man-Machine Stud 21(4):365–375
2. Abowd GD, Beale R (1991) Users, systems and interfaces: a unifying framework for interaction. HCI 91:73–87
3. MacKenzie IS (1995) Input devices and interaction techniques for advanced computing. In: Barfield W, Furness TA III (eds) Virtual environments and advanced interface design. Oxford University Press, Oxford, pp 437–470
4. Coomans M, Achten H (1998) Mixed task domain representation in VR-DIS. In: Proceedings of the 3rd Asia-Pacific Conference on Human Computer Interaction, APCHI'98, Shonan village. IEEE Computer Society, Washington, DC, pp 415–420
5. Brown JNA (2012) Expert Talk for Time Machine Session: Designing Calm Technology "… as Refreshing as Taking a Walk in the Woods". 2012 IEEE International Conference on Multimedia and Expo, vol 1, pp 423
6. Brown JNA, Gerhard Leitner, Martin Hitz and Andreu Català Mallofré (2014, April-May) A model of calm HCI. In: Bakker S, Hausen D, Selker T, van den Hoven E, Butz A, Eggen B (eds) Peripheral interaction: shaping the research and design space. Workshop at CHI 2014, Toronto, Canada. ISSN: 1862-5207
7. Brown JNA, Kaufmann B, Bacher F, Sourisse C, Hitz M (2013a) " Oh, I Say, Jeeves!" A calm approach to smart home input. In: Human-computer interaction and knowledge discovery in complex, unstructured, big data. Springer, Berlin, pp 265–274
8. Brown JNA, Kaufmann B, Huber FJ, Pirolt KH, Hitz M (2013) "… Language in Their Very Gesture" First steps towards calm smart home input. In: Human-computer interaction and knowledge discovery in complex, unstructured, big data. Springer, Berlin, pp 256–264

9. Brown JNA (2013) It's as easy as ABC: introducing anthropology-based computing. In: Advances in computational intelligence. Springer, Berlin, pp 1–16
10. Brown JNA (2015) Making sense of the noise: an ABC approach to big data and security. In: Akhgar B, Saathoff GB, Arabnia HR, Hill R, Staniforth A, Bayerl PS (eds) Application of big data for national security. Elsevier, Oxford, pp 261–273
11. Brown JNA (2016) "…Unseen, Yet Crescive…" The unrecognised history of peripheral inter-action. In: Bakker S, Hausen D, Selker T (eds) Peripheral interaction: challenges and opportunities for HCI in the periphery of attention. Springer, Cham (in Press)
12. MacLean PD (1990) The triune brain in evolution: role in paleocerebral functions. Springer, Dordrecht
13. Miyata Y, Norman DA (1986) Psychological issues in support of multiple activities. In: Norman DA, Draper SW (eds) User centered system design: new perspectives on human-computer interaction. Mahwah, New Jersey, USA, pp 265–284
14. Dawkins R (1976) The selfish gene. Oxford University Press, Oxford, England
15. Sainte-Beuve C-A (1837) Pensées d'août: poésies. E. Renduel

Chapter 11
Applying Anthropology-Based Computing

Smart Homes: Are they?

Abstract I developed my first model of interaction based on the triune brain while working on smart homes in Austria. In this chapter I'll talk a bit about how I based my minor contributions to the Casa Vecchia project on a century-old British non-sense poem, and I'll also tell you a bit about our findings regarding intuitive multi-modal interaction.

We'll close this chapter with a look at the research project I ran in Portugal, and our attempts to apply ABC and the BRAINS model of interaction to the design of smart ringtones for smartphones.

Let's start the chapter with a discussion about a black box, and the story of how my colleagues, my students, and I filled it with a series of apps based on a 50-year old communications failsafe from the early days of satellite networks.

© Springer International Publishing Switzerland 2016

J.N.A. Brown, *Anthropology-Based Computing*, Human–Computer
Interaction Series, DOI 10.1007/978-3-319-24421-1_11

Zapping the SNARK: A Simple Gesture of Understanding

In Which Intuitive, Multi-modal, Human-centered Interaction Proves to Be, Well, Intuitive, Multi-modal, and Human-centered

The DOMUS initiative is a transborder research network in the Alpine/Adriatic region of Europe. There, high-ranking professors, their research staff, and assistants try to chart out a cooperative path for their work in the field of Smart Homes. I was lucky enough to be invited to their first meeting, just after arriving in Europe.

Chatting over coffee during a break, I was asked if had an opinion on how to solve the problem they had been discussing: making interaction with smart homes "intuitive" (Fig. 11.1).

I suggested that one solution, the easiest one I could imagine, would be to replace the technology-centered interface with a formal but friendly butler. Your butler and you would have to have an understanding, right from the start, that he or she was always working in your service and would always try to accomplish what you wanted. That said, he would not always understand, and it would not always be possible to get his staff to do what you want.

I wasn't talking about a butler based on an AI, but the illusion of a butler. While I write these words, my computer pretends to be a typewriter and presents to me the illusion of a piece of paper with letters appearing as I type them. In multipage mode, I am presented with a series of pages, each with borders and edges and a shared font…

Fig. 11.1 We had the chance to promote our research group at a gala ball. We used it to run an informal test of our prototype and of the hypothesis that gestures can actually be very easy to learn

It is an illusion based on someone's conception of helping people get used to typing on a computer.

Why not replace that illusion – not for typing, where it works well – but for inter-acting with a home. I have a mental model of an assistant who helps me run my home. That model is a butler; one who can manage all of my other invisible servants.

Someone in our little kaffeeklatsch shared the idea with their delegation and it was raised during the meeting. It was shot down as being too impractical for short term development. Standing outside of my office the next day a colleague who had been there explained why.

Dr Abdelhamid Bouchachia told me that effective voice-activated controls were still a black box, and I had to ask him to explain.

It seems that many people had worked on the idea of voice-activated systems, including the voice interface for smartphones that became a fad a few years ago. The problem of misunderstandings was bad, even when you held the device in your hand and it was trying to learn to understand your voice and your word choice. Building a system that could teach itself your preferences is his field, but the prob-lem goes further than that in two very practical ways.

First, there is the problem of misunderstandings leading to constant errors that need constantly to be fixed. The first few misunderstandings might be funny, but it doesn't take long for it to become frustrating. Consider the story of Error 404 I shared a little earlier. How much worse would your life be if you encountered that kind of blind resistance as a regular part of your day?

The second problem area is the issue of having a computer listen to you all of the time. People concerned with privacy have one problem with that, but there are also the engineering issues of the need for the system to run 24/7, and the need for the system to be able to understand you even in the midst of all of the background noise of day-to-day life.

People theorizing about HCI often came back to the idea of an invisible major domo [1]. People trying to implement it in real world settings found that these other issues made the idea impossible for now [2]. The result was a black box on many plans for interaction with smart systems: a shorthand code for an obstacle that should just be ignored for now. I thought it was wonderful to learn that engineers and computer scientists were actually applying the principle of the S.E.P. field as described by Douglas Adams in "Life, the Universe, and Everything" [3].

According to Adams, anything within such a field is automatically filtered out of your perception and you can carry on as though it was not there. In your mind, it has become Somebody Else's Problem (SEP).

Well, by the time we'd finished talking we were in my office and I'd drawn the black box on the whiteboard I shared with my officemate. Hamid had drawn arrows going into it and arrows going out of it, and had added another limitation.

The language you and the system use to speak with each other is so stilted that it never feels natural. The generated audio feels alien and every mispronunciation breaks the illusion of natural conversation. Worse, humans don't like to have to use a limited command lexicon. They want to be able to speak naturally, but it takes time for a system to learn your phrases, your word choice, and all of the possible synonyms in natural speech.

I thanked him for making it so clear and we shook hands, and I told him I'd see what I could think up.

In principle, I solved the problem that night.

I should stress that some of the solution came from Gay Deceiver, the smart car in Robert A Heinlein's book "The Number of The Beast" [4], and some of it came from a paper I'd read from the 1960s about the use of triple modular redundancy to effectively communicate with satellites back in the days when reception was uncertain [5]. A large part of the idea came from Lewis Carrol's great nonsense poem "The Hunting of the Snark" [6].

If you want to read about it in detail, my PhD thesis is available in the national registries in Austria, Spain, and Italy, and you can find it online pretty easily [7]. If you can't be bothered to read it all the way through, well, let's just say that you wouldn't be the first person to make that decision. A very short summary of the work is available at the "Reading Room" of the Future and Emerging Technologies Proactive Initiative of the European Commission (http://www.focas-reading-room. eu/intuitive-interaction-with-a-smart-environment/) [8].

My original whiteboard drawing is shown in Fig. 11.2, and you might want to refer to it as I run through this explanation. I'm sorry about the quality of the photo,

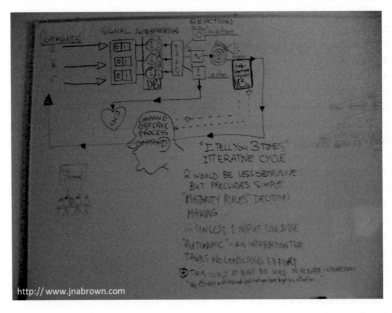

Fig. 11.2 My original SNARK model of the possible means to facilitate human-centered communication between humans and computers

but I was trying to preserve the idea before it was erased, and never thought that anyone would want to see it.

The basic idea is triple modular redundancy, as expressed by the Bellman in the story about the Snark: "What I tell you three times is true". Almost all noise and possible signals are ignored, but if three particular signals are recognized, then the system should prepare for further input and ask how it may help you. If, at any time, the system recognizes two signals and is uncertain about the third, it could query.

I thought that the whole thing could be controlled with a smartphone, using that device's abilities to provide incredibly rich and varied voice output, and to detect input from sound, touch, and movement.

I called the system SNARK or Synchronizing Natural Actions and Reacting Knowledgeably. Prototypical versions were tested and reported in two formal papers co-authored with some of my students from a particularly practical course in Research Methods [9, 10]. Three other papers were also produced in that course, based on the ideas of other members of our research group, and one of the three was also published. The two papers based on my ideas established that we could capture deliberate command sounds in a noisy environment, and that we could use a smartphone to capture unconscious movements – all as computer input. They were the first international publications for four of my students, and I should take a moment to put their names in print here, and to publically thank them for developing and demonstrating their skills so well. Herr Huber, Herr Pirolt, Herr Bacher, and Monsieur Sourisse, you all did a good job, and I hope we will work together again in the future.

Despite this experimental success with multimodal interaction, I still had to convince my supervisors that gestural interaction was not as complex as most researchers seemed to think. I believed that the key to implementing gestures in HCI was an understanding of how humans naturally use them as a data stream that is parallel to but different from the data stream provided by our words [11]. Somehow, it seemed that computer scientists had misunderstood this, and I believed that their misunderstanding was what made it hard to use gestures in HCI. We tested my theory on a bunch of well-dressed drunks.

My friend István Fehérvári programmed a simple game based on my design, and set it up as a downloadable app, the "z_APP". We presented it at the annual Gala Ball of the Alpen-Adria Universität Klagenfurt. The game concept was a simple Rock-Paper-Scissors (Schere, Stein, Papier) structure, but the players wore wizard's hats and stood on a red carpet in front of a big video screen that showed wizardly avatars waving wands in a castle tower.

The player could choose three magic spells as shown in Fig. 11.3. Done properly, each could make either giant scissors, a giant stone, or a giant stack of paper appear over the head of their opponent's avatar with a "ZAPP!". Matched spells would both be defeated, and the game worked according to the normal, well-known rules. A winning stone or pile of paper would crush your opponent's avatar. A winning pair of scissors would cut off the top of the avatar's hat.

We reminded the first players of the rules, and showed them the diagram of the spells and asked them to please teach the next players in line.

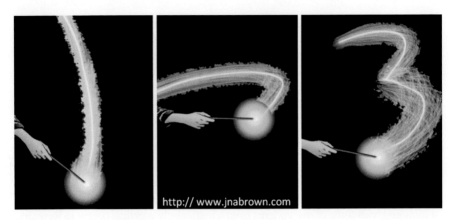

http:// www.jnabrown.com

Fig. 11.3 The gestures for "Rock", "Scissors", and "Paper"

The game was a big success among the tuxedoed and gowned partiers, and it also provided two proofs of concept. The players all found it effortless to apply a familiar mental model to interaction with a computer system, and; the teaching and learning was very successful. The raw data from the server showed that, over the course of the 5 h of gameplay, 649 gestures were attempted and 524 of them were successful. That meant that players who had not been formally familiarized, who were trained in a noisy and distracting setting, and who played while in various (uncontrolled and unmeasured) degrees of sobriety, were more than 80 % successful [12].

Catching the SNARK and Putting Him to Work in a Wise Home

Appropriate technology should be designed in a way that would enable users to freely choose which devices to use for interaction, and in what order and combination to use them; selecting the appropriate means and modality with which to perform any given interaction. This freedom of choice occurs naturally in human to human interaction, where the combination and the change between gesture, tactile, and verbal interaction works smoothly. (Gerhard Leitner, from his 2015 book, *The Future Home is Wise, Not Smart* [13])

At the opening of this chapter I told a story in which I was rescued from criticism by a well-read colleague. That colleague was Gerhard Leitner. By the time I returned to Austria, Dr Leitner had been working for years, with his colleague Anton Fercher, on a wonderful research project called Casa Vecchia [14–17]. This project implemented smart home technology in the homes of rural and suburban seniors in the Alpen-Adria region, and it did so gradually, in sensitive and calculated response to the needs and desires of each household. I advise any readers who are interested in Smart homes to read their publications and to contact Dr Leitner and Mr Fercher directly. Theirs was the only Smart Home project I have ever heard of that was implemented the way that those systems were originally intended to be implemented – through the gradual introduction of technological assistance into the established home and existing routines of the target user [18].

Rather than rest on their laurels, they are trying to help the concept of Smart Homes move on to the next natural stage of their evolution, an idea Dr Leitner calls *"The Future Home is Wise, Not Smart"* [13]. We should all hope that his ideas are understood by the engineers and computer scientists currently working in the field of Smart Homes, as well as in the larger fields of Ubiquitous Computing, Pervasive Computing, and HCI in general.

In applying the SNARK to a smart home setting, I wanted to make the interaction truly intuitive and Calm. In Weiser's words, I wanted the SNARK to disappear. If you're familiar with the original story, then you know – SPOILER ALERT – that the Snark turns out to be a Boojum. I came up with a strategy for mapping technical devices and commands onto names and actions determined by the user's preferences and fit it rather strenuously into the acronym for Brown's Open Ontology for Joint User Management. This would allow each user to have a customised interaction, and it would be fast. Rather than having the system train itself to recognize general identifiable patterns of sound and motion from samples provided by the user, we simply filled in a parallel database in which the user's preferences were associated directly with existing values.

This allowed us to initiate the Bellman's Protocol. To understand, let's look back one last time at the original poem. In it, the captain of the ship, the one who has gathered the crew to hunt the Snark, is also called "the Bellman". This is because he doesn't use maps or any traditional means to navigate or to control the ship. He simply rings a bell – at the time a ubiquitous tool for distant communication – and the ship goes where he needs it to go. He does not have to know how that works, or why, or where they are going. He just has to want to go there. Sounds like intuitive interaction to me.

Anton wrote the next generation of the SNARK as a downloadable app that would fit over the established interface of the Casa Vecchia system, enabling natural multimodal interaction with the visible and invisible tools and devices in a smart home. We called the new app CASA TEVA, which is the ending of the old Catalàn phrase "Casa meva és casa teva" that might be more familiar to the reader as the Spanish "Mi casa es su casa". In this particular case, it was also an acronym for "Customizable Activation of Smart-home Appliances Through Enhanced Virtual Assistants".

Gerhard, Anton, and I worked together to implement the system in the Living Lab at Lakeside Park (http://www.lakeside-scitec.com/). That laboratory was built in an alcove between several offices and labs. It contained the shared kitchen and bathroom for the area, as well as a lounge arranged like a living room. All of the electronic devices, from the radio to the powered blinds above the couch, were hooked into a working model of the Casa Vecchia interface.

Our trials took place in June and July of 2013. They went surprisingly well. In a brief one-on-one, carefully-designed discussion, each participant was reminded of their own mental models of butlers and servants, and each was introduced to the idea of having an invisible butler who would try to help them use the technology hidden in the lab. Some participants were very comfortable with the idea (Fig. 11.4).

Fig. 11.4 During the Gesture-centered trial, one participant was a little more laid back than the others

They each named the butler, and then were shown how to interact with him. Both styles of interaction were multi-modal, but one focussed primarily on audial interaction and peripherally on visual, while the other focussed primarily on gestural interaction with peripheral support in audio, visual, and tactile modalities. To put it more clearly, the participants could either clap their hands and call the butler by name, after which he would offer assistance and ask for their wishes, or they could speak the name of the device they wanted to control and wave their phone like a magic wand casting one of three spells, and the invisible butler would hurry to make the magic happen.

They were allowed to try four tasks, but were not given the time to become familiar with the device. They were then given a list of nine to perform in order. They would have to intuit how to perform the five tasks they hadn't tried with the unfamiliar interface.

We measured a success rate that ranged between 28 and 69 % on the first voice-centered attempt (median 56.3 %), and between 34 and 91 % on the first gesture-centered attempt (median 90.6 %).

By the third attempt, without pauses or retraining, the voice centered interaction was between 66 and 100 % successful (median 65.6 %), and the gesture-based commands were between 78 and 100 % successful (median 93.8 %).

In qualitative terms, the project was also a success. The participants rated the features of the app as desirable with median rankings at the highest or second-highest level possible in all questions. We also used a System Usability Scale to evaluate the experience [19]. The participants rated our prototype as having a higher usability than 80 % of all such systems.

The project that had brought me to Europe was over, and had ended well. To my surprise, I was awarded separate doctoral titles from three universities, and that should have been enough... ...but it wasn't. I wanted to continue to apply my ideas in practical ways. I believed that this model of interaction could be applied to improving day-to-day interaction with computers, and even to saving lives.

The first step towards that was to design an experiment that could gather some empirical evidence that showed the brain operating on these different levels... or to demonstrate that it doesn't.

So I moved to Lisbon.

O Toque Que Toques: Practical Applications of ABC to Personal Alerts

The first experiment of the ABC Ringtones Project took place at the Laboratory of Experimental Psychology at University Lusófona in Lisbon, Portugal, in 2014.

My partner in this work was Professor Jorge Oliveira. Some of the other professors there also offered support, and feedback, and I should make a point of mentioning Rodrigo Brigo, Pedro Gamito, Diogo Morais, and Waldir Moreira. The first paper describing the experiment is currently in press [20]. Whatever its fate, we gathered a lot of data and we are planning several more papers dealing more closely with qualitative analysis of the experience, and associating the experience with different unconscious physiological processes.

Let me walk you through what we did and what we found. Let's start with a cocktail party.

This book started with a description of Mark Weiser's call for Calm Computing [21]. Weiser specified that, in order not to drive us crazy, the computerized devices surrounding us would have to be designed to allow us to easily control the influx of information. More specifically, he said that we should be able to shift the information from the periphery of our attention to the centre of our attention and back again. Unfortunately, he described the idea quite clearly, and quoted experts from several fields in doing so, but he did not describe the mechanism that would make it possible.

Some have argued that he didn't do so because no such mechanism exists, and many have argued – consciously or unconsciously – that the only way for humans to shift their attention is to divide the limited resource of conscious focus. As you know from Chap. 10, I disagree. I believe that our triune brain provides us with the mechanism to filter information through different levels of attention. I believe that an aspect of this is demonstrated in the interrelation between the conscious and the unconscious in the works of scholars and thinkers ranging from Plato to Freud, but I also believe that it is a practical matter, that explains why fast, emotional reactions cannot be explained logically, and why an expert can knit or juggle chainsaws better than she can explain the mechanism of either knitting or juggling chainsaws.

Logic is slow. Learned patterns of coordinated reflexes are much faster, but involve no reasoning. Most of our reactions to the world around us, at least most of the ones we are aware of, happen in between the two extremes. This is the realm of the visceral brain, of pattern recognition and emotion, and the overlap between the two that I believe is responsible for our sense of humour.

It is also responsible for a step in the filtering of information that is largely unknown to most of us. This step was described by Cherry in 1953; psychologists call it the Cocktail Party Effect [22]. It is the human ability to unconsciously or pre-attentively filter information so that, for example, some voices in a loud room are ignored while others are interpreted as spoken words. In 1959 Moray added to our understanding of this phenomenon by demonstrating that one key to the filtration is the emotional value of some components of the speech [23]. Golumbic et al. demonstrated this very well in 2013 by taking advantage of the network of electrodes directly fitted on the brains of volunteers awaiting surgical treatment for epilepsy [24]. Each was shown a video of two storytellers telling two different stories at the same time. The volunteers were instructed to ignore one person and listen attentively to the other. The parts of their brain that process sound responded equally to the flow of both stories, but the parts of the brain that deal with language responded only to the story that was being listened to.

Somewhere between the process of hearing and the process of listening, some other process was filtering the noise.

I believe that we can trigger that deliberate initiation of that process has the potential to "hack" the way we think, and could force us to pay attention when we might otherwise be on autopilot. The question I wanted to answer in Lisbon was whether or not deliberate initiation was at all possible.

It is.

We wired ten volunteers to monitor their heart and respiration rates and their skin conductivity, and we set them the task quickly and accurately typing a string of numbers and symbols. We tracked their eye movements as they did so, and we had them repeat the whole thing with the loud noise of a busy cafè in the background.

We also wired them with five channels of eeg so that we could see the density of the electrical activity in different parts of their brains, and we tracked their word rates as they went along.

After familiarization with the task, and establishing a baseline for all of our data, we made their phone ring. It wasn't just random ringing. We filled their phone with a series of ringtones – their own, a common one, and two different voices speaking to them, one a stranger, and one a very close personal friend or family member. Each speaker said an everyday word that had been chosen because it was ranked as having a low emotional impact, and at the same time as being highly common.

Each speaker also spoke the name of the participant.

Each recording was played at three volumes. One louder than the background noise, one matching the volume of the noisy and crowded café, and one too soft to be heard over the background noise.

To our surprise, we found that the participants were not very distracted by the ringing of their own ringtone. Apparently, they had learned to ignore it while working on a deliberate task – or at least a short-term one being run as a scientific experiment.

More surprising, we saw that when the voice of a loved one softly spoke the name of the participant at 55–65 decibels (dB), in the midst of a background noise of 75–85 dB, the brain reacted differently than it had to any of the other stimuli. The posterior region of the brain lit up with electrical activity, and a small signal was seen to move from the back of the brain to the front, and the participants reported becoming aware of the voice, and the speaker, and of their name. But their word rate didn't drop, and the part of their brain that lit up when something caught their attention… it didn't light up.

Whatever happened, it didn't interrupt their work.

We suggest that the signal we recorded is physiological evidence of the natural act of undemanding attentional transfer that Weiser called "centering". We believe that we have generated a "Calm" output.

We believe that we may have uncovered the process that will allow us to create alarms that will be heard and understood without interrupting one's conscious attention to other matters. Aside from making it less unpleasant to be i a crowd of ringing phones, this has tremendous implications for the use of signals and alerts in hazardous situations and in emergencies.

Imagine a way to always catch the attention of a distracted pilot, or to inform a firefighter of new and vital information without breaking her concentration. I'll talk about possible applications in the next chapter, but first I'd like you to consider something.

Measuring that cerebral process was pretty cool, but here is the cooler part of that story. There was nothing special about those ABC ringtones. They weren't created in a lab or assembled using proprietary software. Without knowing how they would be used, the participants recorded the voices of their loved ones that had such astonishing affect.

You could do the same.

If you'd like to learn how, check out Chap. 17.

Summary

This has been a test of our individualized information sharing system.

If you had been interested in finding information about the early days of Anthropology-Based Computing, you would have had access through the system.

If you are reading this instead of reading the full chapter, then you have made your individualized choice and your performance will be recorded as a successful trial.

If you are reading this simply for the jokes, then you should laugh now, or at least smile.

Go on.

If you finish the chapter laughing, your memory of the entire experience will be more positive.

References

1. Ping A, Wang Z, Shi X, Deng C, Bian L, Chen L (2009, December) Designing an emotional majormodo in smart home healthcare. In: Intelligent interaction and affective computing. ASIA'09. International Asia Symposium on. IEEE, pp 45–47
2. Vacher M, Istrate D, Portet F, Joubert T, Chevalier T, Smidtas S, Meillon B, Lecouteux B, Sehili M, Chahuara P, Méniard S (2011) The sweet-home project: audio technology in smart homes to improve well-being and reliance. In: 33rd annual international IEEE EMBS conference, Boston, MA, USA
3. Adams D (1982) Life, the universe, and everything. Pan, London
4. Heinlein RA (1980) The number of the beast. Fawcett Columbine, Manhattan
5. Kaschmitter JL, Shaeffer DL, Colella NJ, McKnett CL, Coakley PG (1991) Operation of commercial R3000 processors in the Low Earth Orbit (LEO) space environment. IEEE Trans Nucl Sci 38(6):1415–1420
6. Carroll L (1876) The hunting of the Snark. Macmillan, London
7. Brown JNA (2014) Unifying interaction across distributed controls in a smart environment: using anthropology-based computing to make human-computer interaction "Calm". Doctoral dissertation, Alpen-Adria Universität_Klagenfurt; Universitat Politècnica de Catalunya; Università degli Studi di Genova. Retrieved from Tesis Doctorals en Xarxa (tdx.cat)
8. Brown JNA (2015) Intuitive interaction with a smart environment. Fundamentals of Collective Adaptive Systems (FoCAS) reading room, January 2015. http://www.focas-reading-room.eu/intuitive-interaction-with-a-smart-environment/. Last retrieved May 2015
9. Brown JNA, Kaufmann B, Bacher F, Sourisse C, Hitz M (2013) " Oh, I Say, Jeeves!" A calm approach to smart home input. In: Human-computer interaction and knowledge discovery in complex, unstructured, big data. Springer, Berlin/Heidelberg, pp 265–274
10. Brown JNA, Kaufmann B, Huber FJ, Pirolt KH, Hitz M (2013) "… Language in Their Very Gesture" first steps towards calm smart home input. In: Human-computer Interaction and knowledge discovery in complex, unstructured, big data. Springer, Berlin/Heidelberg, pp 256–264
11. McNeill D (1992) Hand and mind: what gestures reveal about thought. University of Chicago Press, Chicago
12. Brown JNA, Féhrevári I (2012) zAPP: gesture learning and transfer in an informal setting. Unpublished report
13. Leitner G (2015) The future home is wise, not smart: a human-centric perspective on next generation domestic technologies. Springer, Cham
14. Leitner G, Fercher A, Felfernig A, Hitz M (2012) Reducing the entry threshold of AAL systems: preliminary results from casa vecchia. In: Miesenberger K, Karshmer A, Penaz P, Zagler W (eds) Computers helping people with special needs, vol 7382, 1st edn, Lecture notes in computer science. Springer, Heidelberg, pp 709–715
15. Leitner G, Mitrea O, Fercher AJ (2013) Towards an acceptance model for AAL. In: Human factors in computing and informatics. Springer, Berlin/Heidelberg, pp 672–679
16. Leitner G, Felfernig A, Fercher AJ, Hitz M (2014) Disseminating ambient assisted living in rural areas. Sensors 14(8):13496–13531
17. Leitner G, Hitz M, Fercher AJ, Brown JNA (2013) Aspekte der Human Computer Interaction im Smart Home. Aspekte der Human Computer Interaction im Smart Home. HMD Prax Wirtschaftsinformatik 50(6):37–47
18. Venkatesh A (1996) Computers and other interactive technologies for the home. Commun ACM 39(12):47–54
19. Brooke J (1996) SUS: a "Quick and Dirty" usability scale. In: Jordan PW, Thomas B, Weerdmeester BA, McClelland (eds) Usability evaluation in industry. Taylor & Francis, London, pp 189–194
20. Brown JNA, Oliveira J, Bakker S (2015) I am calm: towards a psychoneurological evaluation of ABC ringtones. Interact Des Architect 26:55–69

21. Weiser M, Brown JS (1996) Designing calm technology. PowerGrid J 1(1):75–85
22. Cherry EC (1953) Some experiments on the recognition of speech, with one and with two ears. J Acoust Soc Am 25(5):975–979
23. Moray N (1959) Attention in dichotic listening: affective cues and the influence of instructions. Q J Exp Psychol 11(1):56–60
24. Golumbic EMZ, Ding N, Bickel S, Lakatos P, Schevon CA, McKhann GM, … Schroeder CE (2013) Mechanisms underlying selective neuronal tracking of attended speech at a "Cocktail Party". Neuron 77:980–991

Chapter 12
Future Work in ABC

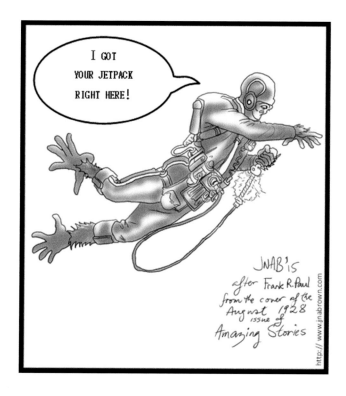

Abstract According to Bardzell and Bardzell (Pers Ubiquit Comput 2:1–16, 2013), Weiser's ideas of ubiquitous computing and calm technology have generated two very different responses. "Calm" was intended to become a fundamental factor in the design and creation of hardware and software. Instead, engineers and

© Springer International Publishing Switzerland 2016

J.N.A. Brown, *Anthropology-Based Computing*, Human–Computer
Interaction Series, DOI 10.1007/978-3-319-24421-1_12

technology-oriented scientists have continued to pursue technology-centered solutions, while psychologists and human-oriented scientists remain on the periphery, chasing a vision of human-centeredness. My work has been an attempt to build a bridge between the two groups Brown (Intuitive interaction with a smart environment. Fundamentals of collective adaptive systems (FoCAS) reading room. Jan 2015 http://www.focas-reading-room.eu/intuitive-interaction-with-a-smart-environment/. Last retrieved May 2015).

I've been trying to create interactive technology that works based on how humans naturally perceive, process, and respond to environmental stimuli. Key to this idea is the understanding that humans perceive reality differently than many of us seem to think. The idea that we filter perceived data has been suggested before, but don't we also rebuild it to suit the mental models of our expectations, hopes, and fears? Isn't that how we see sequential images as movement and why we hear the laughter of those lost to us on the wind at night? This may be why the art that touches us the most is that which lets us fill in the empty spaces – the silence between the notes, the words left unspoken, and the action that happens off-screen.

We never see the whole picture, we never hear the entire song. Our nervous system picks up stray threads of the larger tapestry of life, and we unconsciously knit them together, as best as we can, into recognized and anticipated patterns. Artists understand that. It is time for computer scientists to understand it, too.

Like in a classroom, human-centered information should never be presented "whole cloth": that style of presentation limits how much we can perceive and process. Better to share suitable patterns, as Vannevar Bush proposed Bush (Atl Mon 176:101–8, 1945) and to provide us with threads deliberately designed to suit them. The designer or computer scientist who tries to knit the cloth herself is more likely to elicit an "uncanny valley" experience where unconscious perception of "dropped stiches" make the blanket feel uncomfortable. A good lecture, like a good interface, provides just enough information so that the human on the other side can subconsciously knit the tapestry themselves.

I've already told you about some of the threads I've spun and some of the patterns I've supplied to mental looms across Europe. In this chapter I want to provide you with a few more threads before you to begin to spin your own.

ABC and Design: Addressing Your Audience

I intend to spend part of my research time, over the foreseeable future, trying to formalize the conversion of peripheral information into formats that can be both perceived and processed peripherally – not at the edge of a screen, but at the edge of our perception.

As mentioned elsewhere in this book, I believe that the concept of sidebars is based on a fundamental misunderstanding of the difference between the periphery of our attention and the periphery of our display screen. I also believe that it must be

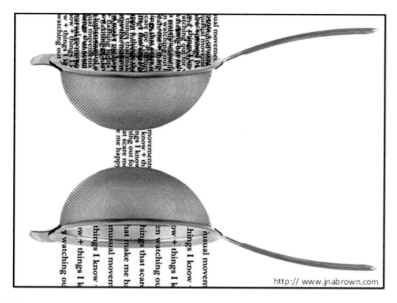

Fig. 12.1 Our minds perceive only a small stream of "signal" in the ongoing rush of "noise", and then rebuild that data into a comfortable flow of information according to our mental models

hard to imagine a significant difference between the two without an understanding of the value of peripheral perception and processing. Let me try to clarify that for a moment, before I start talking about death.

When you are sitting down to a nice cup of tea in the early morning hours, and you close your eyes and relax your shoulders, and just breathe in the cool air while the thousand little sounds of morning wash over you – you are taking a break from deliberate thought to more clearly experience your peripheral input. As you think about and notice these stimuli, they come into focus – the soft snoring of the baby in the crib, and the light rattle of the refrigerator fan; the cacophonous chorus of mixed birdsong from outside and the distant rumbling hum of passing traffic.

All of these impressions have been on the periphery of your awareness, and while they are there, they have been keeping you informed – they have been reas-suring you like the nattering of our primate ancestors and the shared gurgling of "baby talk" (Fig. 12.1).

Like the steady rocking of a train or the rhythmic swell and fade of a boat deck under your feet, these stimuli can be shocking and overpowering at first; impossible to ignore, demanding your attention. But in time you become accustomed to them, and they do not intrude into the ivory tower of your conscious thought. They inform you from the periphery, and so your reactive or limbic or visceral system of infor-mation processing, the anxious little protoprosimian in your head, takes comfort in the pattern. That protoprosimian – let's call her Amygdala, or Amy for short – she's good at patterns, and her thoughts are all emotional. When she has done well, Amy is awash with oxytocin and her emotions are positive.

But then the boat deck lifts a little too high or dips a little too low; the train rocks a little too sharply to one side, or seems to drag a little under your feet. Now Amy the protoprosimian feels that the pattern is broken, and she reacts.

How she reacts will also be based on established patterns. If the train is dragging a little, then you might "realize" that a stop is coming up – the pattern of slowing is familiar and Amy whispers into the open window of the ivory tower. She is calm and you can respond intellectually. You check that the station is not yours and then let that concern fall back to the periphery, reassuring Amy that she's doing a fine job, and she is again awash in oxytocin, happy, and reassured, and calm.

On the other hand, if the train suddenly brakes hard – not a little too hard, which often makes everyone laugh – but much too hard, then your reaction is emotional and full of fear. Amy's expectations of recurring patterns has been badly violated, and she cannot know what to expect next. She is scared, and she is screaming and crying and wants you to abandon everything and run for the hills. Now you have to fight for control of your response and you have to do it under the influence of adrenaline and cortisol and vasopressin that make your muscles tense and your pupils wide, that makes it hard to think coherently, and prepares you for escalating conflict rather than for calm and deliberate thought.

These are our choices, our options: we can respond to the world in a wash of calm that lets us think rationally, or we can respond in a wash of stress that makes cogency almost impossible.

Alerts and alarms are usually designed to disrupt our attention, with the idea that we will then deliberately re-focus our attention according to a rational evaluation of the situation. That is, to quote US Supreme Court Justice Antonin Scalia, "Pure applesauce" [4]. We are triggering a fear response and then expecting rational thought.

I understand cross-generational habit – after all, I came up with the name – but I don't accept that we should continue doing things the way our ancestors did when an easy improvement is at hand. Let's improve our tools so that they can improve our lives, so that this cycle keeps turning.

In the rest of this chapter, I'm going to present a few of the places where I think the ABC approach could be put to good use. First, let's have one slightly silly example – just to drive the point home.

Car alarms don't have to wake the neighbourhood – that will not reduce the risk of theft. Car alarms don't scare thieves, so designers should stop acting as though they do. I think that a good car alarm should politely inform the would-be-burglar that this particular car is being tracked, and that the engine has just been disengaged, and cannot be started again without a password. It could also point out, still politely of course, that cameras in the car and on the street are now streaming the incident on-line and recording it for future reference. If the purpose of the alarm is to stop a thief from taking your car or something in it, then it's probably better to talk with them directly than it is to annoy your neighbours with a lot of beeping and howling. If I were writing the script, I would ask the would be thief to smile for the camera and then move along while the crowd watching on the internet still hasn't seen anything worth mentioning on Twitter.

ABC and HF: Not "Hands-Free" but "Distraction-Free"

In the previous chapter, I spent a bit of time telling you about ABC ringtones which use the natural internal communication system of the brain to alert you to a phone call based on the filtering systems responsible for the cocktail party effect.

I hypothesize that the same kind of filtering process may be in place for the visual data we perceive. In fact, without one, I'm not sure how we could function in a world so rich with visual stimuli, or how we could manage to perceive motion when all we can see is still images.

I would like to develop a formal trial of what I call "fade-ups" or "ABC pop-ups" [5, 6]. These are pop-ups that would contain only easily-recognizable patterns like familiar faces, logos, or avatars. It would be important that the image contain no text, because that might trigger the attention of the wrong part of the brain. You see, the goal here would be to provide only information that can be naturally processed by the amygdalic, visceral, reactive part of your brain.

For the same reason, there should be no abrupt visual changes – rather than "popping up" the image should fade partially into view, and then fade away again without ever becoming fully opaque.

Any kind of a popping sound, beep, or other noise that is usually used to grab attention is right out of the question.

I hypothesize that this kind of ABC pop-up would work like the ABC ringtones, informing the user that a message has arrived, and informing them whether it was sent by a stranger or by a particularly familiar person, and that it would do so without having a disruptive or interruptive impact on their attentive focus.

My intent is to resume my work on these pop-ups later this year. It would be great if a lot of you reading this book should decide to do the same. More of us working on the idea means a greater chance of quickly proving or disproving the hypothesis. At the very least, we may be able to narrow down some of the parameters under which the triune brain can be deliberately used.

Another area where I would like to see this applied may seem at first to be the exact opposite of these calm alerts. Sometimes, as in the cruel old joke about the cruel old farmer and his well-trained mule, "you just have to get his attention". I think that ABC audial and visual alerts and alarms could be extremely useful in safety-critical environments. When overwhelmed by circumstances, imagine the effect (or affect) of hearing your daughter softly call you as though she were there. It could lead to more stress, but I stipulate that it might help you to focus. Especially if she were to combine her call with a short and concise directive based on behaviour patterns you already know, like: "Turn off engine number four" or "Evacuate now".

Conversely, a constant, subtle nattering could reassure a surgeon or a pilot that everything is going all right at other stations. Right now flight safety systems try to automatically fix any problem in an aircraft underway, and turn to the pilot only once the automatic system has failed. The problem is that people are not good at making good logical decisions quickly while under pressure. This is why the ancient

Chinese formally codified their rules of behaviour – so that you would never have to make an important decision about how to behave at the last minute. You could follow the well-rehearsed, ingrained behaviours reactively, which would give you time to reflect on what else to do. As I have mentioned elsewhere, we need could use a modern HCI version of the ancient Chinese Book of Rites [5].

This idea of spending the time to decide earlier when you have no pressure, instead of at the moment a fast decision is needed, is a fundamental part of any preparedness training and is the underlying concept of training in the Martial Arts [7].

I am planning to continue my pursuit of these two ideas as well, and welcome others to do the same. Imagine if we could improve alarms systems to really reach people who are dealing with overwhelming circumstances.

Speaking of overwhelming circumstances, I have written elsewhere about the possibility of using the Dynamic Environmental Focus and interconnected reflective and reactive feedback loops of ABC as a model for improved situational awareness in police and military operations [8]. By deliberately creating a mental model in which the interactions of the people on either side of you become a part of your own feedback loop, we increase the possibility of calm and thoughtful intervention when someone in the field is reacting emotionally rather than according to procedure. This would be good for the forces, and for the general public, for the victims of emotionally-driven misconduct, and for the individual whose loss of deliberate control led them to commit an action they might be able to justify after the fact, but that they never would have willfully and deliberately chosen to carry out.

There's another side to this that I have been looking into but have not yet written. Police and soldiers work in an environment of perpetual perceived threat, and there is a deliberate and willful ignorance in our society regarding how that shapes their pre-attentive, visceral, amygdalic reactions to normal day-to-day events. If they serve and protect us, then we have a duty to help them disengage from that service and return to patterns of behaviour better suited to non-threatening environments.

I believe that the new triune model of the brain can help to isolate some of the overlapping human factors that contribute to the problems facing our sworn protectors. I would like to help protect them in return.

Speaking of human factors, I have proposed elsewhere the use of ABC and DEF in the design of a metric of "calm interaction" [9]. I call the prototype the Classification of Attentional Demands in a Layered Matrix, or the CALMatrix (Fig. 12.2). It is based on identifying the reflexive, reactive, and reflective demands at every stage of the use of a tool or a device. The stages are Preparation; Starting; Normal Use; Flow; Pause; Resume; Stop; Settle; and Emergency. The demands at each stage can be rated as *Negligible*, *Sporadic*, *Constant*, or *Overwhelming*.

This allows us to create a quick illustration of the demands on each tine of our triune brain during the course of using a tool. For example, an intellectual conversation may demand Constant processing at the reflective level, and only Sporadic

CALMatrix			
STAGES	DEMANDS		
	REFLEXIVE	REACTIVE	REFLECTIVE
Preparation			
Starting			
Normal Use			
Flow			
Pause			
Resume			
Stop			
Settle			
EMERGENCY			

Fig. 12.2 The CALMatrix for classification of attentional demands in a layered matrix

processing at the reactive level, while a spirited argument about politics might require the inverse.

The advantage of this model is the layering referred to in the acronym. Now that we have established the demands at each level for a spirited argument about politics, we could overlay it on the chart for driving. That chart would show a Constant requirement for reflexive processing, Constant requirement for reactive processing, and a Sporadic requirement for reflexive processing.

Overlaying the two would show us at a glance that simultaneously driving and arguing about politics can overload the reactive processing system.

You'll have a chance to try out one of these matrices in Chap. 18.

A similar prototype matrix is intended to evaluate the possibility to Perceive, Process, Put off, Deny, Acknowledge, and Ignore alarms and alerts.

Yet another similar layered matrix could serve as a replacement for Reason's Swiss Cheese Model of system failure [10]. I call this prototype Systemic Hazard Intervention through the Evaluation of Layered Displays (SHIELD). This tool is intended to improve hazard identification and mitigation by matching remedial actions to potential system failures. Instead of Reason's mental model of layers of cheese through which an accident might slip, my proposed mental model is of a hockey team working together to achieve goals while avoiding failures and the concomitant results. Unlike cheese slices, these are experts who work together dynamically, supporting one another, and succeeding or failing as a team. They understand that anyone can make a mistake, and that a single mistake should never be disastrous. They also understand that the environment, the tools of their trade, and all of their supporters play a role in their success.

The latest prototype of this matrix is much more complex than the original, but then again, it is intended to perform a very complex function.

I intend to continue my development of these matrices, and hope to have functional prototypes for formal investigation very soon.

--

I have also written elsewhere about the possibility of applying the principles of ABC to the design of emotionally-charged haptics in order to preserve memories of loved ones who are far away in time and/or in space [11]. The basic idea is that a loving couple who go through the pleasant routine of recording a simple haptic interaction – whether it is as complex as a loving caress or as simple as a personally-meaningful series of taps – will be able to evoke the memories of that event and of the shared experience at a later time. This is another case of supplying the few threads that can be fit to the mental loom of the user, so that she can weave her own rich tapestry of evoked experience. A snippet of a forgotten song can plunge you into rich memories of a dance from decades ago, and the whiff of a perfume can remind you of your first meeting with a long-lost love. The same should be true of small but meaningful touches. I don't believe that this would require any technological advances beyond what already exists. The technological factors could be very shallow and simplistic – it is the emotional factor that would be deep and complex.

I would also like to look more deeply into that area. I think that it is possible that haptics holds the greatest potential for ABC-based communication, because our peripheral nervous system uses a wide range of haptic sensors to deal with a constant flood of data about our body and our environment. I would like to investigate the use of deliberately-constructed emotional mental models to trigger the reflexive and reactive branches of our triune brain so that they learn to automatically push some meaningful haptic data directly to the center of our attention.

--

The last future application of ABC that I would like to share with you is an idea based not on Human-Computer Interaction, but on Human-Human Interaction.

Applying the ABC Principles to Human-Human Interaction

My father was a psychiatric social worker who specialized in working with emotionally-disturbed children. John L. Brown advanced his field and won international recognition for his work in some of the royal courts of Europe and, more to his taste, in some of the homes and halls of Canada's First Nations. He wrote extensively about his philosophy, his theories and his methods [12–14] and I will not discuss most of them here, except to point out that I have met Social Workers from around the world who have formally studied his child- and family-centered philosophy and theories, and who apply his methods every day.

In this last part of this last theoretical chapter in this book about my own work, I return to the work of my father, and look to the future from that vantage.

I have mentioned earlier in this book that I believe that almost all of our interaction with the world around us is either reflexive or reactive, and that we are very rarely consciously involved.

You see this when people fall into the same arguments over and over again, or when they become emotionally intense about inconsequential ideas – they are reacting with their amygdala rather than reflecting with their neocortex.

Arguments about politics and religion are examples, as are most recurring arguments at family occasions. If someone seems to you to have an absolutely illogical idea, based purely on their own delusion rather than on any factual evidence at all, and if your every attempt to educate them fails, then you should stop trying. You are probably both arguing with the wrong part of your respective brains.

What's that? You feel certain that you have been absolutely reasonable and logical every single time?

Really, *every single* time?

You see, I believe that arguments of that sort are negative feedback loops in our cognitive systems. It's like when you hyperventilate. For some reason you have over-absorbed oxygen, and a glitch in your nervous system responds by trying to absorb even more instead of less.

In this case, you have over-reacted emotionally, and your reactive system responds by trying to be even more emotional instead of less.

Almost anyone who has lived or worked with overly-emotional people will tell you that you can't do anything about it. They'll say that you just have to avoid their triggers, or be careful not to set them off. This strategy teaches everyone involved that this individual or this type of person needs to rely on someone else to control their emotions… or that no one can control their emotions, so they have to be boxed up and avoided.

My father had an incredible ability to help people assume and maintain self-control when faced with challenging emotional stimuli. When the emotional stimuli were overpowering, then they were encouraged to lose control while held warmly and firmly in a carefully-designed hug that protected them from hurting themselves or anyone else. The latter is a technique my father simply called "holding". You can see samples of both kinds of intervention in the 1967 documentary "Warrendale" by director Alan King [15]. I advise you to look it up though I warn you that the experience is incredibly intense. It is well worth seeing if you're interested in the care of the emotionally disturbed, in *cinéma verité*, or in great documentaries in general -the film won the Cannes Festival award, and was named best documentary of the year by the US and UK societies of film critics.

I wish that I could provide a place for everyone and anyone to let themselves be overcome; to rage and strain and lose control, to "let it all out", safe in the arms of someone who truly loves them unconditionally and will only love them more after witnessing their lack of control. I wish I could, but I know that I can't. That requires a very close relationship, and it requires very specialized training, and doing it wrong will always backfire.

But the other technique – the technique that helps people interrupt their own negative feedback loop of emotional reactions, and reclaim rational, reflective control – I think I might be able to work on that with ABC.

Now you might be wondering why I would be interested in trying to help control emotional over-reactions in a book on HCI. If so, I have to ask, have you ever visited an on-line message board?

The internet can be an incredibly hostile place because a small percentage of the people who use it choose to be emotionally abusive to strangers. Trying to respond to them almost never works, because they seem to be there just to have nasty, demeaning arguments. This is why many sites and many surfers have a "don't feed the trolls" policy.

By the way, "trolling the message boards" originally referred to the fishing technique of dragging your line through water hoping that you could attract the attention of fish you might not otherwise find. It had nothing to do with the trolls we know and love from Norse mythology.

Anyway, I believe that my father was able to interrupt the negative feedback loop by getting the individual's emotional reactive system to query its logical reflective counterpart.

Like the previously unseen communication measured during the use of ABC ringtones, I believe that his technique was not perceived as an external interruption that would trigger reactionary responses, but that it was perceived instead as an internal communiqué. Once the reactive brain has started to query the other cognitive systems, it could well be that the feedback loop is broken.

I don't know if this will prove to be measurable, other than in a removed manner. I don't know if my speculation will result in a truly testable and refutable hypothesis. I don't know either of these things, but I'm very excited by the idea of trying to find a way to put an end to the pointless emotional arguments that add so much stress to our lives and hurt so many people who would probably be much happier if they could all just get along.

Personally, I suspect that a method of triggering yourself or someone else to think logically when immersed in a flood of emotions could have a sizeable effect on society. It might provide a means of resistance to associative (rather than merit-based) advertising. It might do a lot of good in politics by interrupting a lot of what's bad in politics.

It might help people to face up to the lies they tell themselves, blaming others for their own behaviours, fractioning society and the wider world, and the assumption that each one of us is somehow intrinsically better than everyone else.

It might help people face up to the fact that their behaviour affects their children, and their spouses, their co-workers and even total strangers more than they want to admit.

A process like this might help people see that cigarettes are just a slow but certain poison that you buy from billionaires and then administer, via your own mouth and lungs, to all of the people closest to you.

I don't think it could disrupt our use of emotions for emotional purposes, but I don't know. I hope that it won't put an end to love or to laughter, and I don't think it could unless that love and laughter were in violation of your own rational best interest.

…and just think what it might do to religious or political extremism.

What's that? You think that your religious and political extremism is completely reasonable? Well, then you have nothing to worry about.

Me? I'm looking forward to learning what I can.

So, now you know everything I can tell you about the theory and practice of Anthropology-Based Computing, from its beginning, through its philosophy and rationale, and on into my dreams for its future. I encourage you to theorize about it on your own or in small, ambitious groups. If you'd like to try practicing it, too, you'll find a half-dozen projects in the next section of this book.

Please do try these at home.

Summary

In this chapter, I discussed some of the work I hope to do next with the ABC theory and with the tools I've built based on it. In fact, I hope to be doing that work by the time you read this book.

So, if you want to know some of my research ideas, you should go back and read this chapter. If you want to know more of my ideas, and to have some guidance in how to perform them yourself, without professional tools or facilities, then please read the next section of the book.

That's where I'll do my best to help you make use of the principles of ABC. Hopefully, that will inspire you to come up with and test a few ideas of your own.

References

1. Bardzell J, Bardzell S (2014) A great and troubling beauty: cognitive speculation and ubiquitous computing. Pers Ubiquit Comput 18(4):779–794
2. Brown JNA (2015) Intuitive interaction with a smart environment. Fundamentals of collective adaptive systems (FoCAS) reading room, Jan 2015 http://www.focas-reading-room.eu/intuitive-interaction-with-a-smart-environment/. Last retrieved May 2015
3. Bush V (1945) As we may think. Atl Mon 176:101–108
4. King D et al (2015) Petitioners v. Sylvia Burwell, Secretary of Health and Human Services et al. 576 U.S.__, 14–114 (Dissenting Opinion)
5. Brown JNA (2012) Expert talk for time machine session: designing calm technology "… as Refreshing as Taking a Walk in the Woods". In: IEEE international conference on multimedia and expo. vol 1, pp 423
6. Brown JNA (2013) It's as easy as ABC: introducing anthropology-based computing. In: Advances in computational intelligence. Springer, Berlin/Heidelberg, pp 1–16
7. Brown JNA (2011) Martial arts. In: Greenwald SJ, Thomley JE (eds) Encyclopedia of mathematics and society. Salem Press, Hackensack, pp 49–51, 218–219, 582–584

8. Brown JNA (2015) Making sense of the noise: an ABC approach to big data and security. In: Akhgar B et al (eds) Application of big data for national security: a practitioner's guide to emerging technologies. Butterworth-Heinemann, Oxford

9. Brown JNA, Bayerl PS, Fercher A, Leitner G, Mallofré AC, Hitz M (2014) A measure of calm. In: Bakker S, Hausen D, Selker T, van den Hoven E, Butz A, Eggen B (eds) Peripheral interaction: shaping the research and design space. Workshop at CHI 2014, Toronto. ISSN: 1862-5207

10. Reason J (1990) The contribution of latent human failures to the breakdown of complex systems. Philos Trans R Soc Lond B Biol Sci 327(1241):475–484

11. Brown JNA (2015) "Once More, With Feeling": using Haptics to preserve tactile memories. Int J Hum Comput Interact 31(1):65–71

12. Brown JL (1976) The philosophy and rationale of the Browndale treatment process. Family Involvement, 7–13 April

13. Brown JL (1979) Browndale: a new delivery system in the helping services. Canadian Educational Programmes, Willowdale, 159 pp

14. Brown JL (1979) Philosophy and rationale of Browndale: a guide to normal living. Canadian Educational Programmes, Willowdale, 108 pp

15. Warrendale (1967) Film. 110m. Producer and director Allan King, cinematographer William Brayne, editor Peter Moseley

Part III
Citizen Science: Simple Solutions to Improve the Way Your Technology Treats You

How to Stop Your Phone Screaming at You, Use a Computer Without Straining Your Neck or Your Wrists, Listen to Loud Music on Your Headphones Without Going Deaf, and Text Your Friends Without Killing Yourself, Them, or Anyone Else

Darwin's Believe It Or Not...

Introduction

This part of this book is all about citizen science.

In the first section we talked about the history of how humans and their tools co-evolved in response to environmental pressures, and about how our computerized devices have not been around long enough to go through that process.

In the second section we talked about my theory and practice of ABC. The theory is basically a way to look at our computerized tools through the long lens of human cultural, physiological, and neurological factors. The practice is the attempt to deliberately modify those same tools to better suit humans, without having to go through gradual iterations for thousands of years.

Here in the third section, we're going to talk about making changes in your own tool use and – more importantly – asking you to help the world to see the value of making and testing more and more human-centered, citizen-science-based modifications to the tools we all use. Just imagine how much nicer life will be when the interaction with our most ubiquitous devices is based on a combination of creativity and the scientific method, rather than a combination of cross-generational habit and marketing!

Not sure you see a need for that kind of change? Let's think for a minute about how we use our tools. Not any of these flash in the pan, faddish tools like iPhones or horseless carriages; let's consider one that's had a bit of time to prove itself on the market… like, say, an axe.

If you go to your local hardware store, or look on-line, you'll find many types of axe available. There are one and two-headed axes, short and long-handled axes, axes made of different materials and sold for different purposes. For the most part, that is all marketing. We know the best type of axe. The single-headed, curved-blade axe, with a slightly bowed handle, has been around for thousands of years. The ancient Egyptians used it, as did the ancient Baktrians and the ancient Chinese. The Vikings used it as a weapon, and also for building and gardening. Reverse your grip and it becomes a hammer. Grip the head from above and it Is a cane. It is a perfect tool that humans have been using, let me say it again, for thousands of years. And never once, in all of that time, has anyone ever said: "Hey, I'm going to drill some flute holes in the handle so that I can play music while I work".

It would be ridiculous, wouldn't it, to use something as dangerous as an axe while being distracted by something as whimsical as playing music… wouldn't it?

Then why do we play music in cars?

Yeah, that's an example of a technology that really seems to be designed to kill its user. But you can't talk about it with the car companies, they just keep including more and more distractions every year, competing to see who's product can pack in the most bells and whistles. Of course, we bring our own bells and whistles into our cars, don't we? The internet is full of images of teenagers – adults too, but mostly teenagers – who have taken photos of themselves driving. They're pulling faces and grabbing their friends and mugging for the camera, which they are often holding themselves, and they are never, ever paying the least bit of attention to the road. The internet is full of teenagers like that… and so are the morgues.

Again though, it's not just teenagers. We, as a people, have stopped thinking of the car as dangerous. It's just a place where we sit while we get to where we're going. It's not dangerous and it doesn't need our conscious and alert attention any more than our living room does or, for instance, our bathroom.

Have you heard of the distracted driver in Florida? Which one, you ask? Well, back in March, 2010, this particular driver crashed into a pickup truck on a highway in the Florida Keys [1]. Still not specific enough? This driver was only sort of driving. The truth is, she was working the brake and the gas, while her ex-husband leaned over from the passenger seat to handle the steering wheel. Why, you might ask, did her ex-husband have to steer the car? Well, his ex – the one in the driver's seat on the highway – was running late for a date, and she needed her passenger to steer because she was busy, shaving her… "bikini area". Really. Now, I do *usually* encourage people to modify their tool use, but… Of course, for all I know, that *could* be precisely what Fredrik and Otto Kampfe had in mind when they patented the safety razor back in 1880.

Did you hear about the two experienced and heavily trained pilots on Northwestern Airlines flight 188, on October 21st, 2009? They were flying from San Diego, California to Minneapolis, Minnesota, and they decided to work on their laptops during the flight [2]. These professional pilots flew more than an hour past their destination, with alarms sounding and warning lights flashing, and air traffic controllers screaming at them over the radios; with fighter jets doing flyby to try and discover whether they had been hijacked, and 144 passengers wondering what the heck was going on. Seriously. The two pilots admitted afterwards that they had been distracted because they were deep in a discussion about how to use a new crew flight scheduling system, and they lost track of time. It seems to me that they were having a hard time subconsciously deciding which was the important task and which was the distraction.

Then there was the veteran train conductor in Southern California on September 12, 2008 [3]. He was sending and receiving text messages while he sped through warning light after warning light and crashed his commuter train into a freighter, killing 25 people and injuring 135 others.

We cannot multitask with our rational mind. We cannot divide our focussed attention. We do not choose wisely when we subconsciously differentiate between what is important and what is just a distraction.

And we keep building tools based on the idea that we can.

In 2014 the United Nations released a report saying that the leading cause of death for teenagers is no longer alcohol-related driving accidents. The leading cause of death for young men and women 15–29 years of age, is now largely-avoidable traffic "accidents". What's more, if you fall within that age group, you are four times more likely to be involved in a fatal crash while using a phone than if you are driving without one [4]. That means that, if you are between 15 and 29 years old, your phone is literally more likely to contribute to your death than anything else.

This section of the book will help you understand how things like that happen: how it is that our natural mental and physical limitations do not mix well with the constructed limitations of our common tools.

It is my intent that these chapters will also provide you with a simple ways to modify your tools – or your use of them – to make your life less stressful and maybe even safer.

If you want, you can stop there, but there is more. You see, these next chapters are not just recipes or simple life hacks. They're an invitation to help build a community of citizen scientists. Each chapter offers you the chance to record your attempts to improve your personal Human-Computer Interaction. You can run these experiments and then share your results with the community of readers of this book. We can pool the data and learn from it together. If – or rather, when – you come up with improvements on my ideas, you can test them and share the results and make the world a safer place.

It's much more than any one scientist could hope to do, but as a group…

…As a group, we might just be able to make our adaptations so ubiquitous that the manufacturers take notice. Imagine that… like our ancestors who figured out how to put handles on hammers, we could force our computers, peripherals, and computerized devices to take an evolutionary step towards truly Anthropology-Based Computing.

References

1. Linhardt A (2010) FHP: driver lacked razor-sharp focus. Key West Citizen. Retrieved from http://www.keysnews.com
2. National Transportation Safety Board (2009) NTSB issues update on its investigation of flight 188 that overflew intended Minneapolis airport [press release]. Retrieved from http://www.ntsb.gov/news/press-releases/Pages/NTSB_Issues_Update_on_its_Investigation_of_Flight_188_that_Overflew_Intended_Minneapolis_Airport.aspx
3. National Transportation Safety Board (2010) NTSB determines engineer's failure to observe and respond to red signal caused 2008 Chatsworth accident; recorders in cabs recommended [press release]. Retrieved from http://www.ntsb.gov/news/press-releases/Pages/NTSB_Determines_Engineers_Failure_to_Observe_and_Respond_to_Red_Signal_Caused_2008_Chatsworth_Accident;_Recorders_in_Cabs.aspx
4. World Health Organization (updated, October 2015) Road traffic injuries [fact sheet N° 358]. Retrieved from http://www.who.int/mediacentre/factsheets/fs358/en/

Chapter 13
Simple Experimental Design

The great Jean Piaget developed a really cool test that demonstrates
how little we know compared to what we think we know… y'know?

Abstract Not sure you can run your own experiments? Sure you can!

Remember, the scientific method is counter-intuitive. No one should expect you
to be able to use it correctly the first time you try… or even the second. This book
isn't trying to replace real training, it's just trying to introduce you to the idea of
thinking and adapting your technology according to the principles of Anthropology-
Based Computing. Don't let the little protoprosimian in your head convince you to
be afraid… I promise you both that this is going to be fun. Now, maybe what you

both need is to ease into it with a little unofficial experiment. This chapter offers a simple experiment for you to run, just to see what it's like.

You don't need to wear a lab coat or to a spill a bowl of alphabet soup after your name. The scientific method just means doing things carefully so as to make sure that you are only measuring what you think you're measuring, and to describe them fully, so as to make sure that your experiment can be accurately recreated by another knowledgeable and clever person.

But if you have a lab coat, and you want to put it on, go ahead. Lab coats are cool.

Obviously, safety glasses are also cool and can be a great compliment to formal wear.

I Think This Is Boring, But I Don't Know *How* Boring

As an example before we get into the real work of changing your use of technology, here's a fun experiment that will help make your friends feel as though they're stupid and cannot draw.

Sound good?

No?

Well, it doesn't have to make them feel stupid. If you think that advertising it that way might make it hard for you to get people to join in, then you could just say that the experiment will demonstrate that they don't really know some of things that they think they do.

I believe that this experiment actually reflects the way that one part of our brain lies to the rest, giving us a false sense of confidence and a false sense of our own abilities and knowledge. Now, it may be that false confidence was necessary to get us out of the trees, or out into the grasslands, or to allow us to give up migration and try a sedentary lifestyle.

This little test is based on an experimental idea first proposed by Jean Piaget [1]. If you don't know Piaget, you should really look him up. He started off as a natural scientist – specializing in malacology (the study of mollusks) – but became a brilliant theorist in the psychological development of children after finishing his PhD. His work is quite lovely and I recommend reading as much of it as you can.

Before looking at the experiment, I have to talk to you just a little about statistics. Please, stop crying, this won't hurt at all. I used to hate statistics, until I finally had a teacher who helped me see them for the incredibly practical too that they are (Hi Jim, and thanks again!). I think statistics are usually taught by people who either hate their job or hate the topic. That could even make astronomy boring, or swordplay, or learning a new language. We'll spend just a moment now on stats, and revisit them here and there through the next few chapters. I promise to try and make it less boring than you might expect, without exciting you so much that you have to stop reading.

Before starting any experiment, you always have to stop and think about what you are trying to learn, and how it can be perceived and described in the real world.

Thinking about that will help you figure out how to measure it. Deciding how to measure your results tells you what kind of experiment you need to design. There, that's our first lesson in statistics. Not bad, eh?

Just to be a little bit boring, I will reiterate.

If you want to measure how boring a something is, you need to start by figuring out how the boringness is demonstrated in a measurable way in the real world. How you do that is up to you, but there are a few standard ways. Let's use an example that some of you might be able to apply immediately – trying to measure how boring a class is.

1. You could just ask everyone in the room to rate the boringness of the class themselves (without consulting each other) on a scale of 1–5. Then you would have each person's opinion of how boring the class was. Just as a note, we call this kind of a scale a "Likert-type Scale", because it is not quite what Rensis Likert had in mind [2]. Curious? Look it up; research is fun! Anyway, this kind of scale is useful even if the progression of the values isn't even. So we can use a scale for a "ratio value" in which the difference between each step is the same and the value could start at 0. Inches could be one example, (1–5 in.). Alternatively, we could use a "nominal value" scale, where the names mean something but they don't go in order. Imagine a flavour scale where the numbers 1–5 represent "Sweet", "Salty", "Bitter", "Umami", and "Bland". We just have to treat the answers differently when we do our stats.
2. You could also have some impartial observers watch the class and rate it. This would give you the opinion of your observers.
3. You could do both 1 and 2 and compare the results. Figure out some way to measure boringness in the class; if you can figure out a way that will be the same no matter who does it, then you've found a quantitative method.

I once had a professor – a great guy – who was so boring that large numbers of students fell asleep in every class. This leads me to think that we could rank boringness as a measure of the number of people falling asleep.

That would mean that we would have to decide what we would count as falling asleep. It has to be something we can perceive accurately. A change in brainwave patterns would be accurate, but hard to measure in a normal classroom – especially if we want the class to run like it normally does. Maybe we could count that moment when s student's head drops down and then bounces up again? You know what I mean, when they suddenly snap awake?

Or we could count it as falling asleep if a student's eyes close and stay closed for 3 s or longer. Three seconds doesn't seem like a long time when you read it in a sentence, but try it. Close your eyes for 3 s when you're talking to a friend. I bet they'll think you're falling asleep.

Measuring boringness would also mean building a scale. Say if less than 1 % of the students fall asleep, then you could rank the class as "not particularly boring" and if all of the students fell asleep you could rank the class as "the most boring a class can be". Why percentages and not just numbers? So that you can compare classes with different numbers of students in them.

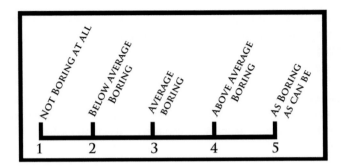

Fig. 13.1 Our "boringness" scale, where you ca see it has numbers and names, but no values, yet…

That would give you two extremes. Usually, we would fill the space between them with roughly equally-spaced options. This way we would end up with a boring scale that looks like the one you see in Fig. 13.1.

Having the scale would help you decide how to run your experiment. It sounds like this experiment would be pretty straightforward, doesn't it? That said, I can think of a few things you will have to take control of so that your experiment will work. The first is to decide whether you are counting if people fall asleep at all, or if they fall asleep and stay asleep. Those are two very different things and they shouldn't be confused. My next thought is that it would be good to have more than one person counting the sleepers. One person might get sleepy herself and make a mistake in her counting. If you have three people all count separately, then you could either average out the answers or, better yet, use "majority rules". If two (or more) of your three agree on a number – then it is correct.

Can you think of any other things that should be controlled? If so, please let me know. After all, as scientists we all have to learn from each other.

Just for fun, I'll add one more. I think that, after the class, you should ask the students if any of them had less sleep than usual the night before. If a student was up all night playing video games, she might be more likely to fall asleep in class. That would be a factor that we didn't control. We could either control it after the fact by excluding her from the experiment, or we could include her but report the additional information so that others reading our work can decide whether or not she should be excluded.

Summing up: the boring experiment would involve having an odd number of trained observers watch a class and count how many people fall asleep. It would also involve collecting a little sleep-related information from the students in order to either control or at least be informed about outside factors. Finally, the numbers would be recorded and compared using our boringness scale. Like I said, pretty straightforward. Actually, you might also want to take informal notes of special occurrences you didn't anticipate. For example, in that class I was talking about, one guy actually fell out of his chair during one lecture. The impact of hitting the floor woke him up. The noise he made when it happened woke me up, too.

The last thing you want to do, having thought up the experiment, and having thought over the experiment, is to formalize your idea as a simple "if-then" statement of what you are going to measure, and how, and why. This is called the Hypothesis, and it should be clear enough that any reasonably intelligent person can understand the logic. They might not know all of the words you use, but they should be able to follow the logic of what you're trying to do. While we're on the subject, though, I should point out that I think too many scientists try to hide their ideas behind complicated or specialized language. Your hypothesis, like the rest of your writing, should really be clear and simple.

If we were to carry out one of the versions of the boringness experiment discussed above, then we could phrase our hypothesis as follows:

> If a lecture happens right after lunch, it will be rated more boring than the same lecture right before lunch.

Feel free to try that experiment, too. If only it were possible to find a boring class somewhere… …maybe you should ask my students if they could recommend a class.

Anyway, I won't *really* suggest that you measure the boringness of your classes – that would be impolite in at least two ways that I can think of – instead we'll go back to Jean Piaget and his bicycle test. Let me walk you through the simple sample experiment we started with. We'll talk about how to measure the results later.

I Think This Is a Good Drawing, But I Don't Know *How* Good

First, get each participant to fill out a personal information form. You'll also want to ask them a few questions about their experience with bicycles. Do they know what a bicycle looks like? Do they know how to ride one? Do they ride sometimes? How often? When was the last time? How many gears are on their bicycle? Do they use the gears? Have they ever had to repair the gears? Did they do it themselves? That should be about enough.

Now, making sure that no bicycles or pictures of bicycles are visible, and allowing them a little peace and quiet, give them 5 min to draw a bicycle as accurately as they can. Oh, be sure that their phones are turned off, and ask them ahead of time not to let anything interrupt them.

After 5 min, thank them very sincerely, collect their picture and put it away so that no one sees it by accident. Before you put it away, mark one corner of the page with a letter or number, so that you can keep track of which drawing was done by whom. You can note the same code on the questionnaires they filled out. If you want to be taken seriously as a scientist, then you should keep the relationship between names and codes a secret. Done? Good, then bring in the next participant. Ask them the same questions, give them the same instructions and, when five more minutes have passed, collect, mark, and store their drawing.

Looking at the drawings, especially the ones by people who ride bicycles, and even those who have reported that they have repaired the gears, should show you

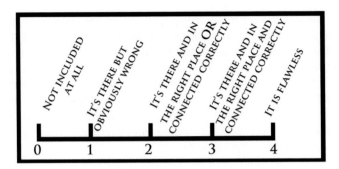

Fig. 13.2 A simple Likert scale to evaluate each of the seven key elements of a bicycle drawing

that humans really don't see everything in front of them, and really don't remember everything they see.

You can evaluate the drawings by just making a personal choice about each one, but that's not very scientific. To be scientific, in this kind of case, you would try to use a grading system that will be consistent, no matter who uses it, and no matter when or where they use it. In other words, you want to find a system that won't give a different grade depending on your mood or your personal beliefs and/or feelings.

On top of those things, your ideal grading system should give you answers in a format that would allow you to compare the results arithmetically. This would mean that you could compare one individual's score to the score of another, or the scores of one group of individuals to the score of other individuals, or groups.

So, let's try it like this. We will evaluate the drawings in terms of seven key elements of a bicycle: the wheels, the frame, the seat, the handles, the pedals, the gears, and the gestalt or whole picture.

Then we evaluate each element on a 5 point scale like in Fig. 13.2

We could consider the brakes but they can vary in location and are hard to show in a drawing. We could also consider the peripherals (kickstand, basket, lights, etc....), but some of our participants might imagine a bike fully tricked out with peripherals, and some might imagine a bike that has none. It would be hard to control for that without spoiling the experiment.

The scale still just measures your opinion of a drawing, but it maps your opinion onto a limited range of possible criteria. The limitations were designed to make the scale impartial, with the intent that many different people evaluating the same drawing, would give it the same score.

In fact, in a big and serious science experiment, our first few studies would be conducted just to evaluate the scale. After all, an inaccurate meter stick can't really be used to measure meters, right?

So, this scale and the process we use with it will give us a score either in numbers or in words. If we use it like a "nominal" scale, then we just report the labels, treating them like descriptive terms. If we use an "ordinal" scale, then the labels have progressive value, but not consistent progression – like in Fig. 13.1. If the progression were consistent, so that the value increased exactly the same amount between a rating of 2 and a rating of 3 that it does between a rating of 1 and a rating of 2, then we would call it an "interval" scale. Now the numbers really mean something, and we could use more complicated statistics to confuse our readers – I mean to tease out more information from our data.

If we use a scale like Fig. 13.2, where we assign points building on measurable values from 0 to 100 % (though we call it 0–4), then it is a "ratio" scale. This kind of scale gives us arithmetically useful values. For example, using that scale to rate each of seven features of every bicycle drawing, will result in a score between 0 and 28 for each bicycle drawing. You can convert the numbers to percentages if you want, or to a score out of 10, if either of those makes things easier for you.

These requirements about the type of results your testing generates are very important if you plan to share your work... ...and all scientific work should be shared. That's one of the key points of science: you have to ask others to check your work.

So, imagine, if you've done a good job of having 10 or 12 people draw bicycles, and you've graded their work, and I've done the same, for five or six others, then we can compare our results and see if we both see the same general pattern. If so, then maybe we've learned something about people in general... or maybe not. Fifteen to eighteen people isn't a very good representation of the seven billion people on the planet, or even of the much smaller number that might read this book.

But if half of the readers of this book were to conduct this experiment on 10 or 12 people, and do it carefully, in a controlled manner; and if they were all to grade the work following the same guideline, and do that carefully too; and if we were to pool all of that data and compare it and find the delicate patterns of information hiding in that pool...

...then we might learn something about the seven billion people on this planet.

What do you think? Does that sound like fun? Conducting an experiment with the possibility of getting to pool your data with data collected by others around the world?

If it does, well then that's what the rest of this section of the book is for! Each chapter offers a little insight into a problem in how computers and humans interact, and each one tries to explain some aspect of that problem in terms that you can try to change. In that way, each chapter is a guide to improving some part of your relationship with your computerized devices.

"But wait, there's more!", as the marketers like to say. Each chapter also offers you a chance to do a little experiment, teaching you how and why to collect some data, and how and why you might learn from it. If you choose to share that data with the other people who are trying the same experiment, then your book has become something much more.

Instead of a guide to improving some small aspect of your life, the book in your hands (either literally or figuratively) could be a guide to improving some small aspect of everybody's life.

Wouldn't that be interesting?

References

1. Piaget J (1927) La causalité physique chez l'enfant. Librairie Félix Alcan, Paris
2. Likert R (1932) A technique for the measurement of attitudes. Arch Psychol 22(140):5–55

Chapter 14
Stop Your Mouse from Twisting Your Arm

"Meh, you get used to it…"

Abstract You've heard the story of the frog in boiling water, right? This is the common fable of how a frog dropped into boiling water will immediately leap out again, but a frog placed in water that warms gradually to a boil will stay complacent until it is too late.

I don't know how frogs actually respond to such stimuli, but I do know that humans ignore some deadly threats because they don't seem immediately threatening. We see this reflected in public policy about distracted driving, smoking, mandatory vaccination, the cost/benefit balance of insurance, and action on climate change.

Immediate needs tend to outweigh long-term needs, even when the immediate need is more of a desire and the long-term need is essential for continued existence.

In this chapter, we will take a look at the computer mouse, a tool that hurts most of the people who use it. Now, it doesn't hurt everyone and, more importantly, those it does hurt are wounded slowly and additively, through what is called repetitive strain. As a result, its usefulness is more immediate than the risk of injury, even though the common injury can cause life-long pain and debilitation. This imbalance is innately ignored, and the relative time frames make it easier to ignore the problem than to respond to it – like the apocryphal frog in the warming water.

Like the frog, we won't know we're in trouble until it's too late.

Once Upon a Time…

…there was a man who wanted to enable people to navigate through layers of data storage without having to think like a computer. He thought we should be able to fly from one file to the next, thinking less like a computer scientist and more like a pilot.

While developing the first computer mouse back in 1959, Englebart had the goal of trying to recreate his air force experience of creating really simple, sequential 2D maps of distant terrain moving closer over time. Pilots had been able to "fly through" these simulations of terrain.

Now, his focus was to create a means by which people could navigate their files like a pilot flying through charted territory, using a controller something like a pilot's joystick. Building his prototype in 1963, Englebart gave very little consideration to the long-term physical effects of using the device. He cut the end off of a two-by-four, hollowed out the bottom to make room for a couple of wheels, and gouged a hole right through for the activator. With three buttons looking like eyes and a nose at one end, and a long tail flowing out of the other, it was dubbed "the mouse" [1].

If you want to know more about this incredible man – and there is a lot more to know then you should look into the Doug Engelbart Institute. As I write this, their website can be found at http://dougengelbart.org/.

I'm not saying that reading about his work and the programmes he founded will lead you into a path that will change your life and improve the world, but I do insist that it's a possibility.

At first, the mouse was just one of several tools for navigating around the new graphic user interfaces (GUIs) that were making the computer seem friendlier. It's hard to imagine, now, that there was a time when keyboard step keys were considered the optimal navigational tool for computer interfaces but, for those not old enough to remember, there is evidence in the archeological record [2]. Since the adoption of the mouse, many studies have been conducted tying it directly to the increase in repetitive strain injuries (RSIs) and Carpal Tunnel Syndrome (CTS) [3–10]. The scientific community responded to this with an approach based on the science of Ergonomics.

If you didn't read Chap. 8, or if you've forgotten our discussion of Ergonomics, here is a quick refresher.

Scientifically, Ergonomics is a focus on understanding how work is done and how doing it affects the worker. The term was coined by Wojciech Bogumił Jastrzębowski in 1857, combining the Greek words for "work" (ergon) and principle (nomos) [11–14]. Ergonomics has improved the usability of simple tools and of complex machinery. The word usability is key. That means that it improves some or all of the factors that allow humans to safely and effectively put the device to the use for which it is intended. That balance is what really makes the science important. Trying to improve safety, for example, without considering how effective the tool is, would result in replacing hammers with pillows. You might never again drive a nail, but you will certainly not be able to flatten your thumb.

The same nonsense results from considering only effectiveness, in complete ignorance of safety. Like fishing with dynamite, this would replace the same hammer with a nail gun. Oh it is possible to use a nail gun without injuring yourself or any-one else, but only because of the addition of safety features after the fact. In fact, even with safety features in place, nail guns remain quite dangerous. Though they are used by only a small subsection of the construction industry, nail guns are associated with more injuries requiring hospitalisation than any other tool [15].

This is where the evils of marketing re-enter our story. A nail gun is made *safer* with the addition of a muzzle cap that must be depressed against a flat surface before the trigger can be activated. That same muzzle cap also slows down the work by preventing "bump firing" (where the trigger is held down and the nail gun is bounced from target to target). That muzzle cap substantially reduces injury (increases safety) but also reduces speed (reduces effectiveness). Where does ergonomics balance out the equation?

Well, thanks to the misappropriation of the word "ergonomic" by the sales department, a nail gun without a muzzle cap can still be labelled as ergonomic, with the simple addition of padding to the handle.

This same logic is behind the marketing of countless "ergonomic" computer mouses. They have been designed with minor changes to shape and acuity, but with no consideration for the underlying problem that some parts of the human body will always be injured if they are forced into some postures and made to repeat some patterns of movement. A device that, when used as designed, will always cause injury, simply should not be called ergonomic.

The failure of industry to provide a safe tool for the public means, of course, that it is up to the public to either abandon the tool or find a safe way to use it.

A Simple Analysis of the Underlying Problem

The people who built the first computer mouse never intended for it to be used for more than a few minutes at a time, over the course of a working day. They simply did not consider, in their design, what it might do to the human body to try and use the mouse for the majority of one's waking hours.

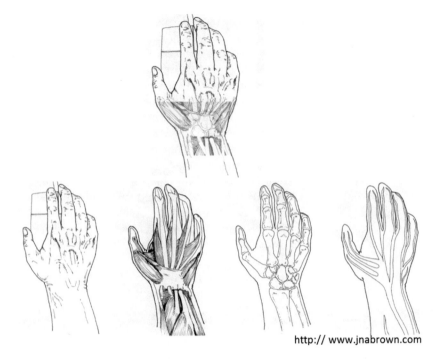

http:// www.jnabrown.com

Fig. 14.1 The hand in a mouse-holding posture, with a look at some of the local internal structures that will have an effect on building or relieving discomfort. Please notice that none of those structures will be affected by minor changes to the shape or to the colour of the mouse

The human body is really quite fragile. Most of our important organs are soft and squishy, with a surprisingly inefficient endoskeleton offering very limited protection to some of them, and no protection at all to others (Fig. 14.1).

Neither the bones nor the skin protect the soft squishy bits we need to keep in working order if we are going to function. Some are better protected than others, but it does seem awfully inconsistent. The brain, for example, is about as well protected by bone as we can manage, but it is very fragile to shaking and to impact and, even with the skull intact, it is much too easy to suffer a brain injury from either of those. An argumentative person might even offer this imperfection of the human body as evidence of the way that humans developed through natural selection which could only select between whichever randomly-generated characteristics were available.

The mechanisms of ovulation and gestation are protected by as much skin and muscle as our bodies can manage, and by the only really flexible skeletal shelter our bodies can offer. That makes good sense, from a purely evolutionary point of view. On the other hand, the mechanisms of spermatogenesis are not nearly as well protected. While this might seem to be unfair to those who anthropomorphize nature, it could instead be taken as a simple reminder of the fact that males are mutants, who only exist because having two sexes provided a successful means to stir up the gene pool. Looking at this obvious factors, it seems clear that the human body is not the result of particularly intelligent design.

The human body is basically strung together like a meat marionette, sealed in a semi-flexible bag of skin. Not sure what I mean? Have you ever hit your funny bone? You're not actually hitting a bone. You're hitting a nerve against an outcropping of bone. This happens where there is nothing but skin and tendon between the big, bad world and one of the three major nerves for your arm. That weird tingling you feel is something like static in a radio or television broadcast... Hrm... How can I explain that to people born after broadband? Well, the nerves are sort of like the wetware version of data cables. There is a constant stream of data flowing between them, like when you're streaming video from an external drive while also backing up another file onto that same external drive.

So, if you can imagine your streaming video getting glitchy because the stream is being interrupted, that's sort of what makes your little finger feel tingly when you hit your funny bone.

What's that? When you hit your funny bone, you feel it in your thumb and first two fingers? Then you haven't hit your ulnar nerve, you've hit your median nerve. Both nerves run out of your spinal cord at your neck, around your shoulder, past your elbow and wrist, and all the way to your fingers. The big differences between the two, for our purposes, is that the ulnar nerve snakes around the outside of the wrist, while the median nerve passes directly through the carpal tunnel.

If you look at Fig. 14.2, you can see a very rough drawing of the bones of the arm and of two of the three major arm nerves running along and around them. When the ulnar nerve (blue) crosses from the upper arm to the forearm (as shown in the inset close-up), it nestles into a protective groove in that particularly pointy bit of the upper arm. When you knock into something that squeezes the ulnar nerve against that outcropping, that's when you get the glitch in your signal.

The outcropping is called the medial epicondyle (middle, well, middle knuckle, I guess) and the forearm bone is the Ulna. The bone in the upper arm is called the humerus, and I've always thought that must be where we got the name "funny bone".

Just as a note, these explanations and drawings are rough, and you should use them only as a crude guideline. Both text and image reflect my beliefs and my understanding far more than they reflect reality. There are great anatomy textbooks and websites out there, but this isn't one of them. For example, the branchings you see in the ulnar nerve are just caricatures of what the branchings are really like. Really, I should be showing more branchings, and more branches at each one. A realistic drawing would show so many branchings, each with so many branches, that the image would look more like it was covered with a blue spider web.

Even with the rough drawing, I hope you can see that the ulnar nerve winds its way around the bones of the arm, on a path from the brachial plexus (the cluster of nerves that connect the arm and shoulder to the spinal cord) all the way out to the tips of the fingers. Well, not all of the fingers.

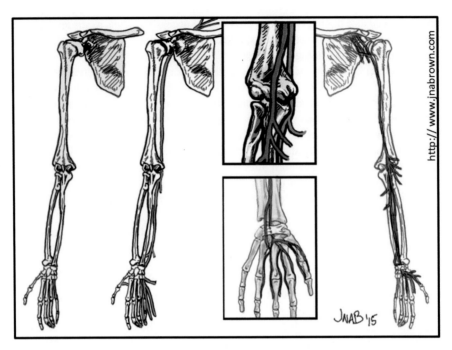

Fig. 14.2 The ulnar and median nerves, shown in close-up at the Medial Epicondyle, the "funny bone", and passing through the Carpal Tunnel at the wrist

As mentioned earlier, there are three major nerves that enervate the arm. They are angled around the same big bones and winding through almost similar paths to different ends. Figure 14.3 provides a rough idea of the relative paths and endings of the three nerves.

You can see there that the ulnar nerve (Fig. 14.3b) ends in the base of the thumb and in the little finger and part of the finger next to it. This is why a sharp and unexpected blow to the "funny bone" makes the area around your little finger and the base of your thumb feel either tingly or like they are buzzing, or even like they are in pain. You're experiencing a temporary neurapraxic injury as shown in Fig. 14.4b.

Kind of makes you feel all tingly, doesn't it?

Here's One Paper That Addresses This Problem

Brown, J. N.A., Albert, W. J., & Croll, J. [16]. A new input device: comparison to three commercially available mouses. Ergonomics, 50(2), 208–227.

The hypotheses tested in this study were

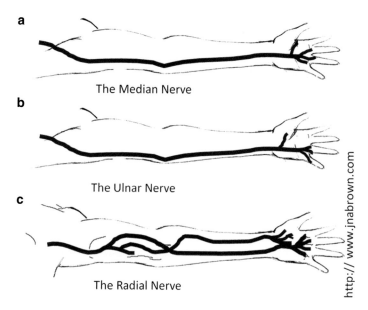

a

The Median Nerve

b

The Ulnar Nerve

c

The Radial Nerve

http://www.jnabrown.com

Fig. 14.3 An illustration of the three major nerve branches innervating the hand, with all muscu-loskeletal structures removed… like that time the new Defense Against the Dark Arts Teacher accidentally made the bones in your arm g- Oh… Wasn't that you?

1. That the use of a new mouse replacement would not result in performance that is significantly worse than the performance elicited through the use of two other, commercially-available mouse replacements, and;
2. That the use of the new mouse replacement would be less demanding than the use of the two others, in terms of requiring that the users move into and hold postures that had previously been related to Repetitive Strain Injuries (RSIs).

Performance was tested using a combination of Fitts' Law Tests and Steering Tests. Static and dynamic postures were captured using an opto-electric motion capture system. But I don't want to talk about the work I set out to do, I want to talk about the work I did accidentally. Let me tell you the story.

More than a decade ago, with the help of friends and colleagues, I recruited a bank of participants for the major research project for my Master's degree. The idea was to test a new device I had invented and prototyped: an ergonomic replacement for the computer mouse. The plan was to get some people to use four different devices, and to measure their speed and accuracy while performing some simple steering tasks at the computer. At the same time, I also captured the static and dynamic postures of their spines, shoulders, arms and hands, using a high-speed, multi-camera, opto-electric system from Vicon™.

One-by-one the recruits came to the laboratory I was using – at the Institute for Biomechanical Engineering at the University of New Brunswick. They filled out

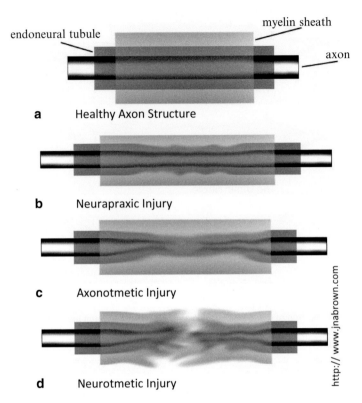

Fig. 14.4 An illustration of three degrees of nerve compression injury: they do look a bit like insulated data cables, don't they?

questionnaires, and they waited while I measured them and adjusted the desk and chair to suit their measurements. Each one showed some interest in the motion capture system, and seemed not to mind all of the small reflective balls that had to be attached to precise locations on their spines and heads and arms and hands.

They all listened to instructions, and asked for clarification if they felt that it was needed. They were a great bunch of people, willing to take the time out of their day so that I might try to make good use of it.

In the end, though, not one of them wanted to work in the "standard, recommended posture" while using the mouse. I started each of them there, but with the instruction that they should feel free to adjust themselves into their preferred working posture before starting the task. There was a lot of variability in the way they sat and leaned and even moved, but there was one thing that every single one of them did. It was subtle. I didn't notice it until I was analyzing the captured data as applied to my 3D model. Then, when I went back and looked at the videos, I could see it clearly. Every single one of them was sticking out their elbow. Some more than others, some stuck it out while leaning in the same direction, and others while leaning the other way. Some did it while sitting upright but with their chair turned about 45° away from the monitor and their starting position.

My intent had been to evaluate my new mouse replacement, and that is what I did. At the same time, though, I had been conducting another experiment without realising it: I had been measuring posture of the entire upper body during use of a standard mouse. Now that part is kind of cool, but it gets cooler. You see, in order to avoid hurting anyone, I had specifically selected people with no history of work-related pain or injury in their arm, wrist or hand. At the same time, for the sake of consistency across the sample, I had selected people who were heavy-duty mouse users. In practical terms, this meant that each one self-reported as using a computer for at least 4 h per day, over the course of at least 4 days per week.

I hadn't realised that, since I had selected people whose personal mousing behaviour had allowed them to avoid injury, I was collecting data on the postural strategies that were keeping these heavy duty mousers from being hurt.

Imagine my shock when I realised that I might have accidentally found a useful strategy to mitigate the threat of repetitive strain injuries from mousing. After all, each of these 24 people had managed to avoid getting carpal tunnel syndrome or any other problem (according to both a self-report and some quick and dirty testing in the lab), despite heavy-duty use, for work and for recreation, over the course of many years.

You can see that strategy in action in Fig. 14.5, which is a screencap from the Vicon™ Bodybuilder™ Software. The view has been rotated so that the markers on the shoulder, elbow and distal heads of the radius and ulna are seen from above. The graphic display windows on each side of the viewscreen show the displacement of the shoulder and elbow markers over time along each of the x, y and z axes.

In the remainder of this chapter, we're going to look at how you might apply that strategy to evaluating your own use of a computer mouse, and see if it might help you to avoid injury. You can also use the same technique to evaluate others and see if the strategy works for them.

Proposed Experiment

This simple experiment is going to involve you using your computer mouse in two different postures as seen in Fig. 14.6, and evaluating both experiences with a Likert scale.

Our hypothesis is straightforward:

If I use a mouse with the manufacturer's recommended posture (MRP – elbow under shoulder, wrist straight ahead and flat on desk) and with the modified strategy (elbow away from body in a relaxed posture), then there will be no difference in the pain or discomfort measured with our pain scale.

Before starting, you should learn how to assume a relaxed posture by sticking out your elbow. Once you've found a comfortable posture, come back and try it a few

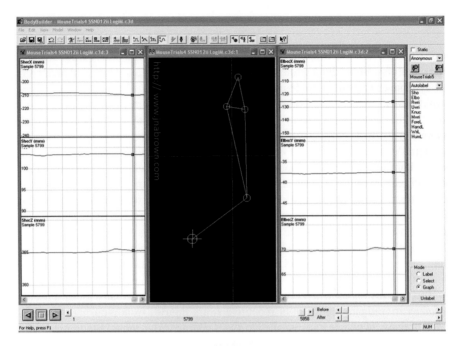

Fig. 14.5 The view from above of the arm of one of our participants after she moved to her preferred posture for mousing. The *dots* show the position of her shoulder (the *bottom* of the screen), elbow, and wrist, and of the second knuckle of her hand. You can see that her elbow is not under her shoulder as recommended by the manufacturer, but has been pushed out to the side

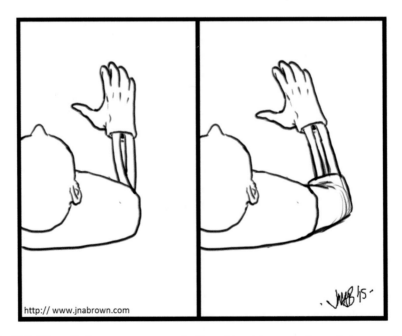

Fig. 14.6 Elbow displacement means you don't need to rotate your radius and ulna around one another

times. Adjust it as necessary before you start the experiment. Once you start, you want that posture to be approximately the same each time you do it.

A couple of tips for comfort: don't hold your arm above the desk; don't rest your arm on any obstacles or uneven surfaces (especially sharp or hard edges); don't rotate your arm at the shoulder to try and put your hand straight in front of your elbow. In the right hand side illustration in Fig. 14.6, you can see how the hand stays (roughly) in front of the shoulder, instead of being straight in front of the elbow. Referring to Fig. 14.7, you can see which part of your elbow should be resting on the desk when using the manufacturer's recommended posture (A) as opposed to when using the modified posture discussed above (B).

Now make some decisions about how to run the experiment. After all, we've talked about your posture, but not about what you're going to do while holding that posture. We want you to perform a task with the computer mouse. We want you to be working hard enough on that task that you stop thinking primarily about the posture of your wrist. That is, we want you to keep holding the correct posture, but we want you to be concentrating on what you're doing with the mouse, not with your wrist.

The task we're going to try is a Fitts' Law Test [17]. Paul Fitts came up with the idea of measuring how well people use a pointing device, like a pencil or their finger, or a computer mouse, by measuring how well they tap back and forth between two targets. If you read the original paper – and I do think you should – then you'll see that there is a formula for grading your performance, based on the size of your targets and how far apart they are.

This formula is good for comparing the difficulty of different Fitts Law tasks, but we can get by with something easier. For your tests, we're just going to count how

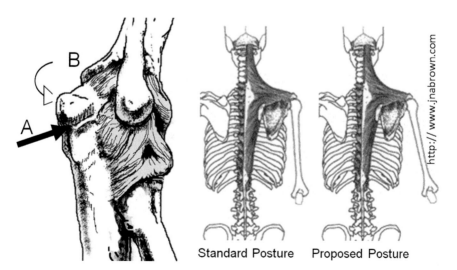

Standard Posture   Proposed Posture

http://www.jnabrown.com

Fig. 14.7 Close up and distance view of the part of the ulna that rests on the desk during normal mouse use (**A**) and during the new strategy (**B**)

Fig. 14.8 Fitts Law Test
-the *top* shows
measurement of radius and
distance between the
targets. The *bottom* shows
a trial with 26 taps and 7
misses

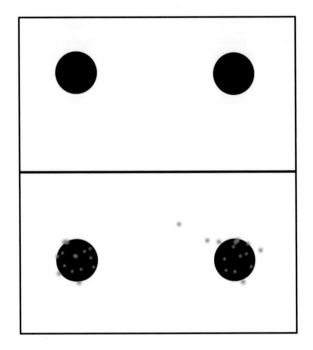

many times you tapped, and how many of those times were outside of the circles. Outside of which circles, you ask? Well, you can just recreate the images in Fig. 14.8 in your favourite graphics programme. Just remember that if you want to be able to compare your data to the data from others, you'll have to note how big your circles are, and how far apart they are. If you want to be able to compare your own data from one attempt to your own data from another attempt, you should remember to use a fresh copy the same drawing (set at the same size in your view) each time.

Before starting, decide which posture you're going to use, and remember to try and stay in that posture for the whole 5-min session. While using the mouse, rate your discomfort on a scale of discomfort like the one shown in Fig. 14.9. You can recreate it digitally, or just refer to this book.

I recommend that you type your choices directly into a spreadsheet, but if you're working with a partner, then they can ask you how you feel every 30 s, and they can type in the letter that you call out. The scale offers you five choices labelled A, B, C, D, and E, where "A" means "no discomfort or pain whatsoever", and "E" means "excruciating pain that prevents me from continuing". If you rank anything as a "D", you can stop. If you rank anything as an "E", please consider seeking medical help.

Rate your discomfort after 30 s, and then again every 30 s for a total of 10 min. If you decide you have to stop because of discomfort, then please take note of how long you lasted. Rest for 20 min and then complete the experiment by switching postures and doing it again.

If you want you can repeat the experiment in order to have data about your experience over time. Take a day to rest and recuperate in between sessions. If you used

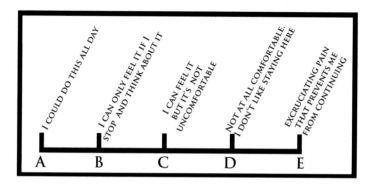

Fig. 14.9 A scale of general discomfort and pain

the Manufacturer's Recommended Poature first, then next time use our new posture first. Change the order like that each time, and record it – just to see if it makes a difference.

You should also take note of where it hurts or is uncomfortable. We aren't measuring that this time, but collecting that data will help us learn more about how the two postures effect someone, and may help us to decide if we should include be measuring something in particular next time.

Be sure to save your answers because we want to see how they change over time.

How to Record and Report Your Results

Now, for every participant, you should have six sets of data, three for each of the two postures. The three are: the notes you wrote out for additional information, your Fitts' Law Test, and the letter grades you assigned to describe your discomfort over time.

The Fitts' Law Tests are going to be the easiest to use, because we're going to simplify the process. Count the number of attempts achieved during the trial, either in real time or after the fact. You can do the latter either by counting the dots you made when clicking the mouse, or by recording the sight or noise of the trial and then counting during playback. Then count the number of dots outside of the targets. What percentage of your attempts were successful?

There are many ways to interpret written notes, but we won't go into any depth about that here. There are specialist books on the topic and specialist courses as well. For our purposes, you could just try to form a negative, neutral, or positive opinion of each trial.

Now, we'll concentrate on how to use your letter grades. If you've logged a score for your discomfort every 30 s over 10 min, then you should have 20 letters for us to consider. Now you have to decide whether you want to:

examine 1 session alone,
examine one posture over time,
compare two postures on one day, or
compare 2 postures over time.

Once you've decided which one you want to do, come to the website associated with this book and sign in to share and compare your results with other citizen scientists.

References

1. Perry TS, Voelcker J (1989) Of mice and menus: designing the user-friendly interface. Spectr IEEE 26(9):46–51
2. Card SK, English WK, Burr BJ (1978) Evaluation of mouse, rate-controlled isometric joystick, step keys, and text keys for selection on a CRT. Ergonomics 21:601–613
3. Brown JNA (2004). A new input device: comparison to three commercially available mouses. Master's dissertation, University of New Brunswick, Canada
4. Aarås A, Dainoff M, Ro O, Thoresen M (2002) Can a more neutral position of the forearm when operating a computer mouse reduce the pain level for VDU operators? Int J Ind Ergon 30(4):307–324
5. Keir PJ, Bach JM, Rempel D (1998) Effects of finger posture on carpal tunnel pressure during wrist motion. J Hand Surg 23A:1004–1009
6. Keir PJ, Bach JM (1999) Effects of computer mouse design and task on carpal tunnel pressure. Ergonomics 42:1350–1360
7. Loscher WN, Auer-Grumbach M, Trinka E, Ladurner G, Hartung H-P (2000) Comparison of second lumbrical and interosseus latencies with standard measures of median nerve function across the carpal tunnel: a prospective study of 450 hands. J Neurol 247(7):530–534
8. Rempel D, Bach JM, Gordon L, Levinsohn DG (1998) Effects of forearm pronation/supination on carpal tunnel pressure. J Hand Surg 23A:38–42
9. Jensen BR, Laursen B, Ratkevicius (2002) Forearm extensor muscle fatigue in young and elderly subjects induced by four hours of computer mouse work. In: Proceedings of the 8th international conference on human-computer interaction, 93–96, Aug 22–26, Munich
10. Dainoff MJ (1999) A fitt's law comparison between two different mouse designs. Proceedings of the 8th International Conference on Human Computer Interaction, Aug 22–27, Munich
11. Jastrzebowski WB (1857) An outline of ergonomics, or the science of work based upon the truths drawn from the science of nature, part I. Nat Ind 29:227–231
12. Jastrzebowski WB (1857) An outline of ergonomics, or the science of work based upon the truths drawn from the science of nature, part II. Nat Ind 30:236–244
13. Jastrzebowski WB (1857) An outline of ergonomics, or the science of work based upon the truths drawn from the science of nature, part III. Nat Ind 31:244–251
14. Jastrzebowski WB (1857) An outline of ergonomics, or the science of work based upon the truths drawn from the science of nature, part IV. Nat Ind 32:253–258
15. Lipscomb HJ, Nolan J, Patterson D (2015) Musculoskeletal concerns do not justify failure to use safer sequential trigger to prevent acute nail gun injuries. Am J Ind Med 58(4):422–427
16. Brown JNA, Albert WJ, Croll J (2007) A new input device: comparison to three commercially available mouses. Ergonomics 50(2):208–227
17. Fitts PM (1954) The information capacity of the human motor system in controlling the amplitude of movement. J Exp Psychol 47:381–391

Chapter 15
Stop Your Keyboard from Taking Your Hands

Maybe they should come with a warning label…

Abstract If you use a computer for writing, you probably use a keyboard for text entry. Now, I know that not everyone does use a keyboard, whether that is by choice or by circumstance, but I have only known two people who didn't use them at least a little.

Yes, my experience is only a small sample of the sum experience of the human race, but I've worked with computers on five continents, and I've been playing with

J.N.A. Brown, *Anthropology-Based Computing*, Human–Computer
Interaction Series, DOI 10.1007/978-3-319-24421-1_15

them so long that I remember when the latest advance was connecting a punchcard reader to a distant computer via telephone through the use of some new tech called a modem.

But, like Peter David, I digress.

You may be thinking that you don't use a keyboard, because you type on a touch-screen. If so, I invite you to take my new distance learning course on Hair-Splitting. It will begin once we have all agreed to a single grading scale.

Sorry.

In this chapter we will discuss a stupid device called a keyboard. It was technologically brilliant in its time, but it has always caused injury to the people who use it, usually in direct proportion to the time they spend on it.

We know, through science, a few things about how to make a keyboard better or worse – less or more injurious. Strangely, the manufacturers ignore this knowledge, and the consumers continue to purchase bad designs – whether due to cross-generational habit, or successful marketing, or – and this seems more likely to me – through blind ignorance and lack of options.

Once you've read this chapter you won't have those last two excuses anymore.

A keyboard under glass – where it can't ever harm anyone again…

Once Upon a Time…

…there was a terrible and crippling medical problem that spread through the land. Women, young and old, were being crippled by unseen forces. It always happened to professional women, usually of lower- or middle-class, which may be why it received so little attention in the press of the day.

Those women were only the first to suffer from this problem. When computers moved from being a rare workplace tool to be a ubiquitous tool for both home and work, the flea that was spreading this plague moved with it. For those of you who are unclear on metaphor and analogy, I don't mean that there was actually a flea. I mean that the cause of the crippling problem moved into our homes and our workplaces with the computer.

That cause? The keyboard.

A Simple Analysis of the Underlying Problem

How could keyboards be responsible for pain in the hands?

Well, you remember that, in the lead-up to the experiment in Chap. 13, we talked about how the position of your elbow (relative to your body) will make a difference in how much your forearm has to rotate in order to hold your mouse, right? And you remember that the rotation of the forearm is one of several factors that can cause you pain or even injury just from the repeated strain of using your mouse the way it was designed to be used, right?

Well, the angle of your wrists when you are typing with your fingers is one of the factors related to pain or numbness or tingling that could feel as though you've hit your funny bone. You're getting another neurapraxic injury. Where you feel the tingling or numbness will tell you which nerve is being "pinched".

The problem isn't that typing or using a computer mouse is going to be like getting the occasional sudden shock to your funny bone, the problem is that the nerve injury could get worse. Some will say that the actual mechanism of injury is not yet scientifically proven. I would recommend that those people read the discussion of science versus faith that happened a little earlier in this book.

Take a hold of your wrist as illustrated in Fig. 15.1 and gently slide your fingers and thumb around your wrist. You'll find the radius and ulna at the sides of your wrist. At the back, you'll find a big bump at the distal head of the radius – that just means the end of that bone that is furthest from the core of your body. Above that bump, you'll find all kinds of little bones (carpals) squeezed together, running up the back of your hand until you get to the longer bones (the metacarpals) that lead out to your fingers, made up of bones called phalanges. Have you ever noticed that your thumbs have fewer phalanges than your fingers?

Under your wrist, everything is much softer. Now you should be able to feel the distal head of the other forearm bone, the ulna, but that end of the radius should be sort of padded over with soft tissues. In between the two bones, you should feel nothing but soft tissue.

If you look at Fig. 15.2, you can see an illustration of that. The top of the carpal tunnel is a whole bunch of hard bones, held tightly together by tendons. The underside of the carpal tunnel is an intertwined mass of tendons and nerves and other soft tissues.

That soft tissue and lack of bones under the wrist is the reason that some people will tell you that it is "ergonomic" to use a wrist rest. In my opinion, it is also the

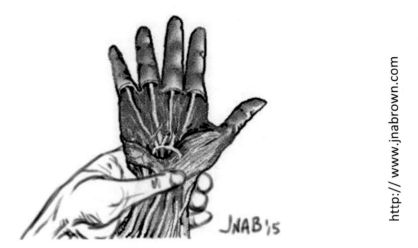

http:// www.jnabrown.com

Fig. 15.1 Feeling the difference between the front and the back of the wrist. Please note: You do not actually have to remove the skin from your hand in order to do this…

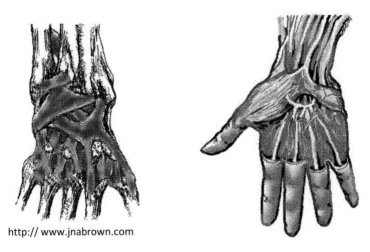

http:// www.jnabrown.com

Fig. 15.2 The barriers on the *top* and the *bottom* of the carpal tunnel: *above*, tendon and hard bone; *below*, tendon and other soft tissues

reason why we should never use them. You should never rest your wrists when typing – not on something hard, and not even on something soft.

There is compelling evidence that wrist extension puts additional strain on the ulnar nerve [1, 2]. There is compelling evidence that resting the wrist on a hard or soft surface puts additional pressure on the ulnar nerve [3]. There is lovely bit of evidence that, once your wrist is in a bad posture, you can radically increase the pressure on you ulnar nerve by working your fingers [4, 5].

So, the posture of using a keyboard, the construction of the "ergonomic" intervention, and the movement of typing are all associated with increased pressure on the ulnar nerve. With or without compelling evidence of association between keyboard use and nerve damage – and I believe that the scientific evidence is compelling – the point is that the injuries are happening.

We're going to take a look now at a paper that proposes a way to find out which wrist angle causes the least discomfort. Once we've looked at their work, we'll modify it a bit and share an experiment for you to try at home. The experiment is intended to help you find out which wrist posture causes you the least discomfort, but we're going to add a couple of modifications based on my research.

I don't know for sure, but I think I can help you find a wrist posture that will cause you a lot less discomfort. I hope that your scientific tests will reveal it.

Here's One Paper That Tries to Offer a Solution to This Problem

Asundi, K., Odell, D., Luce, A., & Dennerlein, J. T. [6] Changes in posture through the use of simple inclines with notebook computers placed on a standard desk. Applied ergonomics, 43(2), 400–407.

Asundi, Odell, Luce and Dennerlein have reported the results of an interesting attempt to find a good angle at which to use your laptop [6]. They literally set laptops on the kind of hard tables you find in coffee shops and elsewhere, and they used found objects (like a three-ring binder or the laptop's transformer) to change the angle of the laptop's keyboard and the height of its monitor.

I like this study very much (I mean, enough to recommend that all of you read and cite it) but that doesn't mean that I agree with every part of it. At first pass, the experiment sounds balanced and clever and easy to reproduce. My opinion of these characteristics didn't change the next time I read the paper. However, I also noticed a fundamental problem with the idea.

They are trying to adjust both keyboard angle and monitor height to suit "ergonomic" guidelines for neck posture, while minimizing discomfort caused by wrist posture. Even if that were a reasonable guideline they would still be trying to meet a vaguely-defined sets of requirements for the neck posture.

The result is that they cannot find an angle at which to set your laptop so that both your neck and your wrists are comfortable, but they recommend a 12° incline as the best compromise and go on to say that "these results also indicate that users of notebook computers may find improved postures with the use of an external mouse… a riser, and external keyboard". We'll come back to that in the next two chapters, with an alternative set up that I wish they had tested. Since they didn't, I'm going to be asking you to test it instead.

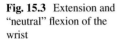

Fig. 15.3 Extension and "neutral" flexion of the wrist

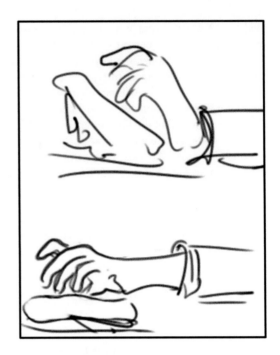

Here and now, we're going to focus on keyboard, so let's take a look at what they did, and then take a look at what they found out, and then take a look at what they decided they could learn from it – all with a focus on keyboard angles.

Basically, they slipped two different risers underneath laptops in order to change the angle of the monitor and of the keyboard. Then they used a nice infra-red 3D motion tracking system to track the postures of the hands, arms, heads and trunks of their participants while they worked at six different set-ups, involving two different keyboard inclinations along with the use of an external mouse and of a manufac-tured laptop riser with external mouse and keyboard. The keyboards inclinations ranged from 25 to 0°, meaning that the wrist could either be extended or neutral, but not flexed (Fig. 15.3).

Proposed Experiment

Their basic experiment was pretty straightforward. Yours should be, too. Basically, we're going to recreate the part of their experiment that involved assessing people's discomfort when working at different keyboard angles, but we're going to simplify it a lot, and we're going to add in one more dimension: angling the keyboard in the opposite direction (Fig. 15.4).

Fig. 15.4 Extension,
"neutral" posture, and
flexion of the wrist

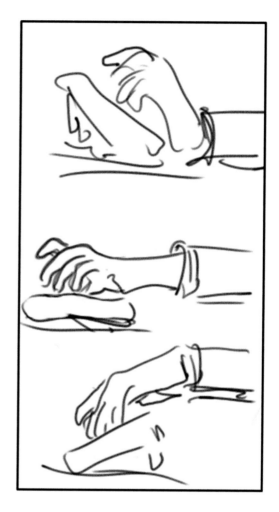

Some Things to Do Before the Experiment

The experimenter(s) find a free on-line typing speed test.

The experimenter(s) recruit some people to participate in the experiment.

The experimenter(s) have to make sure that the participants are all roughly equally familiar with the devices they will be expected to use and with the tasks they will be expected to perform. Otherwise, they will have to be familiarized – given time to learn how to do the task competently. This doesn't mean that they all have to be able to type at the same speed, but it does mean that they should all be used to typing.

The experimenter should collect a description of the detail about each participant that might have an effect on their work For example, if you are testing someone who is 2 m tall (6 ft, 6 in.) and also someone who is 1 m tall (3 ft, 3 in.), then you should make sure that their heights do not have an effect on the experiment – or at least, do not have an effect that is not accounted for and discussed and explained. For this test, the height should only matter if you are trying to specify the height of the desk or of the chair, or if you are trying to measure the distance from the laptop to the chair or to the table's edge, etc… A good solution would be to have each participant sit comfortably the way that they would sit at a table in a coffee shop, in a library, or while visiting friends. The shorter person may want a riser on the chair and a foot rest. The taller may want to sit further back and to slouch. If you do adjust the height of the chair, then just take note of the fact, and of any details you can. Not because we know it will tell us something, but because we know that it might.

The experimenters have to make sure that each participant is capable of performing the task, too. If for any reason, any participant might be limited in their use of the tool or performance of the task, the experimenter(s) should take note of that, and consider whether or not to exclude that participant. For example, needing to use glasses should not interfere in this test. That said, it might interfere if the lighting in your experimental are causes glare on the glasses. Needing to use glasses to read will definitely affect the experiment if the participant has forgotten them at home and can barely see the laptop, much less the words she is supposed to be typing.

The Experiment

A person sits at a standard desk and works on an online typing speed test at a laptop. During the work, ask the person to describe their relative comfort and discomfort using the same discomfort scale we already introduced.

They repeat this with the laptop set flat on the desk, set at an incline (with the charger's transformer set under the back of the laptop), and set at a decline (with the transformer set under the front of the keyboard).

Remember not to worry about the neck angle – we're going to talk about that in the next chapter.

How to Record and Report Your Results

Now, for every participant, you should have nine sets of data, three for each of the three postures. The datasets are: the notes you wrote out for additional information, your Typing Speed Test, and the letter grades you assigned to describe your discomfort over time.

The typing speed tests are going to be the easiest to use, because we're just interested in comparing your word rate, as it was captured by the test, either to your own rate at different wrist angles, or to your to your own rate at the same angle on another day, or to the general sample data we get from everyone else who goes to the website to share what they've done.

As before, we won't go into any depth here and now about "ethnographic methods" or how to interpret your notes. There are specialist books on the topic and specialist courses as well. For our purposes, you could just try to form a negative, neutral, or positive opinion of each trial.

Now, we'll concentrate on how to use your letter grades. If you've logged a score for your discomfort every 30 s over 10 min, then you should have 20 letters for us to consider. Now you have to decide whether you want to:

examine 1 session alone,
examine one posture over time,
compare two postures on one day, or
compare 2 postures over time.

Once you've decided which one you want to do, come to the website associated with this book, and sign in to share and compare your results with other citizen scientists.

References

1. Amell TK, Kumar S (1999) Cumulative trauma disorders and keyboarding work. Int J Ind Ergon 25:69–78
2. Katz RT (1994) Carpal tunnel syndrome: a practical review. Am Fam Physician 49:1371–1379
3. Baker N (2013) The effectiveness of alternative keyboards at reducing musculoskeletal symptoms at work: a review. In: Digital human modeling and applications in health, safety, ergonomics, and risk management. Human body modeling and ergonomics. Springer, Berlin, pp 189–195
4. Keir PJ, Bach JM, Rempel D (1998) Effects of finger posture on carpal tunnel pressure during wrist motion. J Hand Surg 23A:1004–1009
5. Serina ER, Tal R, Rempel D (1999) Wrist and forearm postures and motions during typing. Ergonomics 42:938–951
6. Asundi K, Odell D, Luce A, Dennerlein JT (2012) Changes in posture through the use of simple inclines with notebook computers placed on a standard desk. Appl Ergon 43(2):400–407

Chapter 16
Stop Your Tech from Wringing Your Neck, Breaking Your Back, and Being an All-Around Pain in the … Life

I can't feel my fingers or toes…

Abstract Despite the fact that parents and schoolteachers have been demanding it for generations, the human body is not very good at staying still.

Now, you may be thinking that, even if this is true, the exception is that famous "ergonomic" posture in which a person sits close to a desk with their ankles, knees, hips, and elbows all at about 90 degrees. You know the posture I mean, the one that nearly everyone uses…

Well, it's wrong.

I mean, it's wrong to expect humans to sit still for more than a few minutes and still have healthy functioning bodies, but I also mean that the famous posture has been misappropriated and is not a valid strategy for sitting at a computer.

In the last two chapters we've looked a little at remedial changes you can make to the way you use your mouse and the way you use your keyboard. In this chapter we'll tie both of those together and give you a couple of whole-body postural recommendations based, in part, on how your eyes work.

Really.

Go on, give it a try.

Once Upon a Time…

…there was a woman who walked everywhere.

She carried her children with her, in all weather and over all terrain. In time, they walked beside her, returning to her arms only for rest or for comfort.

She didn't walk every minute of the day, only most of the time. Her body functioned best when moving, and felt limited and restricted when she had to hold it still. Her skeleton was interwoven with a vast network of interconnected and cross-balanced muscles and tendons that moved together well when she ran or jumped or swam; that they should all be locked at one length was not natural. This was true for standing still and for lying still, for lounging without moving and for crouching without moving, even for perching or for sitting.

She might do any of those things for a time, but almost never holding still, always with some shifting of her weight to keep the blood moving, always with some dynamic tension to keep her coordinated muscles taught or relaxed in balance with one another.

Her family walked for 200 generations, and then they sat down.

Somehow they got the idea that sitting still was a good idea, and that to do so for hour upon hour every day was… normal.

They lost the coordination and tone of their muscles, and their blood pooled, and their bodies suffered…

…and their minds…

…I don't even like to think about what happened to their minds once they had given up on their bodies.

The Underlying Problem

The human body works best when it is moving. It did not evolve in static postures, it has just always been easier to study and discuss in static postures. Dissecting corpses taught us where nerves and veins ran through and around the bones, muscles and tendons of the arm or the leg, but it taught us nothing about how they move and stretch and twist when that arm or leg is being put to use.

Decades ago, experts began to claim that sitting in a 90-90-90 posture was "ideal", but it's not. I've heard two stories of where that idea comes from, and both confirm that it started with an illustration labelled "optimal". In both versions of the story the image has been denounced by its creator who specifies that he never intended it to be used as a specific illustration of the way a human should work or even sit.

I don't want to spread a false story, and I haven't been able to confirm one version over the other, so I'll hold off putting the details in writing. If you'd like to talk about it sometime though, and happen to see me on the street or between presentations at a conference, I'd be happy to fill you in on what I've heard. Maybe by then I'll have confirmed one story or the other, or a different origin altogether.

The point is this. The research reported in the Asundi et al. paper is based in part on a false understanding of where a monitor should be located in order to avoid neck strain. Don't get me wrong; they cite good literature and they have designed and conducted a good research experiment based on those citations, it's just that the work they cite started in the wrong place.

Let me try to explain it with a story. If you wanted to find a buried treasure, you could start digging in your local garden or in the street, or anywhere at all. It would be better, I think we could all agree that it might at least save you some time, if your choice of where to dig could be limited to places with evidence of treasure. Ideally, it would be nice to have some directions that at least directed you to the right general area. But what if those directions were written by someone who copied it from a copy of a copy? What if, somewhere along the line, someone read the phrase "somewhere in that region, but closer to the mountain than the beach" and abbreviated it as "in the region close to the mountain".

Do you see how, several copies later, you might be digging too close to the mountain?

This kind of mistake happens all the time when people don't think scientifically, and it still happens some of the time when we do. We all make mistakes, every day. That's why it's so important to have people check your work. I shudder to think how many mistakes I'm making in writing this book, and I'm very happy to working with such good editors. In fact, I wonder if they'll let this story through...

So, to cut to the chase at last, your monitor should not be elevated. It should not be at eye-level, it should be somewhere lower than 15° below your eye level, maybe as low as 60° below. Here's a fun and simple test I learned from Denny Ankrum when he was keynote speaker at the first Ergonomics conference I ever attended.

Hold a business card at arm's length and at eye level. Now slowly bring it closer to your eyes until the letters begin to blur. Don't move your head at all, but keep your eyes on the letters as you slowly lower the card. What happened to the letters?

If you moved slowly and lowered your gaze without tipping your head, the letters should have come at least partially back in to focus.

This is because our eyes naturally focus better on close things when they are lower, and on far things when they are higher. This makes good evolutionary sense, too. When you're standing in the waving grass of the African Savannah, you would have to raise you head to see things that are further away.

When you live in tall grass, looking down always means seeing close things; to see something far away, you have to lift your head

Here Are Two Papers That Address the Problem

Ankrum, D. R. (1996). *Viewing distance at computer workstations.* Workplace Ergonomics, 2(5), 10–13.
Ankrum, D. R. (1999). *WORKPLACE ERGONOMICS SUPPLEMENT Visual Ergonomics In the Office.* Occupational Health and Safety, 68(7), 64–70.

In the papers cited above, Denny Ankrum explains in clarity and detail just why it is a bad idea to set your monitor according to common "ergonomic" guidelines. The muscles that control the position of your eyes have to strain more when you try to overlap their focus while looking up. The natural shape of the muscles and of the eyes works better for overlapping focus when the eyes are looking down. Don't take my word for it: read those two papers. In fact, read as many more as you can find… I mean, you know, *good* ones.

The natural neck and eye postures for looking at something that is close and looking at something that is far away are illustrated in Fig. 16.1. Their application to monitor height – and monitor angle – are illustrated in Fig. 16.2.

Proposed Experiment

Now we're going to expand the previous experiment on discomfort related to wrist flexion and extension, by adding a simultaneous look at neck discomfort. In this way it is again like the original experiment by Asundi et al. [1], but with another major difference (Fig. 16.3). As we saw in Ankrum's papers [2, 3], it is not a

Fig. 16.1 Look down to see what's in your hands, look up to see what's far away

Fig. 16.2 According to Ankrum's application of the natural limitations of human vision, natural monitor height should be between 0 and 60°. Proximity should be based on text size and vision

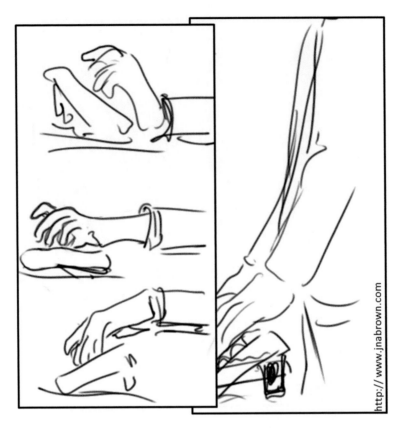

Fig. 16.3 We'll expand the previous experiment to incorporate neck discomfort based on monitor visibility – not monitor height

question of elevating the monitor as much as possible, but of angling it to suit a height that reflects the natural parameters of human vision. We hypothesize that postures related to mild wrist flexion and no neck flexion or extension at all will be the most comfortable.

Generally, I'd recommend that you shift your position all day long, but for this study we're going to try to control your postures and how often you change them. First, the two postures:

The first posture is shown in Fig. 16.4, with a happy fellow is sitting with his laptop on his knees and his mouse on an upside-down garbage can. He'll shift his height and the degree to which he is reclining to suit his comfort and his furniture. If his chair is too high, he could set the mouse on an old computer tower, instead. Please note that his mouse may be sitting just a little too far forward for his comfortable reach, I would advise him to move it closer to his hip, so that his hand could naturally fall onto the mouse if his arm is relaxed.

Fig. 16.4 First posture – remember to shift your weight around. Really, learning to balance your laptop should take care of that

Fig. 16.5 Again, remember to shift your weight, and to find the right height for your reach and for your vision. The woman in the illustration has decided to use a touchpad instead of a mouse, which gives her room on the small table for a donut. Not as useful as a mouse, perhaps, but one might expect it to be tastier

The second posture standing at desk with laptop tipped back and mouse beside (if you use a mouse). Figure 16.5 shows the posture in use, but cannot show the importance of adjusting the set up to suit one's own height, reach, and vision.

Follow the same experimental methods as before, but this time go long…

Incorporate this trial into your regular computer time. Try to alternate between the two postures every 40 min. Before you switch, rate your discomfort on our scale, and take note of anything in particular that you've noticed, like that your feet are sore from standing for 40 min. If they are, though, it may be because you were standing too still. It may not, it may be that you have sore feet for some other reason that I can't evaluate remotely, and that I wouldn't be qualified to evaluate even if I were in the room with your feet at the time. I can suggest this much: if your feet hurt when you do this, then stop doing this.

If you want, you can design your own experiment to rate your productivity and compare how well you produce in your normal sitting posture to how well you produce switching postures every 40 min. My own personal studies gave a clear answer as to which is more productive. I'd like to hear what you find.

How to Record and Report Your Results

This time, for every participant, you should have three sets of data, one series of discomfort scores for each of the two postures, and your notes on the experience.

As before, you have to decide whether you want to:

examine one session alone,
examine one posture over time,
compare two postures on one day, or
compare two postures over time.

Like always, once you've decided which one you want to do, come to the website associated with this book, and sign in to share and compare your results with other citizen scientists.

References

1. Asundi K, Odell D, Luce A, Dennerlein JT (2012) Changes in posture through the use of simple inclines with notebook computers placed on a standard desk. Appl Ergon 43(2):400–407
2. Ankrum DR (1996) Viewing distance at computer workstations. Work Ergon 2(5):10–13
3. Ankrum DR (1999) Workplace ergonomics supplement visual ergonomics in the office. Occup Health Saf 68(7):64–70

Additional Reading on Related Topics

Aaras A, Fostervold KI, Ro O, Thoresen M, Larsen S (1997) Postural load during VDU work: a comparison between various work postures. Ergonomics 40:1255–1268

Birch L, Graven-Neilsen T, Christensen H, Arendt-Neilsen L (2000) Experimental muscle pain modulates muscle activity and work performance differently during high and low precision use of a computer mouse. Eur J Appl Physiol 83(6):492–498

Bracker MD, Ralph LP (1995) The numb arm and hand. Am Fam Physician 51:103–116

Brown JNA, Albert WJ, Croll J (2007) A new input device: comparison to three commercially available mouses. Ergonomics 50(2):208–227

Burgess-Limerick R, Plooy A, Ankrum DR (1998) The effect of imposed and self-selected computer monitor height on posture and gaze angle. Clin Biomech 13(8):584–592

Cook CJ, Kothiyal K (1998) Influence of mouse position on muscular activity in the neck, shoulder and arm in computer users. Appl Ergon 29:439–443

Fernstrom E, Ericson MO (1996) Upper-arm elevation during office work. Ergonomics 39:1221–1230

Kleinrensink GJ, Stoeckart R, Vleeming A, Snijders CJ, Mulder PGH (1995) Mechanical tension in the median nerve. The effects of joint positions. Clin Biomech 10:240–244

Matias AC, Salvendy G, Kuczek T (1998) Predictive models of carpal tunnel syndrome causation among VDT operators. Ergonomics 41:213–226

Neuhaus M, Healy GN, Fjeldsoe BS, Lawler S, Owen N, Dunstan DW, … Eakin EG (2014) Iterative development of Stand Up Australia: a multi-component intervention to reduce workplace sitting. Int J Behav Nutr Phys Act 11:21

Van Niekerk SM, Fourie SM, Louw QA (2015) Postural dynamism during computer mouse and keyboard use: a pilot study. Appl Ergon 50:170–176

Chapter 17
Stop Your Phone from Screaming at You (and Everyone Else!)

http:// www.jnabrown.com

Abstract When a phone rings, what is it supposed to do? Well, the original idea was that it should get the attention of the intended person, so that they can decide whether or not to postpone or stop what they're doing and answer it. We've all seen how a crowd reacts when they hear a popular or default ringtone in a crowded room: everyone checks their phone. It might be funny the first time it happens, but it gets annoying pretty quickly, as do most customized ringtones. How many times can your best friend's phone play your favorite song before you learn to hate both the song and the friend?

I've come up with a simple way to improve the function of your ringtones, based on a psychological phenomenon called "The Cocktail Party Effect". It's been observed that a person in a crowded and noisy room can hear their own name more clearly than anyone else can – even if it is spoken at low volume. A familiar voice is also easier to hear. So… how about replacing your ringtone with the voice of your favorite (and least favorite) callers softly speaking your name?

Not only do you hear the ring clearly at a volume too low to bother the people around you, you also know who's calling without having to stop and check.

Let's have a look at how your brain reacts when the phone rings, and why that might be dangerous. Then we can look at some alternatives that cause different reactions.

Once Upon a Time

In Xanadu did Kubla Khan
A stately pleasure-dome decree:
Where Alph, the sacred river, ran
Through caverns measureless to man
Down to a sunless sea. [1]

Do you know that poem? Have you read the incredibly vivid description of Xanadu? Have you read the last verse?

No, none of us has, and the poet himself told us why. According to Coleridge, the writing of the poem was interrupted by a salesman knocking on the door.

The knocking did not subside for some time, and even then it was only after the poet had gone to the door and told the blighter repeatedly to leave. By then it was too late, the deep thought in which he had been writing had been lost, and with it the imagery, the flow of words, the deep and visceral creative experience were all lost, too.

Modern science tells us that when we are interrupted, it can take up to 20 min to regain the degree of focus, "the flow", in which you had been working.

That's if you can get it back at all. Sometimes the idea is as lost as Xanadu.

Despite that, we all have phones and we are all distracted by them. In this chapter we'll look a little at why and how that happens and what we can do to stop it immediately. That remedy, which I call ABC ringtones, actually makes your phone more efficient by allowing you to know who is calling whenever it is important to you. Not good enough? Research shows that these ABC ringtones not only inform you without interrupting you, it could well turn out that the people around you won't hear them at all.

The Underlying Problem

A phone rings in a crowded room. What happens next?

Well, you can try it out yourself to see. I've done it myself, just to make sure that I wasn't remembering it wrong. What happens is that a whole lot of the people in the room react by moving their heads. Some of them look around, and some of them pat their pockets or their purses, or even turn over the phone that's already in their hand. Several go so far as to take out their phones and check them.

From an anthropological point of view, I suspect that some of them are not actually checking their phones, but are displaying to the others present that it is not their phone that is ringing. I can't say without proper testing or consultation, but it would make sense as an untested hypothesis. This kind of behaviour is done to show social inclusion, much like making a face and moving away when you smell a fart while standing in a crowd. You're letting the other apes know that you're not the one who's been uncouth.

If the ringtone is a really unique song or an unexpected but familiar cartoon voice or something like that, then the people in the room may even react positively by laughing or singing along, or speaking in response.

Positive or negative though, unusual or common, when a phone rings in a crowd, everyone is interrupted to some degree.

If it keeps ringing, what happens? Huh? Huh?! What happens, hunh? What? What happens? What happens when the phone just keeps ringing?

We tend to anthropomorphize the ring, and to project onto it the behaviour we would associate with a human who keeps making inappropriate noises in the wrong place and at the wrong time. Maybe we even resent it a little, because we would never just let our phone ring unanswered. Generally, we take offense.

I can imagine a response from a colleague who doesn't care to question such things. Okay, okay, it bothers people to have phones ringing all the time. But that's just the price you pay for having ubiquitous phones, right? I mean, if it's going to be loud enough for you to hear it, then others are going to hear it too, right?

Wrong. There is a way to generate noises that one person will hear better than everyone else. There are several technological solutions out there or in development – vibrating phone instead of ringtone (ever hear one that's sitting on a metal desk?), multiple directional speakers that only make a coherent noise when they overlap (and so have to stay in perfect orientation to everyone in the scene), small earbuds or even bone induction speakers that are simply too soft for anyone else to hear, and even neurological implants.

The solution I'm proposing is not technological, but neuropsychological and, if you have a smartphone, you can implement it today without any financial outlay.

But phones ringing don't just bother everyone else, they also interrupt our own work, regardless of whether the call is important or not. Some people have tried to fix this by putting different ringtone on their phones for different people – now you can discern your buddy from your boss, a call you must answer from a call you can let go to voicemail.

But both classes of call still interrupt you and everyone around. The solution I am about to teach you is less disruptive and yet more informative.

Let's talk about how and why that is possible.

The Cocktail Party Effect is what you are experiencing when you hear your name spoken from across a crowded and noisy room, even though you had not heard or noticed early components of that conversation. This was first described in 1952 [2], with an affective advance offered in 1958 [3], but it has rarely been applied in day-to-day situations [4, 5]. Basically, it is the natural ability of the human brain to focus on a single auditory input in the midst of cacophony. This is an active, on-line auditory filtering process that cannot currently be equaled by computerized systems [6].

The underlying neurological mechanism behind the cocktail party effect was measured in a study on volunteers awaiting surgery for epilepsy. In preparation for the surgery, these people had been fitted with networks of electrodes directly on their brains [7]. This provided a unique opportunity to measure brain activity directly. Golumbic et al. showed these volunteers videos of two people simultaneously telling separate stories.

The areas of the brain that are responsible for processing sound responded to both voices. The parts of the brain that deal with language responded only to the story on which the listener is focused. Current studies on this effect may have an impact on therapies for attention deficit disorders and even on strategies for the digital recognition of natural language, but we believe that there is another application.

We propose that the effect should allow a mechanism by which to avoid the presumed fact that, in order to be detectable by the intended recipient, a ring tone or audible alert must also be detectable by those others working, playing or resting nearby.

This proposition became the hypothesis for a series of experiments conducted in 2014, in Lisbon, Portugal [8].

Here's One Paper That Addresses the Problem

Brown, J. N. A., J. Oliveira, S. Bakker. (2015) "I Am Calm": Towards a Psychoneurological Evaluation of ABC Ringtones. in Bakker, Hausen, van den Hoven and Selker (Eds) Special issue of IXD&A Journal on Designing for Peripheral Interaction: seamlessly integrating interactive technology in everyday life. Interaction Design and Architecture(s) 26, pp. 55–69.

In 2014, I moved to Lisbon, Portugal, to conduct research based on my theory of Anthropology-Based Computing (ABC). Specifically, the plan was to implement two experimental designs in order to see whether or not it might actually be possible to make a phone ring so that only the intended recipient can hear it.

That wasn't the hard part of the idea.

The hard part of the idea was that I wanted to find a way to do so, without any kind of special technological intervention. I wanted the whole thing to work based on the natural workings of the human mind.

Now, I had an idea that it should be possible to make use of the cocktail party effect.

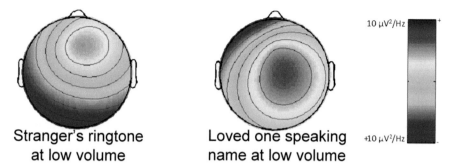

Stranger's ringtone   Loved one speaking
at low volume   name at low volume

Fig. 17.1 Density of beta-wave activity in the brain when a normal ringtone is heard, and when an ABC ringtone is heard

In the end, we found that – even if you were busy, and even if you were in a very noisy room, you will hear and recognize the much softer sound of a loved one whispering your name.

What's more, you perceive and recognize the voice in a different part of your brain (Fig. 17.1). Which may be why you do so without any interruption of your work at the time.

Now, this needs a lot of follow-up study before we can make any claims that we are actually triggering the brains natural information filters and using the cocktail party effect to make truly Calm ringtones. It may even be that we aren't managing to do that at all. I hope that my own tests will bring me closer to the truth, and I hope that you'll run some tests of your own on the idea, too. "Many hands make light work", and many minds catch more errors.

Proposed Experiment

This time I'm going to propose that you work with a group of friends. You don't have to, you can do it alone, but with a group it will seem more like a game.

Beforehand, you should find an on-line typing test that lets you compete with others for speed and accuracy.

You should also find a website that offers free streaming of background noises, and choose a noisy café or bar. It's better if it doesn't have discernable speech in any language you and your friends understand.

You can do that a day or two before you start, just so you don't keep everyone waiting.

The other thing you should do ahead of time is have everyone send you a copy of their usual ringtone, and also a copy of a sound file of someone they love whispering their name. Both should be set at 55–65 decibels (dB) – you should be able to check the volume either on your phone or with the default music player on your computer. Now, if they can't think of (or won't admit) who that might be, then they could just get someone they spend a lot of time with – a very close friend, a partner at work, even the roommate they hate, but hear all of the time. Just make sure that you have a list of that information somewhere so that we can see if different outcomes might be related to different types of relationships.

If you want to be more complex, you can have the loved ones provide four recordings: saying the name of the person who asked them, saying someone else's name, saying an important word like "fire", and saying a totally unimportant word like "car".

Please use some common sense here. If a recorded name matches one or more people, you should have a note of that somewhere, so that we can see if the two people with the same name responded the same way to both loved ones. You should also be careful in your choice of important or unimportant words. The word "car" may have a low emotional impact for the most part, but it might really catch the attention of anyone in your group who plays shinney in the street. By the same token, the word "fire" spoken at normal volume will have a very different effect on a line cook than on someone recently escaped from a firing squad.

Having received all of the files, you want to compile them into a playlist on your own phone. Please put each one in there two or three times and add one or two other ringtones. You'll notice that it gets to be a pretty long list, this is why it's best to use a small group.

Please randomize the order of the ringtones, and leave about 10–20 s between each one. It would also be good to leave 5 or 10 s of silence at the beginning.

Now place your phone in the middle of a round table, seat everyone around it at roughly equal distances, and have them turn on their laptops, tablets or other digital, internet-enabled typing devices and open the typing test.

On another computer, access the website with the noises, set it to 75–85 dB, and start it playing.

When everyone is ready, you can start the playlist and everyone can start typing… but there's a catch. Every time a ringtone plays, you should type whose voice it is and who it's for. Just type it right into your test. If you don't know one or both of the people, then just type "dunno": "Ernie calling Bert; London calling dunno, dunno calling Blondie, etc…)

Be sure to save your typing before closing the test or starting again. If the test you found doesn't allow you to save, then you can screencap it.

Now, whoever won the typing test should be applauded, but our real interest is in seeing if people heard each other's or their own whispered names.

How to Record and Report Your Results

Now, for every participant, you should have two sets of data, their score on the typing test, and their written record of who called when.

You should go through each typing test and extract the series of pairs of names (Frankie calling for Johnny; Jeanette calling for Nelson; Hannibal calling for Clarisse, etc…). This is why we asked everyone to at least type "dunno calling dunno", so that we can easily match up the order.

Some of the lists won't match up… some people may not hear some ringtones and some people may imagine they heard ringtones that never played. I'm not criticising your friends, I just think that might happen. It would be nice if the lists had time stamps as they went along, but even if they didn't you can match them up. It will be easiest if you all go through the lists together at the same time.

For each participant, you should end up with a list of 1 and 0 s, a 1 every time they got it right, and a 0 every time they missed one. Be sure to play fair. If the ringtone in question was just a normal ring, then the correct answer should be "dunno calling dunno". If you put in a ringtone from one of your friends, you can't fault the people at the table who don't know that she uses that tone.

Take special note of whether people hard their own whispered name.

Now you have to decide whether you want to:

examine one person's success at hearing their own whispered name, or
examine one person's success at hearing the whispered name of others, or
examine one person's success at hearing all ringtones. You can just count up how
   many they heard versus how many they missed and convert it to a percentage.

The you should decide whether you want to compare two people to each other, one person to everyone, or everyone to everyone else.

Once you've decided which one you want to do, come to [the website associated with this book], and sign in to share and compare your results with other citizen scientists.

References

1. Coleridge ST (1908) Kubla Khan. In: Quiller-Couch A (ed) The Oxford book of English verse. Oxford University Press, Oxford, pp 1250–1900
2. Cherry EC (1953) Some experiments on the recognition of speech, with one and with two ears. J Acoust Soc Am 25(5):975–979
3. Moray N (1959) Attention in dichotic listening: affective cues and the influence of instructions. Q J Exp Psychol 11(1):56–60
4. Brown JNA (2012) Expert talk for time machine session: designing calm technology … as refreshing as taking a walk in the woods. In 2012 IEEE international conference on multimedia and expo, vol 1, p 423
5. Brown JNA (2013) It's as easy as ABC: introducing anthropology-based computing. In Advances in computational intelligence. Springer, Berlin, pp 1–16
6. Brown JNA (2015) Making sense of the noise: an ABC approach to big data and security. In: Saathoff, Arabnia, Hill, Staniforth, Bayerl (eds) Application of big data for national security. Elsevier, Oxford, pp 261–273
7. Golumbic EMZ, Ding N, Bickel S, Lakatos P, Schevon CA, McKhann GM, Schroeder CE (2013) Mechanisms underlying selective neuronal tracking of attended speech at a "Cocktail Party". Neuron 77:980–991
8. Brown JNA, Oliveira J, Bakker S (2015) I am calm: towards a psychoneurological evaluation of ABC ringtones. Interact Des Architect 26:55–69

Chapter 18
Stop Your Text Messages from Killing You (or Your Friends, or Total Strangers)

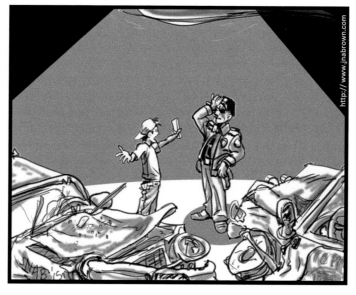

It's not *my* fault! Look at the text she sent me!!

Abstract As we discussed in the last chapter, your phone is designed to get your attention. Just because it is designed to do that, and just because people have been using it to do that for a long time, that doesn't mean that it does the job well… …or even in a way that won't kill you.

We also discussed the UN report about how the combination of smartphone and driving has become the number one killer of young people around the world. Well, the primary source of driver distraction is text messaging.

Please remember our triune model of the brain: Your reflexive system perceives all of the internal and external data that it can, and either filters out most of what it senses, or deals with it reflexively. A small portion of that sensory information is passed on to the thinking parts of the brain for processing.

The limbic part of your brain is the part that wants to see recognizable patterns in that data and becomes emotionally-stimulated by unanticipated change. It seems to me that this is why we have such strong reactions to broken patterns. We, as a race, find some pattern interruptions challenging and upsetting, and we find others funny. I think both of those are reactions of surprise, and I think that both happen in the limbic or emotional or reactive part of our brain… but that's a discussion for another time. In this chapter we are going to look at the way that you have learned to react when your phone buzzes at you, or beeps, or boops, or sings a song that you used to like.

The point is that, right now, the parts of your brain that react to an SMS alert are not logical, or sensible, and they react much faster than your conscious brain. Your well-trained limbic brain treats an instant message as though it's a reward, and it anticipates the opportunity to sink into a nice comfortable environment of instant gratification where you and your circle of friends natter at each other like digital protoprosimians reassuring themselves that they are safe and clever and cared for.

It doesn't care – it cannot care – that your conscious brain is trying to carry on a conversation, or read, or drive, or perform brain surgery. When the phone buzzes it will react,

The only way to stop that is to train that part of your brain to react differently about SMS alerts. In this chapter we're going to try and do that in a measurable way.

Don't worry, you'll still enjoy texting with some of your friends, and you'll still hate getting texts from others. All of the feelings will still be there, they just won't be as likely to kill you or someone else.

Once Upon a Time…

….there was a group of relatively hairless apes who had turned nattering into an art form. Actually, they had turned nattering into several art forms, and even the worst of them were pretty good at it.

They nattered better than anyone else on their planet and they were way beyond what had ever been done with it before. They still used nattering as a constant low-level reassurance, like so many of their cousins did – a sort of reverse alarm that says: "Hey, if you can hear this, then I haven't been eaten yet, so you're probably not under attack from this side". In this way nattering helped them control their fears and impulses. They were constantly reassured that they were in the right place and doing the right thing.

Sometimes, like a few of their cousins, they also used nattering more consciously; to call out specific messages of warning or welcome, of found food or hunger, and of several particularly relevant types of danger.

What made this group of apes special wasn't that they sometimes did it for no reason at all, and it wasn't that they did it so well, what really made them special was their proclivity for putting their young into settings where nattering wasn't allowed.

Most of these sat for hours every day, dreaming of nattering; longing for the comforting reassurance of constant low-level contact with their peers. But to do so was forbidden. They were forced to sit alone, surrounded by row upon row of their peers, but drowning in the roaring silence, barely able to control their impulsive need to escape to some unknown place where they could fit in.

Then something magical happened and they didn't have to be alone any more.

A Simple Analysis of the Underlying Problem

Have you ever seen any of those on-line videos of "cats training their humans"? They show something about the nature of living creatures. The cats in question have learned how to get some very low-level, very fundamental satisfaction or pleasure… maybe comfort is the better word. Anyway, they've learned how to get it, and there are compilations of clips of different cats signalling humans to pat them or stroke them or give them head bumps. The cats want that, they know how to get it, so they get it. If all cats did that all of the time, there would be fewer people on-line.

But that's not the point I want to make. The point is that, when the cat feels the need – for whatever reason, and I am casting no aspersions on the needs of cats here – then the cat does what is necessary to get it.

There's a great video, too, of codfish swimming in a loop, triggering a feeding device that was supposed to attract them temporarily. There's a delay on the device that is intended to shape their behaviour, and it did… …just not in the intended manner. Each fish triggers the device, then swims around while the next one eats the food and then triggers the machine in turn.

This is one of those iterative feedback loops that we looked at early on in the book, and it is fundamental to all of the animals I have ever gotten to know. I've personally witnessed it in mammals and birds and reptiles and fish, including the pets of friends, my own pets, and farmed animals I have later helped to slaughter and eat.

A moment ago you were experiencing some anticipatory pleasure at the thought of those animal videos, relating my words to the memories you have of enjoying similar videos. My mention of slaughtering and eating animals likely interrupted that thought in a less than pleasant way. If you were disturbed by this, please accept my apology and know that I was only using those words to try and communicate with you. It's been many years since I have killed my own food, and I promise you that no food was killed in the writing of this book.

If the change in imagery didn't upset you, well… I'm not sure I want to know why. I'll just assume that it's because you're a butcher or a fisherman and leave it at that.

The point is that it is natural for us to want to have visceral pleasure and comfort, and it is natural for us to seek it out unconsciously and irrationally; whether it is by nudging someone so that they will scratch us behind the ears, or whether it is by watching a seemingly endless stream of cat videos.

In fact, not getting the reassurance we viscerally crave is stressful. Continued non-responsiveness makes it worse and the visceral craving gets stronger.

Why should it be any different with the reassurance of digital nattering? When a group send each other a steady but irregular stream of messages that just read "'sup" and "l8r" and other symbols of relatively minimal semantic content, it is because the words and phrases are not the important part of the message. The important part is the contact… the nattering.

They are reassuring each other at a very fundamental level. "You exist. You belong. You are part of my group and I am part of yours."

At least that's my opinion. I could be wrong. It wouldn't be the first time today. If you think I'm wrong about this, please contact me and let me know. Or, you know, you could contact me if you think I'm right about this, too.

Please…

…anybody…

…hello?

Here's One Paper That Addresses This Problem

Thomée, S., Härenstam, A., & Hagberg, M. (2011). *Mobile phone use and stress, sleep disturbances, and symptoms of depression among young adults-a prospective cohort study.* BMC public health, 11(1), 66.

A team from Gothenberg decided that, since mobile phones have become so ubiquitous among young adults, and since they have a "vast effect on communication and interactions", it would be a good idea to see if using them is in any way associated with mental health symptoms ([1]).

They conducted a survey, using the kind of Likert-style scales that we've been using in earlier experiments. They were, however, operating on a larger scale – that is, with a bigger pool of participants. Their final cohort numbered 4,156. Those are the ones who responded to the first questionnaire and then also responded to the follow-up a year later. That's a good-sized sample, and their methods are solid, and their results are worrisome.

If you're up for it, you should read their paper. Including references and an elaborate abstract, it is only 11 pages long, and reading it may change your relationship with your phone.

You see, they found a strong relationship between frequent mobile phone use and symptoms of depression among both men and women. They also found an equally high association with sleep disturbances among men, and many other interesting associations that it would be worth your time to read.

But it's the link to depression that worries me, and I want it to worry you.

This study shows us that using your phone increased stress without increasing perceived access to social support at all. This means that even though the limbic system insists that digital nattering provides social cohesion and comfort, the people in the study were not actually able to find that support.

I'm afraid that this is another demonstration of how our reactions with the world are irrational, and it sounds as though it may even be another negative feedback loop of the sort discussed in Chap. 12.

You have a subconscious and visceral craving for constant contact with your circle, and so you keep you phone on and learn to react immediately to every incoming message. The reactions are limbic and amygdalic and visceral – which means that they are highly emotional, and that they happen before you have time to think consciously about what you are doing.

This is why you can put the phone down and decide not to check it and then find yourself reading the next message before you've even realised that you had picked it up again.

That is what causes car crashes and bus crashes and at least one train wreck that I know of. You convince yourself that it can't happen to you, and you are certain that the constant use is a choice, and that it feels good, and that you're in control, but you can't discuss it without becoming upset.

The visceral part of your brain wants the constant contact because it believes that this will satisfy some need that for reassurance that you barely know you have. But intellectually we can see that the constant contact will not provide that reassurance; instead it does just the opposite.

This experiment is going to be all about taking conscious control of your visceral reaction to the digital nattering of your network of friends.

Proposed Experiment

Turn off your phone.

Right now.

Don't check your messages and don't check the time, just turn off your phone and set it down and don't pick it up until you've gone back and re-read the story in this chapter's "Once Upon A Time…".

Done?

Great turn your phone back on and check your messages, but please don't answer them just yet – we're in the middle of something here.

Were you able to turn your phone off and leave it off while you read that one-page story?

Were you able to turn the phone back on and then sit and read this without checking your messages?

Check them now.

Please, go ahead; check your messages right now and then come back, because I have an important question for you.

You're back? You checked your messages? So, if you tried this little exercise, then you just spent a couple of minutes without checking your messages. Now tell me; while you were out of touch, did anybody die because they couldn't reach you?

If your answer is no, and I sincerely hope that it is, then please think about that very deliberately for a moment, because I want you to try the same thing again, and I want you to learn that trying it does not cause anyone to die.

It might cause some of your friends to be upset with you. If they are upset that you were unavailable for 3 or 4 min, then you must have a very strange relationship. I suggest that you offer to compete with them in the following game. In fact, invite a few people to play. It might be funny to watch them go from being very confident to squirming in anxious discomfort.

Try the exercise above, the one where you turn off the phone and read one page of text. You can read one story in the newspaper or on Boingboing.net, or you can read the back of a cereal box or the back of this book.

Whatever you choose, turn off your phone and don't turn it on again until you and the others are done reading. Jot down your results. You all lasted – what – 1 min? That's a great start. Once you can do that with one page of text, up the ante.

Go in small steps, and keep careful notes about how it makes you feel, but try to reach an hour of reading, or of watching a TV show, or of sitting down to a phone- and tablet-free meal. You could try to work your way up to 2 h of playing a board game or watching a movie. See who can go the longest.

Try to keep it light-hearted, but try to keep it going. You'll sleep better if you can relax about missing any messages before morning. You'll be more popular at the movies if you can turn off your phone before you go into the theatre and leave it off until you leave.

And you'll be much more likely to survive if you can do the same when you're driving.

You'll see that it becomes less stressful with time, even easier, and you can start to use it to convert your friends to a happier and less stressful life. It'll be like Dianetics, but without the risk of serial marriage to some old movie star whose ancient soul came from outer space to live in a volcano.

How to Record and Report Your Results

These results are really for you. Keep them as a reminder and as a motivation. If competition helps you, then you can compare your numbers with an equally com- petitive friend or stranger.

If recognition helps you, then let me know. I'll be happy to read about your progress.

If you think that you would benefit from writing up this process in a formal and scientific manner, well, I would love to see how it all comes together.

If you want, please sign in to the website associated with this book, where you can share and compare your results with other citizen scientists.

Reference

1. Thomée S, Härenstam A, Hagberg M (2011) Mobile phone use and stress, sleep disturbances, and symptoms of depression among young adults-a prospective cohort study. BMC Publ Health 11(1):66

Chapter 19
Stop Your Dashboard Navigator from Driving You to Distraction

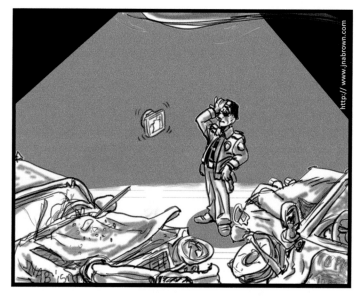

It's not *my* fault! I distinctly said "Turn right in *260* meters", not *250* m

Abstract It's hard for us to admit it, but we're really not very good at being consciously in control of ourselves or of the things around us.

We like to think that we are, some of us are certain of it, but generally speaking, we are very bad at focussing on anything at all. What we're good at is convincing ourselves that we're good at those things. Remember the new triune brain model from Chap. 10? Your conscious and deliberate self, the one that's reading these words and making sense of them, is getting all of its visual information from the two other layers of the brain.

Before you even start to think about the words, you have to have the chance to see them and to recognize them as a language that you can read. Even then, your mental experience of the words is going to be coloured by the emotions that you put on them. This is separate from my intent in writing, and it is separate from your intent in reading – it is a purely irrational and emotional bias that is also purely internal.

Remember that your nervous system doesn't shape your reflexes to your environment. If it did, then we could avoid most industrial accidents. You know, the sort where someone swats at a fly or reaches for a dropped pencil and gets their hand stuck in the machinery.

Well, the same is true of our reactive or limbic system. It is going to respond faster than our intellect. Worse than that, it is going to do so with the blind certainty that comes from a complete inability to be reflective or thoughtful. Still worse than that, afterwards it is going to defend every decision emotionally, which leaves no room for a rational discussion. If you can't admit to yourself that you're behaving irrationally, then you won't have the self-awareness to try and fix it.

We can work around it – but learning to react intellectually instead of emotionally takes the same kind of conscious and deliberate intervention that we use in the scientific method.

It's not a question of learning not to react emotionally, it's a question of admitting to yourself that you are not consciously and intellectually in control of the way you react to some things at some speeds.

When your sunglasses start to slide across your dashboard, consciously and deliberately prepare yourself to let them fall. If you don't, you're going to find yourself cranking on the steering wheel in order to have the leverage to try and reach over to catch them… and cranking on the steering wheel is a bad, bad thing to do by accident.

Back in Chap. 11, when I described the development of that smart home interface, I talked about my idea of the perfect navigation system. I based my Bellman's Protocol on the system of navigation used by the ship's captain who leads the *Hunting of the Snark*.

You decide where you want to go, ring a bell, and arrive. To avoid confusion, your only map is completely blank. This form of navigation is ideal for an automated system, and it is almost completely the opposite of the typical in-car navigation system of today.

With the modern system I still have to do all of the driving myself, without any concept of the larger picture, and under the added burden of the constant threat of a sudden command to change course based on reference points that are foreign to my way of thinking.

Coming over a bridge, I'm told to "turn left in 230 meters." If there are four turns there in rapid succession, which one does it mean? I can't tell at a glance which one was 230 m from the car at the moment of speech and which one was 240. I would prefer something like "After the next crossing, there will be four turns to your left. Please turn at the second one".

In my opinion, these commands and this insistence on using computer-centered references is not the behaviour of a navigator helping you find your course, but the behaviour of a ship's master telling you what to do in the expectation of immediate and error-free obedience.

Don't agree? Please reflect on it. When a group of people are in a car (or a boat, or a bar, or a classroom), how can you tell who's in charge? It's not a question of who's behind the podium or at the rostrum, of who's buying or selling, of who is the loudest or of who talks the most. The person in charge is the one who can interrupt anyone else at any time without raising their voice.

That's the way the Lord interacts with the serf, the Captain with the Crew, and that's the way that the computerized navigator in your car interacts with you.

And *that* is *a bad design choice*. If you feel (not think, but feel) that you have to react quickly, then your limbic system will try and obey. It will *react* faster than you can *reflect*, and it will make an emotionally-charged and illogical decision because it cannot possibly work any other way.

In this chapter I am going to introduce you to one of the prototypical tools I've been developing based on ABC. I mentioned it in Chap. 12 as one of the projects I'm currently pursuing, and I'd like your help in testing and improving it. This prototype is intended to help you decide whether an interaction is reflexive, reactive or reflective, and to evaluate how safe it is.

It seems to me that we really need to find a way to measure that.

Once Upon a Time...

...automobiles were brand new. They hadn't become really commercial yet, and were still at the stage where a rich man might drive his car to the car park so that he could run it around a little bit without annoying the people and animals in the street. In those days streets still belonged to people, and cars were expected to run along the sides, and yield to all comers.

In those days it wasn't very difficult to add new features because cars were hand made. Automating the assembly process didn't make it easier to innovate, it made it harder. Now any change requires shutting down the line and retooling.

It took decades for safety belts to be introduced, and they were literally saving lives. Now, someone suggests on board navigation and suddenly a dozen companies are putting products next to your steering wheel. The most successful companies in the world cannot implement a Human-Computer Interaction that will always provide a crash-free service for people who are depending on it. Why on earth are we introducing that HCI model to cars? (Fig. 19.1)

As mentioned earlier in this book, Error 404 frustrates me. Similar interactive strategies build my frustration and force me to react when I should be reflecting, or to reflect on something that needs a much faster reflexive response.

Fig. 19.1 Is it reasonable to design technology specifically to distract the user when they are doing something dangerous?

And now I get to have the same experience while trying to guide a ton of fiberglass and aluminum through traffic at high speed?

Oh, the humanity…

A Simple Analysis of the Underlying Problem

It used to be that a lot of plane crashes were caused by bad communication skills.

If you've never been in a high pressure environment under military protocol, then the statement above sounds ridiculous the first time you hear it.

If you have operated under military-style protocol, where rank instills immediate control and "the captain sets the tone of his ship", then the statement above sounds inevitable.

People make mistakes. No matter how good you are, no matter how hard you train; everyone makes mistakes. This is why scientists publish papers *after peer review* – so that their peers can find their mistakes before the information goes out to industry and the general public.

What's that? You don't believe that's true? You've read that you can become an expert at anything with 10,000 h of practice, or you've heard that there is a ritual that will remove error from your life, or you just disagree because of some innate knowledge that perfection is possible?

I was having that argument once over dinner with a friend, and he was insisting that practice could indeed make perfect. You just had to spend a lot of time at the skill you wanted to perfect, use it every day, make it a normal part of your life. He was certain of this and passionate about it and got quite worked up and, while making the point for the 7th or 8th time, he spilled some soup on his shirt.

Practice makes you better. Nothing makes you perfect. Perfection is a false standard. It is the kind of false standard that can only be maintained by delusion – like when a billionaire surrounds himself with sycophants and begins to believe his own press, or when any of us starts to believe the whispered amygdalic propaganda that reassures us that everything is fine.

In aviation, human factors experts introduced a concept called CRM – Crew (or Cockpit) Resource Management [1]. It was a formal way to address the deeply-rooted and unspoken rule that the "Captain is God". He can interrupt you and yell at you and do whatever he pleases, and you cannot answer or offer advice or even, as in one tragic true story, point out that the plane is running out of fuel.

Seriously, planes crashed because of this and people died, and the solution was better communication. It had a great effect at reducing fatal accidents in aviation, and has since been applied in surgical teams as well [2, 3]. These are both situations where teams have to work well together, support one another, so that they can all contribute to the success of their endeavour.

It's not a case of whether a team member has skills or knowledge, it's a case of whether they can communicate that knowledge and share those skills in a way that is useful to the person who needs to access them while concentrating on other things. It is a structured and artificially-generated environment replete with subtle but deeply important peripheral interactions. The same is true between surgeons, technicians, anesthesiologists, and nurses and the same is true between pilot, and co-pilot, and navigator.

And the same is true with whoever is helping you navigate while you drive.

Your dashboard navigator may have all the maps and directional updates it needs, and it may be able to speak clearly in a dozen languages, and show your route in brilliant high resolution colour according to several different display protocols. But if it doesn't share the information so that you can reach for it, find it, process it and respond to it peripherally – all without interrupting your focus on driving – then it is not doing its job safely and well.

Here's One Paper That Addresses This Problem

Brown, J. N. A., P. S. Bayerl, A. Fercher, G. Leitner, A. Català Mallofré, and M. Hitz. (2014, April). A Measure of Calm. In Saskia Bakker, Doris Hausen, Ted Selker, Elise van den Hoven, Andreas Butz, Berry Eggen (Editors) Peripheral Interaction: Shaping the Research and Design Space. Workshop at CHI 2014, Toronto, Canada. ISSN: 1862–5207

This short paper proposes that it should be possible to define and measure the qualities that make an interaction fit Weiser's concept of "Calm" [4]. It offers three prototypical iterations of the concept, each focussed on its own type of interaction: the generic model is called Classification of Attentional demands in a Layered Matrix or "CALMatrix". The second variation is called "CALMatrix for Alerts and Alarms", and focusses on that type of one-way communication. The third variation is intended to help assess and deal with potential threats, or hazards. It is called Simple Hazard Identification through the Evaluation of Layered Displays, or SHIELD.

For the exercise in this chapter, we will be using a modified version of the CALMatrix, but I encourage you to read about all three systems, and to experiment with them and improve them. If you come up with a better idea, then please try it out. If you don't mind, please let me know about your improvement, too. I love it when others improve on my ideas!

The people who design, build, sell, and use computerized devices need to know that their devices can be made to communicate well with humans. My hope in developing these matrices was to take the first steps towards making "Calm" an empirically-measurable quality.

Please help.

Proposed Experiment

This experiment is going to be based on a game. This game is going to be loud, and fun, and silly.

At the end of each round of play, every player should rate their experience. Then you should all switch roles, and play again, and fill out another survey.

You'll compile the data to try and build an understanding of each round of the game, and a separate understanding of each role.

Interpreting this data is going to be a little more challenging than it has been in our earlier experiments, but we'll address that after I tell you about the game.

To prepare for the game, you should do four things.

First, you want to write out a series of directions that could come from an automated navigator: simple commands like, "turn left" or "take the next turn on your right", or "you are here". The directions should all be clear and easy to understand, with simple words in short sentences. You should write them on a series of slips of paper that can be mixed together. You can repeat them, but you should have at least 20 pieces of paper. You should put them in a bag so that, during the game, the navigator can draw them out at random. If you're up to a little coding, you could write an app that would make the directions appear in random order at the press of a button, and install it on the navigator's phone.

Second, you should prepare copies of the questionnaire that appears after this description. You will want to have enough copies for everyone and a few spares.

Third, you should find a large space that is not open to either vehicular traffic, or in use by those you may hurt by accident. It would be best if no one is using it (very much) that day. I'd recommend a public park, an unused parking lot, or the common area of a university on an early Sunday morning. If you know someone who has a particularly big yard or an unused grain field that might be fun too, but be mindful of gopher holes and snakes in the grass.

Speaking of snakes in the grass, the last thing you want to do before starting is to gather some players. You should have at least four people to play this game, and it will be more fun with five or more. Ten is a lot of fun. I've never tried it with more than 20 people, and can't decide if that would be horrible or the best version ever. You can use friends and family members, team-mates, classmates, co-workers, and friendly strangers. For the game to work, everyone involved has to be actively supporting the group, trying to make it work. If someone is trying to make it fail, it will be less fun for everyone else, and it will spoil the experiment.

Here's how it works.

Two people stand facing each other. One is the driver and the other is the navigator. The navigator has the bag of directions and will draw from it later.

The other players mob up into a group around the driver and the navigator, all of them facing inwards. They should each put one hand on the shoulder of the person next to them, and one on the shoulder of the person in front of them. Try to hold on, but don't be rude about it. If you don't like touching others in this way, everyone could wear a small backpack, and you could all take a hold of shoulder straps or handles instead.

Because you are all in a bunch like that, walking could prove problematic. To make the experience both safer and funnier, you will all take little tiny steps, almost staying in place. It also helps if you all make little "vroom-vroom" noises.

When everyone is ready, the driver will begin to "drive" the group. That means that she begins to move in the direction, and at the speed, that she wants, and everyone else should be trying to go along with her. No one should resist. No one should exaggerate. Only the driver can steer.

Every 6 or 12 or 18 s, the navigator should whisper a direction clearly into the ear of the driver, and the driver should comply.

After you've used up all of the directions, or after the group has fallen three times, please take a break and fill in the questionnaires. Every player should fill one in during each break, and they should all be collected for processing later on.

Then switch roles and play again.

One alternative version of the game has everyone in the group – except the driver and navigator – talk loudly to each other about some sporting event or TV show. No spoilers, though, please.

Another alternative is the distracted driver – this can involve having the driver tell a long story while she drives, or it can have the driver on her cell phone or holding a cup of water that is pretending to be a cup of extremely hot coffee. Please only use pretend-extremely-hot-coffee.

The game can be a lot of fun and, I think, and it may inspire you all to resist the urge to use a computer that gives you real-time advice while you should be concentrating on keeping yourself, your passengers, and everyone nearby alive and healthy (Fig. 19.2).

Fill in the forms by writing whether each stage required:

"No Demand At All"; "Some Demand"; "As Much As I Could Handle", and; "Too Much For Me".

Each player should fill out two of these for each turn as a driver – one about driving and one about obeying the navigator.

CALMatrix			
STAGES	**DEMANDS**		
	REFLEXIVE	REACTIVE	REFLECTIVE
Preparation			
Starting			
Normal Use			
Flow			
Pause			
Resume			
Stop			
Settle			
EMERGENCY			

http:// www.jnabrown.com

Fig. 19.2 The CALMatrix (http://www.jnabrown.com)

THE DEMANDS

REFLEXIVE: Without thinking, like putting up your arms when you start to fall
REACTIVE: Fast emotional, illogical, like laughing or screaming
REFLECTIVE: Thoughtful, logical, like thinking clearly or anticipating

THE STAGES

Preparation: Before you start to move
Starting: Actually starting to move
Normal Driving:
Flow: Driving without thinking about it
Pause: Interrupting the drive to slow down and maybe to stop
Resume: Getting back to normal again after pausing
Stop: Coming intentionally to a full stop
Settle: Disconnecting from the drive once it is over
EMERGENCY: When something goes wrong

How to Record and Report Your Results

Now, for every participant in every round of play, you should have a questionnaire. You're job, and you can do this on your own or with friends, is to convert the information on those questionnaires into information on a CALMatrix.

What was the most common answer to each of the cells in the CALMatrix on driving? This will tell you the reflexive, reactive, and reflective demands of driving.

What was the most common answer to each of the cells in the CALMatrix on listening to and obeying the navigator. Overlay this values of this matrix on the values of the driving matrix to see the demands of doing both at the same time.

Once you've done that, please come to the website associated with this book and sign in to share and compare your results with other citizen scientists.

References

1. Helmreich RL, Merritt AC, Wilhelm JA (1999) The evolution of crew resource management training in commercial aviation. Int J Aviat Psychol 9(1):19–32
2. Helmreich RL (2000) On error management: lessons from aviation. BMJ Br Med J 320(7237):781
3. Sexton JB, Thomas EJ, Helmreich RL (2000) Error, stress, and teamwork in medicine and aviation: cross sectional surveys. BMJ 320(7237):745–749
4. Brown JNA, Bayerl PS, Fercher A, Leitner G, Mallofré AC, Hitz M (2014) A measure of calm. In: Bakker S, Hausen D, Selker T, van den Hoven E, Butz A, Eggen B (eds) Peripheral interaction: shaping the research and design space. Workshop at CHI 2014, Toronto. April, ISSN: 1862-5207

Chapter 20
Stop Your Noise-Blocking, High-Volume Headphones from Stopping Your Ears

I see a small, dark hearing aide in your future…

Abstract Wearing earbuds or headphones has only recently become something that a person might choose to do for more than an hour or so. The truth is that we really shouldn't do that.

Please, don't have a quick and emotional reaction to what I'm saying. We already know that the little protoprosimian that lives in your head is not happy with any challenges to the status quo. That little darling will try to convince you to be either upset or disparaging or angry or dismissive – before it gives your rational mind a chance to reflect and consider the matter.

This is why parents used to teach their children to count to ten before responding to anything that upset them. It's supposed to give you time for your rational brain to participate in your decisions. Of course, if you spend that time raging, and feeding that rage back into your limbic system, then you will build up your rage and further inhibit rational thought.

In this chapter we're going to talk very briefly about the fact that your triune brain is putting you in danger of losing your hearing and suffering permanent injury. It may surprise you to know that our ability to recover from loud noises has a lot to do with how long we are exposed. The corollary of this is that even a low-volume noise can damage your hearing if it goes on long enough.

This is another one of those things that should have been included in the uses' manual for the human body.

So, we'll take a quick look at those things, and we'll also look at a solution for the problem, but I don't think you're going to like it.

Once Upon a Time…

…there was an entire generation of frogs sitting in slowly-warming water. Unlike their parents, these frogs didn't have to sit in a lab or in some sadist's kitchen in order to sit in slowly-warming water, they carried their tanks with them.

Some of them made the water so hot that it would bother the other frogs passing them on the street or sitting near them on the bus, but most felt that they were being reasonable when it came to just how warm they let their own water get.

They were wrong.

They hadn't stopped to really consider how the hot water affected them.

They understood that long exposure to very hot water would cook them, and they had all heard stories about some unlucky tad who had lost track of time and gotten cooked. But each and every one of the frogs in this generation knew that they themselves were above average, and capable of insights that others didn't have. Each and every one of them felt unique and special and, sometimes, immortal… just like every previous generation had once felt.

They didn't take the simple measure of looking up how heating works in frogs. If they had done the research, they would have learned that longer exposure to lower temperatures would cook them just as surely as short exposure to higher temperatures.

Instead, they stuck with their irrational beliefs, because that allowed them to go on doing what they really wanted to do. They ignored the long-term threat because, well, because it didn't feel real to them.

Are you waiting to hear how this story ends?

So am I.

The Underlying Problem

If you are exposed to loud noises, it damages your ability to hear. I'm sure you've heard that a single loud noise can make you deaf, but do you know that lower volumes can do the same?

The simple truth is that your ears need time to recover from noise. They need silence sometimes. If you wear your earbuds as much as the average person you know, you are probably damaging your hearing.

Really.

If you don't stop, you'll go deaf… and it's worse than you might think. Deafness from hearing damage doesn't mean silence. It means an unending noise in your ears; a painful whistling scream that never stops – not when you are trying to sleep, or trying to concentrate; not ever.

The math is pretty simple. If you are exposed to 85 dB (decibels) for eight hours a day, and then have 16 h to recuperate, you should be fine. If your earbuds, tucked in tight where so little sound can escape, are hitting your ear drums with 100 dB, you can only avoid damage if you stop within 15 min.

In 2015, the World Health Organization reported that, in middle and high-income countries, 50 % of people between 12 and 35 years old are hurting themselves with their earbuds and headphones and might be making themselves permanently deaf [1]. That's 1.1 billion people. Are you one of them?

Listen, use ear buds and headsets, etc., if you want to, but turn down the volume and take long breaks so that you're not crippling yourself.

What's that you say, you need to be able to hear your music? Yeah, that's my point.

Here's One Paper That Addresses This Problem

"Hearing loss due to recreational exposure to loud sounds: a review". Published by the World Health Organization [1].

This paper is available as a free download from the WHO Institutional Repository for Information Sharing: (https://extranet.who.int/iris/restricted/handle/10665/154589).

Please get yourself a copy of it and read it today. The hearing you save could be your own.

Proposed Experiment

I have no magical cure, no technological intervention, no clever repositioning of a device to save you from this technology.

As a result, there is no experiment about this, except the very general experiment of seeing if you can defray your immediate self-gratification in return for the long-term goal of not suffering permanent hearing loss and the terrible discomfort of tinnitus.

Fig. 20.1 It's entirely up to you to make the best decision you can...

Well, can you deliberately and logically take control of that, or are you going to let your visceral brain make excuses? (Fig. 20.1)

It is entirely up to you to decide.

How to Record and Report Your Results

Really, just follow the guidelines and save your hearing. It's better than paying strangers to deafen you.

Do feel free to drop me a line and let me know how that works out for you.

Reference

1. Hearing loss due to recreational exposure to loud sounds: a review. Published by the World Health Organization (2015) It can be downloaded from: https://extranet.who.int/iris/restricted/handle/10665/154589

Chapter 21
Your Chapter

Where do old-fashioned values come from?

Abstract This is the chapter that you get to write.

I'll start you off with this little introduction, but the future is yours, not mine, and this book is all about helping you deal with the problems around you that can be solved through experimentation.

© Springer International Publishing Switzerland 2016
J.N.A. Brown, *Anthropology-Based Computing*, Human–Computer
Interaction Series, DOI 10.1007/978-3-319-24421-1_21

In the hope of inspiring you to study and take action on a problem of your own, I'm going to tell you one more story. My last story for you, at least, my last story for you in this particular book, is the story of a maker who is also a baker.

Jakob Schupp comes from a long line of bakers. He runs a small family bakery and café and variety store on the edge of a town called Klagenfurt, in a valley in the Austrian Alps.

Jakob's story, or at least, the one story I am going to tell you about Jakob in this book, is a story about Cross-Generational Habit, and about adaptation to technology, and about adapting technology to suit your needs.

Jakob is not a computer scientist, or any kind of a professional scientist at all, but he is a clever man. I want to tell you about one particular clever thing that he showed me one day when we were talking in his shop.

I had stopped in for herring salad, a delicious Carinthian concoction of fresh, smoked and pickled fish, mixed with chopped vegetables and home-made mayonnaise. It is a seasonal food, traditionally eaten only in the part of winter that traditionally Catholic Carinthians mark as Lent. In a land of delicious food, Herring Salad is one of my favourites.

When I learned that Jakob makes his own mayonnaise, I was duly impressed. I've done it before and – while it is not terribly hard – it takes the full attention of one or two people, and keeps them occupied without possibility of interruption until the work is done.

Jakob and I had talked before about innovation and adaptation and about some of the inventions I've built over the years. As I was sympathising with the demands of making mayonnaise, Jakob offered to show me his invention.

Jakob's story is a story of an adaptation – a small deviation from a cross- generational habit. Making mayonnaise traditionally involves two roles: one person mixes egg yolks in a large bowl, while another slowly drizzles oil into the mixture. The speeds have to match or the oil does not react with the egg and make mayonnaise. Instead, you end up with a ball of mayonnaise-like pudding in a puddle of oil. In his grandfather's day the job changed.

That was the advent of safe electricity! When electricity came into the kitchen, it became possible to put an automated stirring arm into a bowl. Now the stirring could happen without a human attached, making it a one-man job! That seems like a great improvement from a technical standpoint, but let's think about the human factors. Now the human pouring the oil doesn't get to rest from time to time, or to vary the speed a little in order to keep from falling asleep or developing cramps in his arms. The electric stirrer is unconcerned with your human weaknesses, and you must match its pace or fail!

Until one day when Jakob was trying to work in the store and make mayonnaise at the same time. Like many new parents, he needed to find a way to safely and productively divide his attention. I have an unconfirmed and untested idea, that it might have been parenting that inspired him.

He made a hole in the cap of a small plastic bottle and dribbled oil through it into a bowl. Experimentation got him the right size of hole for the oil he was using. Then he strung the bottle up from the shelf above his mixing machine. The oil dribbled at

Fig. 21.1 The mayonnaise making modification by Jakob Schupp

the right rate, directly into the puddle of soon-to-be-mayonnaise. He used a simple but clever adaptation to commonplace technology to make the hardest part of his task easy – now he can do his job while making mayonnaise. Eventually, he improved the design again, cutting the base from his inverted plastic bottle so that he can add oil when needed (Fig. 21.1).

I like to think that the lovely woman who taught me to make mayonnaise is still making it the old-fashioned way, with her children and, maybe now even with her grandchildren. Me, a long time ago I switched to buying it in a jar or doing without, but I still break out a whisk sometimes if I want to impress someone in the kitchen. For us, making mayonnaise is a rare event, and we can grant it the time and care that a rare event deserves.

For Jakob, making mayonnaise is a chore – one of many chores that all have to be done quickly and without error, and all while baking, and manning the cash register, and making the sandwiches and the conversation that keeps his customers coming back for more.

In all, it's a pretty "Calm" process now. He uses his natural Dynamic Environmental Focus (DEF); keeping a rough sense of time's passage, and glancing at the clock and at the machine while centering his attention on his customers and on other immediate needs. Occasionally, he decides whether to make the mayonnaise the center of his thoughts, or whether to push it back out to the periphery. He's not worrying about it because he has confidence. He has confidence because his limbic brain – the little protoprosimian – is constantly checking everything. Has it been long enough? Should I add oil now, while I'm thinking of it?

Otherwise he goes on about his work, focussing on his customers and on the tasks immediately at hand – like helping his father teach their family traditions to the next generation.

…

Now it's your turn to find and solve a problem in your day-to-day routines. Please consider writing up your project as it develops. When you're ready, please share your chapter with me and with the world.

To start yourself along the path of experimentation, you could try the experiments laid out for you over the last few chapters. As I've mentioned more than once, Springer has arranged a website to host your results for each of these experiments.

We'd like to share your results with the world. You can register with a user name in order to post your results and in order to comment on the results of others. Now, don't be a jackass about it. Abusive posters will be publicly humiliated… either directly or through being ignored.

Maybe I'll consult with the good folks at Boingboing.net to see how they manage to keep their boards so civilised.

I'd also like to hear from you personally, about your experiences with the experiments and about any other problems you have tried to solve using similar methods, like my Carinthian friend Jakob and his mayonnaise making modification. The hard work for him was getting the hole in the cap to be the right size. The improvement to his life was immediate.

So, which new technological challenges are you solving today?

Afterword

Thank you...

A few final words about ABC

ABC is not the first theory to propose that the human brain has three separate, evolved processing systems, or that the human mind is divided in a similar way. Aristotle shared Plato's belief in three separate souls that live and die with each human body – one that is internal and occupied with the metabolism of growth and survival, another that deals with emotion and perception, and a final, separate soul of reason or intellect [1].

Freud proposed the "ego", "superego", and "id" [2], and Jung proposed the "collective unconscious", "self", and "persona" [3]. More recently, Tversky and Kahneman linked two separate processing styles to either fast or slow thinking speeds, deliberately ignoring specific physiological association with either [4, 5].

© Springer International Publishing Switzerland 2016
J.N.A. Brown, *Anthropology-Based Computing*, Human–Computer
Interaction Series, DOI 10.1007/978-3-319-24421-1

Have you seen the castellers in Catalunya? This is a traditional sport in which communities of men and women of all ages compete to form the highest and most complex human towers. Imagine, if you will, a vast tower with uncountable partici- pants. Weiser [6], Kahneman [5], Golumbic [7], and Csikszentmihalyi [8] are standing on the shoulders of MacLean [9], Cherry [10], Freud [2], and Jung [3] – the last two facing away from each other while themselves perched on the famously broad shoulders of Plato [1] and his anachronistic team of Aristotle [1], Broca [11], and Descartes [12].

Countless others are there in the tower. My friends Leitner and Bakker have climbed this tower with their ideas of *The Future Home is Wise, Not Smart* [13] and of Peripheral Interaction [14]. I hope to lock arms with them there, providing addi- tional support for their work and for all future work in this field. I look towards that future with my feet planted on the shoulders of the giants who have gone before. They've provided the foundation. If I should slip and fall, it will be my own fault.

...

Thank you for reading this book.

I hope that you feel inspired to go out into the world and do better science than I have ever done, and to think better thoughts, help more people, and have more fun.

If the ideas, words, or pictures in this book help you to do any of that, I would be grateful to hear about it, and I would ask that you please pay it forward when you can.

If you feel that anything in this book has hurt or inhibited you in any way, then I am sincerely sorry, and I hope that you recover soon.

If you are one of the thousands of people who has influenced my thoughts and helped to shape my ideas, then I thank you for that, too, and wish I could tell you so in person.

If we haven't met yet, and I haven't encountered your ideas in print or online or through some other means, well good – that gives me something to look forward to.

Be Well and Do Good,

July 11, 2015   John
Klagenfurt, Austria

References

1. Aristotle H (1902) Aristotle's psychology (trans. of the De Anima and Parva Naturalia, w. Introd. and Notes.). Swan Sonnenschien and Company, Ltd, London, 339 pp, 8vo
2. Freud S (1961) The ego and the id. In: Strachey J (ed & trans) The standard edition of the complete psychological works of Sigmund Freud. Hogarth Press, London
3. Jung CG (1969) The structure of the psyche. In: Read H, Fordham M, Adler G, McGuire W (eds) (R. F. C. Hull, Trans.) The collected works of C. G. Jung: Vol. 8. The structure and dynamics of the psyche, 2nd ed. Princeton University Press, Princeton
4. Tversky A, Kahneman D (1974) Judgment under uncertainty: Heuristics and biases. Science 185(4157):1124–1131

5. Kahneman D (2011) Thinking, fast and slow. Farrar, Straus and Giroux, New York
6. Weiser M, Brown JS (1997) The coming age of calm technology. In: Denning PJ, Metcalfe RM (eds) Beyond calculation: the next fifty years of computing. Copernicus, New York, pp 75–85
7. Golumbic EMZ, Ding N, Bickel S, Lakatos P, Schevon CA, McKhann GM, … & Schroeder CE (2013) Mechanisms underlying selective neuronal tracking of attended speech at a "Cocktail Party". Neuron 77:980–991
8. Csikszentmihalyi M (2014) Flow and the foundations of positive psychology: the collected works of Mihaly Csikszentmihalyi. Springer, Dordrecht
9. MacLean PD (1990) The triune brain in evolution: role in paleocerebral functions. Springer Science & Business Media, Berlin/Heidelberg
10. Cherry EC (1953) Some experiments on the recognition of speech, with one and with two ears. J Acoustical Soc Am 25(5):975–979
11. Broca P (1865) Sur le siège de la faculté du langage articulé. Bulletins de la Société d'Anthropologie de Paris 6(1):377–393
12. Descartes R, Veitch J, Lévy-Bruhl L (1903) The meditations and selections from the principles of René Descartes. Retrieved from http://www.gutenberg.org/ebooks/4391
13. Leitner G (2015) The future home is wise, not smart: a human-centric perspective on next generation domestic technologies. Springer, Cham
14. Bakker S (2013) Design for peripheral interaction. Doctoral dissertation, Technische Universiteit Eindhoven